C PROGRAMMING

A COMPLETE GUIDE
TO MASTERING
THE C LANGUAGE

C PROGRAMMING

A COMPLETE GUIDE
TO MASTERING
THE C LANGUAGE

AUGIE HANSEN

Addison-Wesley Publishing Company, Inc.
Reading, Massachusetts Menlo Park, California New York
Don Mills, Ontario Wokingham, England Amsterdam Bonn Sydney
Singapore Tokyo Madrid San Juan

Library of Congress Cataloging-in-Publication Data

Hansen, August.
    C programming : a complete guide to mastering the C language /
Augie Hansen.
       p.   cm.
    Includes bibliographical references.
    ISBN 0-201-19444-9
    1. C (Computer program language)   I. Title   II. Title: Complete
guide to mastering the C language.
    QA76.73.C15H364   1989
    005.13'3--dc20   89-17825
                                         CIP

Production Editor: Amorette Pedersen
Cover Design by: Doliber Skeffington Design
Set in 11-point New Century Schoolbook by Benchmark Productions

ABCDEFGHIJ-AL-89
First Printing, November, 1989

Hi Mom!

ACKNOWLEDGEMENTS

First, and quite deliberately, I thank my family for their tolerance, understanding, and love. Each time I convey the happy news about another book contract, they smile politely and give each other that glance that says "Uh oh, here we go again!" But they never fail to support me in every way. Thanks Lindsey, Reid, Corri, and especially you, Doris.

On the technical front, my thanks to Alan Southerton for his timely review and helpful suggestions. Also, I would like to thank Marc Rochkind for illuminating some of the early UNIX and C history for me.

The folks at Benchmark Productions have been a joy to work with. Chris Williams continues to maintain a bizzare sense of humor in spite of advancing age and having to deal with authors whose idea of on-time delivery is "sometime this year."

The success of a book is often determined as much by the efforts of a caring and capable editor as by the skill and ability of the author. Amy Pedersen has certainly done her part to make this book a success. Thanks, Amy. Thanks also to Allison Cox for her help in many aspects of the process that turns the bit patterns on the disks into printed pages.

I would be remiss if I didn't say that my years at Bell Laboratories and AT&T/Infomation Systems were the best I ever had working for someone else. It was both a great job and a fantastic educational experience.

Last, but not least, I express my appreciation to Professor Robert Haas at the University of Rhode Island, Department of Electrical Engineering. He was the best teacher anyone could hope to have and a caring advisor.

TABLE OF CONTENTS

INTRODUCTION   **xiii**

   Machine Talk   xiv
   Assembler Languages   xiv
   High-Level Languages   xv
   The C Programming Language   xv
   Organization of This Book   xvi
   Portability Issues   xvii
   Typographic Considerations   xviii

CHAPTER 1
C LANGUAGE AND
PROGRAMMING ENVIRONMENTS   **1**

   An Overview of C Language   1
   Programming Environments   6
   C Compilers and Interpreters   7
   C Programming in a UNIX Environment   8
   C Programming in an MS-DOS Environment   11

CHAPTER 2
WRITING C PROGRAMS   **15**

   A Simple C Program   15
   Creating a Program File   16
   The main() Function   18
   Program Layout   19
   Getting User Input   19

C Program Connections   22
Summary   24
Questions and Exercises   25

CHAPTER 3
DATA AND MEMORY   **27**

Computer Memory   27
Keywords   35
Identifiers   35
Variables   37
Basic Types   37
Character   39
Integers   43
Floating Types   48
Storage Requirements and Value Ranges   52
Data Input   53
Summary   57
Questions and Exercises   58

CHAPTER 4
EXPRESSIONS AND STATEMENTS   **61**

Introduction   61
C Operators   63
Operator Precedence   64
The Assignment Operator   67
Arithmetic Operators   68
The sizeof Operator   74
Relational Operators   75
Bitwise Operators   79
Additional Assignment Operators   82
Increment and Decrement Operators   83
Address and Indirection Operators   84
Sequence Operator   85
Questions and Exercises   85

CHAPTER 5
PROGRAM FLOW AND CONTROL   89

Flow of Control   89
Making Decisions with if Statements   91
Multi-way Branching with switch   99
The while Loop   104
The for Loop   108
The do Loop   111
An Additional Jump Statement   113
Sequence, Selection, and Iteration Combined   114
Summary   116
Questions and Exercises   117

CHAPTER 6
FUNCTIONS AND
PROGRAM ORGANIZATION   119

The Purpose of Functions   119
Function Declarations   123
Function Parameters and Arguments   126
Recursion   135
The C Preprocessor and Macros   140
Portability   147
Summary   148
Questions and Exercises   149

CHAPTER 7
ARRAYS AND POINTERS   153

Array Types   153
Multidimensional Arrays   162
Pointer Types   165
Pointers and Arrays in C   169
Pointers and Functions   177
Portability   185
Summary   185
Questions and Exercises   186

CHAPTER 8
STRUCTURES   **189**

    Introduction to Structures   189
    Structures and Functions   195
    Pointers and Structures   200
    User-Defined Types and typedef   206
    Enumerations   207
    Unions   210
    Bit Fields   211
    Portability   214
    Summary   214
    Questions and Exercises   215

CHAPTER 9
INPUT, OUTPUT, AND FILES   **219**

    Input and Output   219
    File Input/Output   226
    Summary   241
    Questions and Exercises   241

CHAPTER 10
THE PROGRAM DEVELOPMENT PROCESS   **245**

    Problem Analysis   245
    Program Design   248
    Coding   249
    Testing   250
    Maintenance   251
    Questions and Exercises   252

CHAPTER 11
STACKS AND QUEUES   **253**

    Stacks   253
    Queues   260

Summary 266
Questions and Exercises 267

CHAPTER 12
LINKED DATA STRUCTURES 269

Singly-Linked Lists 270
Doubly-Linked Lists 288
Summary 291
Questions and Exercises 291

CHAPTER 13
COMMUNICATING WITH
THE OPERATING SYSTEM 293

Command-Line Arguments 293
Environment Variables 298
Portability 303
Summary 304
Questions and Exercises 304

CHAPTER 14
FILE CONVERSION UTILITIES 307

Understanding the Needs 307
Designing a Solution 308
The Manual Page 309
Coding the Program 311
Programming Exercises 319

APPENDIX A
KEYWORDS AND RESERVED IDENTIFIERS 319

APPENDIX B
C LANGUAGE OPERATORS 329

APPENDIX C
ASCII CHARACTER SET 335

APPENDIX D
THE C PREPROCESSOR   **341**

APPENDIX E
ANSWERS   **343**

INDEX   **349**

INTRODUCTION

You are embarking on a journey that can take you a long way into the future. I can say this with great confidence because it's the feeling I had during my initial explorations into C programming back in the last half of the 1970s. It is gratifying more than a decade later to see what a tremendous impact C language has had on the computer industry and it is exciting to ponder the future.

The important thing for you to realize is that learning a computer programming language is a long-term process and not an isolated event. You have to work at it regularly and you have to challenge yourself if you are to advance your knowledge and skill level. There are no free lunches and no pills that will make you into a brilliant programmer overnight.

C Programming is designed to teach you the C language, show you how to write working programs in C, and demonstrate through fully developed programming projects how to apply what you learn to real-world programming jobs.

If you have prior programming experience, you will find converting to C to be easy or difficult depending on what languages you already know and how willing you are to make adjustments to the way you think. Some of you, no doubt, will resist change, but many of you will welcome the refreshing freedom of expression and the incredible flexibility afforded you by C.

Those of you who are learning to program for the first time may have heard that C is hard to learn, and you may approach this endeavor with trepidation. Don't. C is no more difficult to learn than any other language (faint praise, but true), and it can really be a lot of fun. I'll take the responsibility of trying to make it so. All I ask is that you give it a good effort. Fair enough?

Machine Talk

When a computer talks to itself what does it say? Probably something like "00110011 10100011 11101011 11110001 1001010." A computer has a limited alphabet (0 and 1) and a correspondingly small vocabulary (typically a few hundred "words"). It's not much of a trick for a human to learn the language of a computer (given a good memory and some practice). But to talk to a computer in its own tongue is a monumental yawn and something you really don't want to do for too long.

Over the years, hardware designers and programmers have produced a vast array of tools that make the task of communicating instructions to a computer a lot easier than it used to be when flipping switches on the front panel represented the state of the art.

Assembler Languages

Closely related to native machine language is assembler language. The major change from the world of 1s and 0s is the use of mnemonic names to represent instructions

Assembler is a convenience to a programmer and it is a relatively simple task to automatically translate assembler codes into machine instructions. This task falls to an assembler program.

A problem with both raw machine language and assembler is that instructions are intimately tied to the host processor, so moving a program to a different processor usually involves complete manual recoding of the program. If you have to support a program in a variety of operating environments, this poses substantial burdens in training, program coding, and ongoing maintenance. In addition, assembler languages, although mnemonic, are difficult to read, and programs of any significance require many instructions.

High-Level Languages

High-level languages offer you an attractive alternative because they tend to be easily read by mere mortals, and programs written with care in some high-level languages can be moved among disparate operating environments with relative ease.

If the choice is yours to make, you have a wide range of high-level programming languages from which to choose. FORTRAN, COBOL, BASIC, and other old standbys have been in use for many years. The majority of all programs ever written were done so in one of these languages. Even today, it's estimated that more than half of all currently operating programs were written in COBOL, but that situation is changing rapidly.

Newer languages such as Pascal, C, Modula 2, and other derivatives of Algol have built strong followings. Of these newer languages, C has probably had the greatest impact on modern programming.

The C Programming Language

C is the result of a personal effort by Dennis Ritchie, a Bell Laboratories researcher. It was not designed by a committee (Ada anyone?). The resulting freewheeling spirit of C has made a significant contribution to its success.

Originally designed as a systems programming language for making UNIX the first "portable" operating system, C had a long gestation period with the Bell Labs. It has grown up rapidly since becoming available outside the Labs, initially benefiting and being hurt by its cult following. Now almost everybody is jumping on the bandwagon.

The language was introduced in the seminal book *The C Programming Language* by Brian Kernighan and Dennis Ritchie (Prentice-Hall, 1978). The book is generally referred to as "K&R". It contains the original formal definition of C in Appendix A, *Reference Manual*. The book is now in its second edition, reflecting the changes to C that have taken place in the past decade.

An updated and extensively revised definition of C has been formulated by the X3J11 technical subcommittee of the American National Standards Institute (ANSI). The draft-proposed standard should be officially adopted by the time this book is printed. Therefore, *C Programming* emphasizes ANSI C. For compatibility with current C implementations, the book also includes guidelines for running programs in ANSI and pre-ANSI environments.

Organization of This Book

C Programming is composed of four major parts. The first part introduces you to the C programming language. The second part describes numerous techniques that you will use in real-world programming situations. The third part presents several programming projects that walk you through the process from concepts to finished programs. The last part is a collection of important C-related information in handy reference form.

Part 1: An Introduction to C

This part introduces you to C language, the lingua franca of a majority of developers of software for microcomputers and minicomputers. The coverage includes basic concepts of programming, data, expressions and statements, execution-control flow (branching and looping), functions, arrays, and pointers.

You will obtain a working knowledge of C that will get you started. This part stresses the fundamentals. Learn them well before moving on.

Part 2: Programming Practices and Techniques

Designing a program and coding it are very different tasks. They are related tasks, but they happen at different levels of abstraction in your brain. Program design requires an understanding of the problem being solved, knowledge of techniques for solving problems, and the ability to express a solution in terms that humans can understand. **Coding**, the process of writing source code in a particular language, is a translation task that converts the language-independent solution into a working program.

When a programmer says he or she is having trouble writing a program, you can safely bet that the real problem is designing a suitable solution. Writing the code, once a programmer understands the language, is usually not a significant problem. Consequently, I have designed this part of *C Programming* to help you analyze problems and formulate workable solutions.

Part 3: C Programming Projects

After you know the language and have acquired or sharpened your problem-solving skills, you can work your way though a set of representative programming projects. The projects in this part take you through the entire design and development process of some programs that should be of general use to you.

Part 4: Appendices

The last part contains tables and other reference information in handy, carefully organized appendices.

Portability Issues

You'll encounter some striking similarities and important differences among currently popular operating environments. Where appropriate, chapters include discussions of system and language implementation differences that might affect the portability of your programs.

In addition, we'll examine design and coding practices that can have an impact on program performance and promote efficient use of computer resources. There are usually many ways to solve a given problem and a solution that works is a good solution. We will explore ways of developing solutions that work and that are efficient.

Typographic Considerations

Here is a summary of the typography used in *C Programming*:

- Variable and function names are shown in Courier typeface [count, ShowLine()].

- Pseudocode listings are shown in italics.

- C source code listings are presented in monospaced type.

Here is a small section of pseudocode from a sample design:

...
for each named file
        open the file
        if file opening error
                display error message
                continue with the next file, if any
        read the file into the internal buffer
        ...
        close the file
...

The pseudocode description cannot be compiled and linked into a runnable program, but it shows the proposed structure and substance of a solution. The indentation of lines indicates subordination, which we'll cover in detail in later chapters.

Program source code in C that is derived from the pseudocode design is presented like this:

```
...
/* read the files into the buffer */
while ((name = GetName()) != NULL) {
    fp = fopen(name, "r");
    if (fp == NULL) {
        fprintf(stderr,
            "Cannot open %s\n", name);
        continue;
    }
```

```
    while (fgets(linebuf, MAXLINE, fp)) != NULL)
        AddLine(editbuf++, linebuf);
    ...
    fclose(fp);
}
...
```

With the preliminaries out of the way, let's get down to business by taking a broad view of C language and a few of the environments in which it is commonly used.

CHAPTER 1

C LANGUAGE AND
PROGRAMMING ENVIRONMENTS

This chapter contains an overview of C language and descriptions of two of the most popular programming environments in which C figures prominently. The purpose is to show you what C looks like and to help you get started using C quickly in the environment that is available to you.

Although the details of a particular implementation of a C programming system vary from one operating environment to another, C looks essentially the same everywhere. C is fast becoming the universal language of computers in much the same way that English has become the universal language of radio communications.

An Overview of C Language

You can only appreciate the full form and beauty of an impressionistic painting from a proper distance. Similarly, you get an overall appreciation of C only when you step back to see the language in its entirety. After you have the big picture, you can focus on the details by stepping closer to the canvas, as we'll do in the remaining chapters of this book.

Feature Summary

Let's step back then, and take a wide view of C language by looking first at its primary features:

- C is a small language, which makes it possible to grasp it in full (unlike Ada and other large languages, which most programmers can only hope to learn as subsets of the whole).

- C is widely portable to environments as diverse as stand-alone microprocessors and the fastest supercomputers.

- Although initially used for systems programming, C is suitable for a wide range of programming tasks including applications programming.

- Possessing a clean set of control statements, C encourages and facilitates structured programming.

- C has a rich set of operators that accounts for its expressiveness and flexibility.

- C is fully recursive, permitting you to create elegant solutions to many problems that lend themselves to recursive rather than iterative solutions.

- C has a set of data types that reflects the underlying architecture of most modern computer systems, while not being shackled to any particular computer architecture.

- One of C's more salient features is its pointer mechanism and the close relationship of pointers and arrays.

- A standardized and versatile run-time library of often-used routines provides a common, well-defined programming interface.

- C has features that permit machine-level operations, permitting system programmers to use C as a high-level assembler.

Next let's take a closer look at C language by examining some of its primary attributes in a bit more detail. The following material describes the elements of a C program, the statements that control the flow of execution of a program, the use of subprograms (functions and macros) to divide programs into manageable units, and other attributes of the language.

Elements of C Programs

C is a relatively small language. It reserves a set of only 32 words ("keywords" or standard identifiers). In addition, the names of standard library functions and macros are now effectively reserved. The ANSI standard allows a compiler vendor to reserve additional words as long as there is no conflict with standard identifiers. Appendix A summarizes the reserved words and standard identifiers.

A comprehensive set of operators, 40 in all, gives C its great power and flexibility. C has all of the expected operators for doing arithmetic, for performing relational and logical evaluations, and for managing data in various ways. In addition, it has low-level operators for manipulating data at the bit level, permitting programmers to program at the systems level and the applications level with equal facility—without having to resort to machine-specific assembly language programming.

You use C's reserved words, operators, and standard routines, together with your own data items and routines, to compose programs. Each program consists of one or more functions, optional data, and possible additional elements, which we'll discuss later. These items exist in a source file or a set of source files. C programs must be converted into executable machine instructions. The process is generally called **translation** and can be achieved either by **interpretation** (translating each C statement every time the program runs) or by **compilation** (translating C statements into machine instructions before the program is run).

Later in this chapter, you'll see how some of the primary C programming environments are organized, and you'll learn how to use them.

Flow-Control Statements

The default behavior of a program is to execute a series of statements in sequence. Some programs contain nothing but sequentially executed statements. Most problems however, are more complicated than that and therefore, most involve alterations to the flow of execution of statements.

Aside from function calls (see the section about subprograms), the mechanism by which the flow of execution of a set of program statements is altered, is a set of flow-control statements.

In many computer languages, a basic decision-making statement (if or test) and an absolute jump statement (jump or goto) form the flow-control mechanism. Nothing else is required because anything else that is needed can be constructed from these basic statements. There is a problem, however.

Absolute jump statements permit (and unfortunately encourage) an unstructured kind of programming technique that produces programs that are hard to read and understand, and that are often difficult to debug (find and fix errors). Languages with such limited flow-control mechanisms usually depend on the use of labeled statements (names or line numbers) as targets of the jump statements.

The problem is that you can write programs that jump all over the place in seemingly random order. If you visualize the jumps as strands of pasta, you end up producing what looks like a bowl of spaghetti. Not a pretty sight in a computer!

C provides sophisticated flow-control constructs that facilitate and encourage a structured approach to programming. There's no guarantee that you will write great programs even with such constructs available to you, but at least you've got a chance. The primary flow-control statements in C can be categorized as branching (decision) statements and looping (iteration) statements. In addition, C provides three jump statements.

The branching statements are the if statement, which can have an optional else clause, and the switch statement. The if statement provides a basic two-way branching capability—the fundamental decision-making capability. The switch statement, together with its case and default labels, provides a flexible multi-way branching capability.

The C language looping statements include the while, for, and do...while statements. These statements provide a way to execute a program statement or a block of statements repeatedly as long as a control expression is logically true. Loops figure prominently in many programs.

Although C programmers eschew absolute jumps, favoring the discipline of structured control statements, C provides the break, continue, and goto statements that are restricted forms of absolute jump statements. They are typically used sparingly in C programs, but each has its place, as we'll see in later chapters.

Subprograms

One of the major tenets of structured programming is that a program should be broken into a collection of subprograms, each of which does a single, carefully-defined task. In C, subprograms take one of two forms: functions and macros.

A **function** is a subprogram that involves a call/return mechanism supported by modern stack-oriented computer systems. A stack is an abstract data type that represents a region of memory used for communication between parts of a program. Functions use a stack to receive inputs from and return values to their callers. A function's instructions appear once in an executable program and can be called any number of times.

A **macro** is a name, preferably short, that stands for something that is usually larger and more complex than the name itself. You create macros by defining them and letting the C compiler's preprocessor expand them. Each occurrence of a macro name in a program is replaced by the macro's full definition. This produces instructions that are executed in-line rather than by the call/return mechanism used by functions.

You will initially create programs that consist of a single function called `main()` to introduce the essential elements of the language and to see how programs are compiled and run. After you have been shown how to write C functions, your programs will take on a more modular form involving multiple functions and, where appropriate, multiple source files.

Other Attributes of C

Certain tasks, such as reading and writing data in disk files, copying text, and calculating the length of a string of characters, occur often in programs. Many functions and macros have been written and refined during the better part of two decades and collected into what has come to be known as the standard C subroutine library.

A library is composed of linkable object modules. Each object module can contain a single function or a set of related functions. When you compile a program, the compiler converts your source files into object files and then calls a linker program to hook your object files together with selected object modules in the standard subroutine library to produce an executable program file. Only modules that resolve external names which you have used in your program or which provide required run-time support are linked. This minimizes your final program size by not dragging in instructions that are not needed.

In addition to the compiler and linker, most C programming systems provide other support programs that aid the programmer in preparing and testing programs. Syntax checkers and debuggers are representative of these tools. Some C programming systems provide other tools, such as syntax-directed editors and on-line help features. Anything that helps to simplify the programmer's job without getting in the way deserves praise.

Programming Environments

As noted in the Introduction, C is supported across an amazing range of computing environments. I cannot possibly cover them all in this book. Although the details of a given implementation vary from one environment to another, the core of a C programming system is essentially constant, so this book should serve the needs of a wide audience.

Two popular operating environments in which C is used are specifically addressed in this book:

- UNIX

- MS-DOS

UNIX and other UNIX-like systems represent open systems in typical minicomputer and mainframe environments and, to a growing degree, in some microcomputer environments. MS-DOS (and IBM's Personal Computer DOS) is representative of the IBM Personal Computer and work-alike microcomputer systems, which are considered, for the most part, non-proprietary. I have purposely avoided giving coverage to blatantly proprietary and closed computer programming environments.

The programs in this book have been developed and tested under the Santa Cruz Operation's XENIX/386 System V, running on an Everex STEP 386/20 and MS-DOS 4.01 on an IBM PC/AT. Programs are written to the ANSI standard for C in order to obtain the greatest degree of portability. Conditional compilation is used to permit the programs to be compiled by C compilers that are not fully ANSI-conforming implementations.

OS/2, a multitasking operating system for Intel-based microcomputers, has features derived from both MS-DOS and UNIX, plus a few of its own unique features. After you are familiar with the basics of programming in C, you may wish to refer to *Advanced C Programming for OS/2* by Augie Hansen and Vaughn Vernon (Addison-Wesley, 1989) for information about programming the OS/2 kernel interface in C.

C Compilers and Interpreters

A program that accepts human-readable source statements and produces machine-readable instructions is called a **translator**. C translators take one of two primary forms: interpreters and compilers. In any operating system environment, C can either be interpreted or compiled. Traditionally, C has been a compiled language, but interpreters for C have become popular in recent years as a way of teaching C and speeding the development process.

Interpreters for C give the language a BASIC-like interactive feel that helps programmers learn C and create program prototypes, but they usually do so by limiting program size and by placing other constraints on the programmer. Compilers tend to take longer to produce running programs, but they can usually handle large, multi-module programs, provide optimization of program size and speed, and offer other benefits.

For the purpose of learning C, you will find interpreters and compilers to be different in some ways, but any C translator will be of value to you (certainly better than none). We will concentrate on learning the language and on applying it at the application level while avoiding system-level issues that would reduce or preclude program portability.

C Programming in a UNIX Environment

C was originally developed as a way of converting UNIX from a hardware-specific operating system into a portable operating system (the first). The language permitted researchers from Bell Laboratories to write system software that could be moved easily to other hardware environments. Had UNIX remained in its original assembly-language form for the DEC PDP-7 hardware, it would have been necessary to completely rewrite it for other processors—not an inviting prospect.

Although C has features that allow programmers ready access to the underlying hardware, it is not tied to a particular processor. Thus, versions of UNIX for Interdata minicomputers, the DEC VAX series, and a wide range of other computer systems were written with modest programming efforts. Try that with systems written for specific hardware families. DOS, for example, is an Intel microprocessor operating system, written in assembly language. To move DOS to a Motorola 68000 microprocessor would require either a complete rewrite or a very sophisticated emulation of an Intel environment on the 68000. Most vendors take the easy (but expensive) way out and install an Intel coprocessor board to run DOS.

Overview

The process of compiling and linking a C program under UNIX is depicted in Figure 1-1. A typical C program involves at least one C source file and possibly some header files. A program of average complexity often involves a set of C source files.

The figure shows a program that is created from two source files, **pgm.c** and **support.c**, and a single header file, **stdio.h**. You use a text editor (**ed**, **vi**, **emacs**, etc.) to create the C source and header files. The **.c** filename extension is required for C source files. The **.h** filename for headers is a convention that we use, but it is not a requirement. You could use **.inc**, for example, as long as you use the name consistently in source files that include the header.

Headers are called that because they are usually referred to ("included" by a preprocessor directive) at the beginning or head of a source file. Many headers are already prepared for you and reside in a special directory on your computer system. On a UNIX system, the directory is **/usr/include**. In addition, some header files used in UNIX system-level programming are placed in the **/usr/include/sys** directory.

The crosshatched boxes in Figure 1-1 represent programs that compile source files into object form and link objects files and library modules into an executable program file. The compiler box represents one or more programs (called passes or phases) that comprise the compiler.

Figure 1-1: Compiling C Programs under UNIX

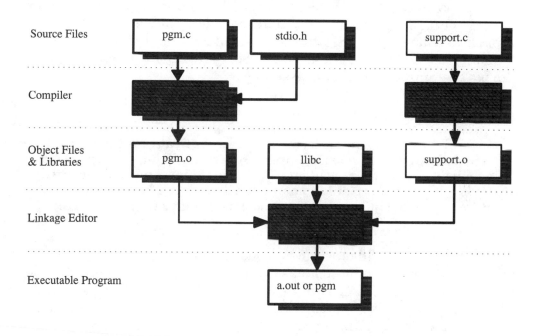

The first pass is typically a C preprocessor that performs text replacements to convert symbolic names and macro names to their definitions before the actual C compiler sees the source files. The compiler proper may be a single program that handles all lexical analysis, parsing, semantic analysis, and code generation tasks. The more common approach is to use a set of separate programs for each phase of the translation process.

In a UNIX environment, the preprocessor is cpp. The preprocessor is C-specific. The compiler resides in files named **ccom** (VAX) or **c0**, **c1** (PDP-11), and **c2**, which is an optional optimizer pass.

You can also create assembly language source files and call the assembler program, **as**, to assemble them, producing additional linkable object files. The assembler is a machine-specific program.

The linkage editor, usually **ld**, is responsible for combining object files and library object modules into an executable program. The linkage editor is not source language-specific. It takes object files produced by any compatible language translator, resolves all external linkages (function names, global variables, and so on), and prepares an executable program image containing a relocation table.

✍ **Programmer's Notebook**

In a UNIX environment, letter case is significant and it is traditional to show filenames in lowercase letters. Using all uppercase or mixed case causes problems. If, for example, you use uppercase letters in your source file to name the header (STDIO.H instead of stdio.h), the compiler can't find the header and reports an error.

The output of the **ld** program is saved in a file called **a.out** by default. You can use command-line options to control the name that is given to the linker's output file, such as **pgm** shown in Figure 1-1. The file is used when the program is run to initialize the code and data segments of what becomes a running UNIX process.

The cc Program

Although several steps are involved in compiling and linking a program's components, the process is highly automated and controlled by the use of **cc**, which is called the compiler-driver program. You usually do not need to call individually the preprocessor, compiler passes, the assembler, or the linkage editor. Instead you use **cc**, which transparently calls the needed programs for you. From a UNIX programmer's perspective, **cc** is the UNIX C compiler.

The C compiler driver controls the compiler, assembler, and linker steps to produce an executable program. You identify the component parts of a program and its name, and **cc** does the rest.

C Programming in an MS-DOS Environment

Several good C compilers have strong positions in the MS-DOS market. In preparing and testing programs for this book, I used Borland's Turbo C 2.0, the Microsoft C 5.0 Optimizing Compiler, and Microsoft QuickC 2.0.

You should be able to use one of the dozens of DOS-based C compilers with little or no change to the source code because virtually all C compiler suppliers for DOS computers are converging quickly on the ANSI C standard and I have tried to avoid non-portable C features in the example programs. If your C compiler is not able to compile the programs in this book, encourage your supplier to catch up with the industry or switch to one that is current.

Overview

As shown in Figure 1-2, the process of compiling a C program under MS-DOS is nearly identical to the way you do it in a UNIX environment.

The primary differences involve source and object filenames and compiler/linker program names. Filenames under MS-DOS are treated internally as all uppercase. You can type such names in lowercase if you prefer—they are converted on input. In addition, compiler suppliers choose their own program names, so you will need to use names that are appropriate for your compiler.

The figure shows names that are suitable for use with the Borland Turbo C command-line compiler (**TCC**) or the integrated compiler (**TC**) that automatically calls the linker when it is needed. Equivalent QuickC program names are **QCL** and **QC** respectively. The C 5.0 command-line compiler is called **CL**. Let's take a closer look at each of these C compilers.

Figure 1-2: Compiling C Programs under MS-DOS

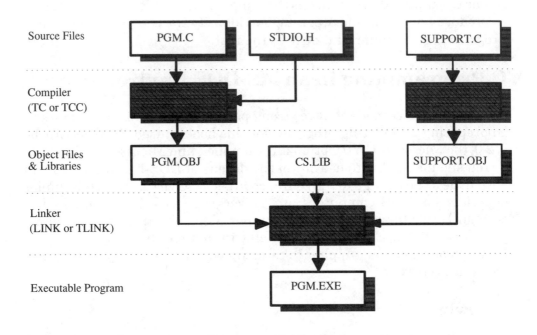

Integrated C Programming Environments

Turbo C was the first integrated C programming environment for MS-DOS computers, combining a full-screen editor, compiler, and help system in a single program. It was soon followed by a similar product, QuickC, from Microsoft. QuickC had similar capabilities and added a symbolic, source-level debugger to the integrated environment. Turbo C's latest incarnation now sports a symbolic source-level debugger, too.

For our purposes, the products are nearly identical because they both track the ANSI standard, provide approximately the same set of features, and produce nearly equivalent object code in terms of speed and size given comparable option settings and identical source code. The compilers have different default settings and you may prefer the operation of one over the other, but reactions to differences are usually personal and often trivial.

Microsoft C 5.0 Optimizing Compiler

The Microsoft C 5.0 Optimizing Compiler is a full-featured compiler that is suitable for large program development projects. It features a command-line compiler, several programming support tools, and a version of the QuickC compiler.

One of the support tools is the CodeView symbolic, source-level debugger. CodeView gives you a convenient means of testing and debugging programs. A comparable symbolic debugger is available for Turbo C and is included in the Professional Turbo C program development system.

A primary reason for using the optimizing compiler, which I will refer to as C5 from now on, is the ability to optimize your program for speed, size, or both. This is of little consequence when you are learning to program in C, but it is of great value to those who are writing commercial software. Shaving a little off the running time or size of a program can have an important impact on its reception in the highly competitive microcomputer marketplace.

I have found that initial program design and prototyping, experimenting, and just playing around is most easily done using an integrated environment. The built-in help systems are great assets in the early going. If a program is likely to go into commercial service, I recompile it with a full optimizing compiler.

CHAPTER 2

WRITING C PROGRAMS

We'll get started with C programming by analyzing some examples of working programs. Although you may not immediately appreciate or understand all of the elements of C programs, it helps to see real programs to get a frame of reference.

By dissecting the programs shown in this chapter, you will encounter many of the major elements that occur in virtually all C programs.

A Simple C Program

Let's start out with an easy one. The **greet1** program prints a message and quits. Not much to it, really. The C source code is contained in the file **greet1.c**, which you can create with a text editor (a stand-alone program, such as **vi**, or the editor part of an integrated C programming environment). If you use a word processor, be sure to save the file as an ordinary text file (no special formatting).

```
main()
{
      puts("Greetings. Welcome to C.");
}
```

The program consists of a `main()` function and a call to the standard library output function, `gets()`.

The standard library is a collection of many highly refined subprograms (functions and macros). We will make extensive use of the standard library in the programs of this book.

The name of our program, **greet1**, provides a handy way for us to refer to it, but there is no need to have a function called `greet()` in the program. We could write one, but we are not required to do so. We must, however, have one function called `main()`.

Creating a Program File

Before you can run the **greet1** program, you must compile and link it. The process is the same in most C programming environments, but the details differ.

The following descriptions show how to compile and run this simple program under UNIX and DOS. If you are programming in a different environment, you may need to modify these descriptions.

UNIX

The UNIX `cc` command runs the necessary preprocessor and compiler passes and the linker to create an executable program file.

For our discussions of UNIX and C, I will assume the use of the standard Bourne shell, but you can use the Berkeley C shell or the AT&T Korn shell if you prefer. Your command-line prompt may be something other than the standard UNIX system dollar sign (do you think Ken Thompson knew that UNIX would become a big commercial success?).

```
$ cc greet1.c
$ a.out

Greetings. Welcome to C.
$
```

This command sequence shows that you compile and link by using the `cc` command. If the source code is syntactically correct, the command produces a file called **a.out** and gives it execute permissions. You can run the program by typing the name **a.ou**t as a command. If you prefer, you can rename the **a.out** file, to **greet1** for example, and run the program by typing its new name.

You can bypass the renaming step by using a compiler command of the form:

```
$cc-0 greet1 greet1.c
```

which uses the -0 option to provide an object filename.

If your program source is defective, the compiler will display some error messages (possibly helpful, but don't count on it) and create an output file that is not executable (execute bits off). If this happens, examine your source file for typing errors. Look carefully at the opening and closing braces (they must be paired) and be sure the line containing the puts() function is properly terminated with a semicolon. If necessary, edit the source file and try the compiler step again.

When you run the program, the output is simply the message "Greetings. Welcome to C." on a line by itself.

DOS

If you use a command-line program, such as **TCC**, **QCL**, **or CL** (**C5**), the process of compiling and linking under DOS is virtually the same as that described for UNIX. Only the compiler driver program name changes.

If you use one of the integrated C programming environments, type TC, QC, or whatever your environment requires, and use the command menus or shortcut keys to control editing, compiling, and program execution steps.

Figure 2-1 shows the **greet1** program about to be run in the Turbo C environment. QuickC has a different command menu organization, but it operates similarly. Both of these integrated C environments show output on a user screen that is separate from the compiler screen. The user screen is kept in memory and you can switch to it with a simple keyboard command (Alt+F5 in Turbo C and F4 in QuickC).

Figure 2-1: The Turbo C Compile Menu

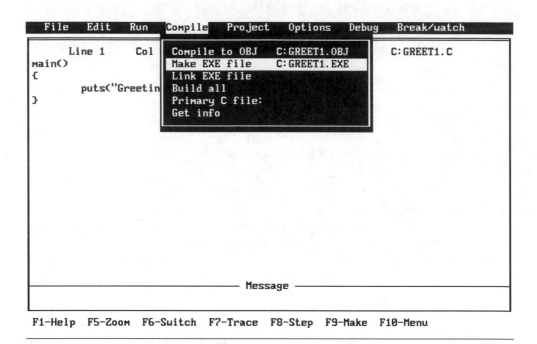

The main() Function

Every C program has one `main()` function, which is the starting point of the program. A C system does some initial setup work, such as processing command-line arguments before turning over control to your program code.

Because the `main()` function is the designated starting point, there can only be one such function in a program. However, you can have as many other functions as you need in your program. The **greet1.c** program source file consists of `main()` and a call to one other function, `puts()`, which prints a message. A more complex program could involve many other functions; typically a mixture of library calls and programmer-defined functions.

In later chapters, we'll explore command-line argument processing and other features of the run-time startup aspects of a typical C system.

Program Layout

C is free form. It does not have a prescribed line structure. Indentation, for example, has no special significance. White space (space, tab, or a new line) is not significant either, except that it is not allowed in a few multi-character operators.

The alarmist program (**alarmist.c**) is an example of a program that is hard for a person to read comfortably, but it compiles and runs just fine:

```
main(){puts("The sky is falling!");}
```

By compressing all the source code together onto a single line, the programmer has saved space at the expense of program readability. This is never a good idea. Use white space, including indentation, to set off elements of your programs. The program sources will be both easier to read and easier to maintain.

Getting User Input

Here is our first revision of the greeting program. The source code contains a few new elements:

- Comments (block and in-line)

- `#include` and `#define` directives

- An array of characters for buffering

- Additional library functions.

We'll discuss each of these elements after looking at the source code:

```
/*
 * greet2.c
 *
 * Get the user's name and print a personalized greeting.
 */

#include <stdio.h>
#define NBYTES     15

main()
{
        char name[NBYTES];          /* input buffer */

        /* prompt user for a name */
        printf("What is your name? ");

        /* read the user's input */
        gets(name);

        /* print a personal greeting */
        printf("\nGreetings, %s, and welcome to C.\n", name);
}
```

This program prints a prompt message and waits for the user to type a reply. Whatever the user types is used as a personal name and printed as part of the output message text. The \n characters inside the control string symbolize a new-line character.

Comments

Comments contribute nothing to the final program. They are stripped out during the compilation process. However, carefully written comments make a tremendous contribution to the readability of a program. Because of C's terse syntax, comments play an even greater role in C source files than in some of the more verbose high-level languages.

The characters /* introduce a comment and the characters */ terminate a comment. Anything between these comment delimiters is the comment's body.

Short comments can usually be contained within a line and are typically typed like this:

/* comment text */

If you need to type a long comment, you can put the comment delimiters on separate lines, creating a block comment. To help keep a block comment together visually, programmers often use a vertical array of asterisks or some other character, as in the following example:

/*
* comment text
* more comment text
* still more comment text
*/

Some programmers place boxes drawn with dashes and vertical bars or other symbols completely around block comments to make them really stand out. You can mix commenting styles any way you like, but try to use comment style in a meaningful way. I recommend block comments at the start of each file or function definition and in-line comments to describe non-obvious program statements that may have meanings or purposes which are not apparent.

Array of Characters

A **buffer** is a place in memory where you can store data for later use when it is received. The statement:

```
char name[NBYTES];
```

is a declaration of an array of characters that is NBYTES long. This statement introduces several new terms and concepts.

The C keyword `char` indicates the data type of a variable, in this case, `name`. An **array**, indicated by the square brackets, is a collection of two or more objects of identical type. The symbolic name, NBYTES, is a defined constant (see the next section for details), which in this program has a value of 15.

Therefore, the statement declares an array of 15 characters. This array is used to hold a name that is typed by the user.

Preprocessor Directives

The **greet2.c** program contains an `#include` directive. An `#include` directive causes the contents of a named file or memory region to be brought into the including file, effectively replacing the directive line in the source file.

Definitions of a set of useful input and output routines are contained in the **stdio.h** header.

The **greet2.c** also contains a `#define` preprocessor directive. In this program, the `#define` directive creates a symbolic name, NBYTES, for a constant value. With certain exceptions, such as the number 0, it is bad practice to code literal numbers in your program source code. For several reasons that we'll explore later, it is far better to use symbolic names that are defined by preprocessor directives.

Standard Library Routines

The **greet2.c** program contains some new functions and macros from the standard library: `printf()` and `gets()`.

The `printf()` function provides formatted printing. It gives you a way of printing text strings; possibly intermixed with numbers in various formats and other variable information.

The `gets()` routine is implemented as a macro. A macro is usually a short name (the macro name) that stands for something larger or more complex (the macro definition). The `gets()` macro reads a "string" of characters from its "standard input," which by default is the user's keyboard.

C Program Connections

Programs can communicate with their operating environments. Two of the primary means of communication are command-line arguments and return values. Both are optional features of programs and functions, and they are under your control for any functions that you write.

Command-Line Arguments

Command-line arguments are values that a user can type on the command line at the time the program is invoked. A reason for using them is to permit a single program to operate on different data each time it is started. A filename in an editor command such as:

```
vi myfile.c
```

is an example of variable data passed by a command-line argument.

To understand how command-line arguments work, you need a sound understanding of function arguments, pointers, and character strings, so we'll come back to this topic later.

Return Values

The purpose of return values is to return a single data item to a calling function or program. In **greet3.c**, for example, `main()` returns an integer value to indicate success or failure to the operating system.

Let's look at the source code:

```
SOURCE CODE =
/*
 * greet3.c
 *
 * Get the user's name and print a personalized greeting
 * (revised version).
 */

#include <stdio.h>
#include <stdlib.h>

#define NBYTES     15

int
main()
{
        char name[NBYTES];          /* input buffer */
```

```
/* prompt user for a name */
printf("What is your name? ");

/* read the user's input */
gets(name);

/* print a personal greeting */
printf("\nGreetings, %s, and welcome to C.\n", name);

return EXIT_SUCCESS;
}
```

This program includes another header file, called **stdlib.h**, which defines a symbolic constant called EXIT_SUCCESS (and another called EXIT_FAILURE, which is not used in this example). We should use these symbolic names instead of literal values of the traditional 0 (zero) for success, and a nonzero value for failure because the conventions may differ on some systems.

Our program always returns an indication of success, but most programs will have return paths that indicate failure. We need to learn about conditional branching and error checking before we can write code that checks for errors and returns appropriate failure indications. Conditional branching is one of several means of controlling the flow of program execution, which is a major aspect of all significant programs.

Summary

This chapter gives you a broad-brush look at C programs. It identifies the required elements of all C programs, such as the `main()` function, preprocessor directives, bracing to show grouping of statements, and calls to other routines such as those in the standard library.

This chapter also hints at things to come, such as command-line processing, execution flow-control mechanisms, and error checking.

Questions and Exercises

1. What is wrong with the following program?

   ```
   test()
   {
     puts("This is a test.");
   }
   ```

2. What are standard library functions and why are they useful in writing programs?

3. What must the user do to a program before it can be run?

4. In C, is it possible to write an entire program in one line? If so, why would this not be a good practice?

5. Using comments:

   a. helps organize a program.
   b. adds unneeded space and clutter to a program.
   c. makes it easier to change a program.
   d. both a and c.

6. Describe two types of commonly used comments and give two examples for each.

7. What does the following statement do?

   ```
   char name[20];
   ```

8. What purposes are served by the #define preprocessor directive?

9. Which preprocessor directive allows a source file to incorporate the contents of a specified file or header? Show an example of this preprocessor feature.

10. List the standard library functions you have learned so far and describe what each does.

11. What are command-line arguments and what are they used for?

12. Explain the purpose of return values and how they might be used in a program.

Additional Exercises

A. Rewrite the **greet3.c** program to allow full names (about 30 characters) and to print a different message.

B. Write a program that asks for two character string inputs and uses both in an output message.

CHAPTER 3

DATA AND MEMORY

The ways in which a computer stores data of various kinds are mirrored rather closely by the ways in which C represents data. This chapter looks at data, from individual bits to higher-level groupings of bits that represent numbers, characters, and strings.

When you have completed this chapter, you will know how to recognize and use data in various forms. You will be able to recognize and use C data types and type modifiers, how to represent data as constants and variables in your programs, and how to print (or display) data.

Computer Memory

Computer memory is an important and essential part of a computer system. The memory of a computer system consists of two types: **primary memory** and **secondary memory**.

Primary memory is typically random-access memory (RAM) that is directly addressable by the computer's central processing unit (CPU). Primary memory is usually fast and volatile. Its contents are lost when the power is turned off—unless some form of battery backup power is provided or special nonvolatile memory devices are used. All program text (instructions) and data exist somewhere in active primary memory while a program is executing.

Secondary memory resides on disk, tape, or some other medium. Such memory is not within the address space of the computer. It has the virtue of (relatively) permanent storage in the absence of power. Secondary storage is typically much slower than primary memory by one or more orders of magnitude, but the ability to retain information for long periods of time is an important benefit.

Another type of memory called **read-only memory** (ROM) has attributes of both primary and secondary memory. It can also be placed in the address space of a processor. As its name implies, ROM can be read but not written, which makes the program instructions and data stored in ROM available without the danger of them being accidently or purposely modified. And the contents of ROM are permanent.

Bits

At the heart of computer memory, whether primary or secondary, is the **binary digit**, more commonly called the bit. An individual bit can have one of two possible states: on or off. These states are often referred to as 1 and 0, respectively. Thus, a single bit has a range of two values. See Figure 3-1.

Figure 3-1: The bit is the fundamental unit of storage.

A bit has one of two possible states.

Bit Value	Indicators	
0	◯ (OFF)	(OPEN)
1	☼ (ON)	(CLOSED)

Inside a computer's memory, the states are represented by voltage levels or direction of current flow. Only the value indicated by a bit's current state is important to us. Figure 3-1 also shows how a bit's value might be viewed as a light that is either on or off or as an electrical circuit that is open or closed.

Combinations of Bits

By combining bits into groups, we can specify greater ranges of values. If we use two bits to represent a value, we can specify one of four unique values ranging from 0 to 3, as shown in Table 3-1.

Table 3-1: Bit Values

BIT PATTERN	DECIMAL VALUE
00	0
01	1
10	2
11	3

In the above table, the bit patterns are formed by using two adjacent bits with the bit on the right having a "weight" of 1 and the bit on the left having a weight of 2. To calculate the value represented by the pair of bits, multiply each bit's weight by its corresponding value (0 or 1) and add the individual bit values together. Following the practice established for decimal numbers, bits toward the right have lower weights and those toward the left have greater weights.

Thus the bit pattern 01 represents 0(2) + 1(1), which is a value of 0 + 1, or 1. The parentheses in this context indicate multiplication, which is done before addition. Similarly, the bit pattern 11 has an equivalent decimal value of 1(2) + 1(1), which yields a value of 3.

Notice that the values represented by a pattern of bits start at 0 and not 1. This is quite natural because all bits off means 0 times the weight of each bit in the pattern, resulting in a 0 value for the number represented by the bit pattern. Therefore, the highest value representable by a pattern of bits is one less than the range.

Octal Numbers

With only two bits, the range of values is limited to four (0 through 3), as you have seen, but by adding just a single bit to the pattern, we can double the range to eight values (0 through 7).

Table 3-2 shows the decimal and octal values of three-bit patterns.

Table 3-2: Decimal and Octal Values		
BINARY	DECIMAL	OCTAL
000	0	0
001	1	1
010	2	2
011	3	3
100	4	4
101	5	5
110	6	6
111	7	7

For the first eight bit patterns shown above, the decimal and octal values are identical. To represent larger numbers of bits as octal numbers, we need to use additional octal digits. Therefore, the decimal number 8 is 10 octal, 9 decimal is 11 octal, and so on. To distinguish octal numbers from decimal numbers in C programs, we must use a leading of 0 (zero). Thus, 4 is a decimal number and its equivalent octal number is 04.

Hexadecimal Numbers

If we add a fourth bit to our collection of bits, we can specify 16 unique patterns having values of 0 to 15 decimal as shown in Table 3-3.

Table 3-3: Hexadecimal and Decimal Bits		
BINARY	DECIMAL	HEXADECIMAL
0000	0	0
0001	1	1
0010	2	2
0011	3	3
0100	4	4
0101	5	5
0110	6	6
0111	7	7
1000	8	8
1001	9	9
1010	10	A
1011	11	B
1100	12	C
1101	13	D
1110	14	E
1111	15	F

Also shown in the table is an alternative representation of the values called hexadecimal. By using the letters A through F (or a through f) in the number, we can express all 16 values of a 4-bit pattern in a single digit. This gives us a more compact and convenient way of representing values.

To distinguish hexadecimal numbers from decimal and octal numbers in C programs, we use a leading 0x (zero followed by letter "x") notation. Thus, 5 decimal can be shown as 0x5 hexadecimal and 12 decimal has the same value as 0xC.

Bytes

A computer keeps track of memory objects by using addresses. It would be too burdensome to address each and every bit in memory, so computers maintain addresses of bytes.

A byte is a collection of bits that is large enough to hold the value of any member of the basic character set of the environment in which a C program executes. The number of bits in a byte is implementation-defined, with eight bits being a common size for a byte in microcomputer settings. The bits of a byte must be contiguously arranged in memory.

Figure 3-2 shows a pair of 8-bit bytes. Let's examine the low byte, which contains bits numbered 0 through 7.

Figure 3-2: Bits are organized as bytes and words.

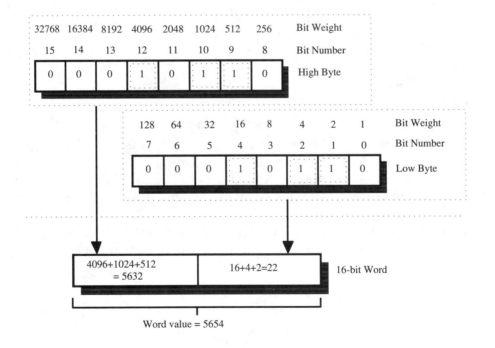

Because of its greater contribution to the overall value of a byte, the left most bit is called the most significant bit (MSB) or the high-order bit. Conversely, the right most bit makes the smallest contribution to the overall value, and is called the least-significant bit (LSB) or the low-order bit.

Only bits 1, 2, and 4 contribute to the value of this byte, so the byte's value is the sum of the weights of these bits: 16 + 4 + 2, which equals 22. The number of unique values that can be represented by an 8-bit byte is 256. Of course, other byte sizes can represent greater or lesser ranges of values.

Objects and Addresses

As you can see in Figure 3-2, we can use collections of bytes to form entities called **objects**. An object (except for bit fields) is a region of memory composed of a contiguous collection of bytes, one or more, that can represent values. A bit-field object, which is a collection of contiguous bits, cannot be directly addressed. We'll examine bit fields in detail in Chapter 8 after covering structures.

In the figure, a pair of 8-bit bytes form a 16-bit word. The significance of a byte depends on its position in an object. The low byte, as we have seen, contributes a value of 22 to the overall word value in this example. The high byte, which for discussion purposes has the same bit pattern as the low byte, contributes a value of 5,632 to the word value.

Notice that the bit numbers of the high byte of the 16-bit data word go from 8 through 15 and that the bit weights are correspondingly higher than those in the low byte. The byte value is, therefore, 4,096 + 1,024 + 512—or 5,632. For the case of 8-bit bytes, we can arrive at the same value by taking the ordinary byte value for the bit pattern (22) and multiplying it by 256.

With the exception of bit fields, all objects have addresses. The address of an object is the address of its first byte in memory. Whether the first byte is the low-order or high-order byte of the object is implementation-defined and is the basis of some serious portability issues.

Figure 3-3 shows an example memory layout for a 16-bit microcomputer typified by the original IBM Personal Computer (PC). I'll refer to this memory layout as the Intel architecture because of the 8088 micro-processor that is the heart of the PC. On the right, we see memory as a logical succession of bytes with successively higher addresses being further down the page. This is the normal page presentation. Some documents show higher addresses toward the top of the page, but either presentation is acceptable.

Figure 3-3: A representative memory organization.

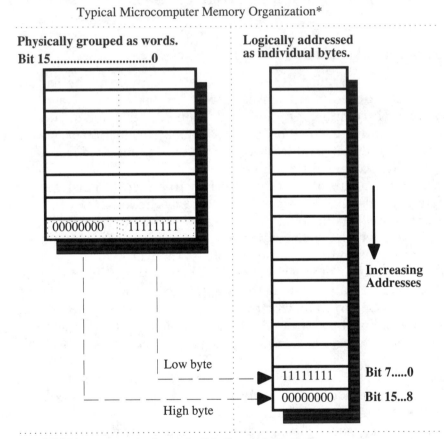

Typical Microcomputer Memory Organization*

Physically grouped as words.
Bit 15..............................0

Logically addressed as individual bytes.

00000000   11111111

Increasing Addresses

Low byte

High byte

11111111   Bit 7.....0

00000000   Bit 15...8

* **16-bit memory is shown in this figure, but other native word sizes are used in many microcomputers.**

For the Intel architecture, memory is physically organized as 16-bit words—as shown on the left in the figure. Notice that the most significant byte of the word is at the higher address. Because an object is addressed by its first byte in memory, the bytes of the word are effectively reversed in memory. This word order is called "little-endian" storage because the addressed byte contributes the least to the word value.

Other architectures, such as that of the Motorola 68000-series micro-processors, are referred to as "big-endian" because the high-order byte is the first byte of the object. Our C programs must be written so as to eliminate considerations of byte order. Problems occur most often when we try to move data to a machine with a different architecture. The portability sections of this book describe issues such as byte order and offer suggestions on how to avoid portability problems in your programs.

Keywords

The following tokens are reserved as C language keywords. They cannot be used for any purposes other than those specified by the standard. Keywords must be typed entirely in lowercase letters.

You will encounter these keywords in groups and individually throughout the remainder of this book. Each is explained in an appropriate context and used in example programs.

auto	double	int	struct
break	else	long	switch
case	enum	register	typedef
char	extern	return	union
const	float	short	unsigned
continue	for	signed	void
default	goto	sizeof	volatile
do	if	static	while

Identifiers

An identifier is a sequence of characters (a token) that denotes an object, a function, or various other elements of C programs. An identifier consists of letters (a through z and A through Z), digits (0 through 9), and underscores (_). It must start with a letter or an underscore to distinguish it from a number.

Although the length of identifiers is not specifically limited by the standard, each implementation is permitted to place limits on internal and external names. An internal name is one that has no external linkage; an external name has external linkage. External linkage refers to the means by which names in different program modules are made to refer to the same object or function.

Each internal name must be unique in no less than the first 31 characters and letter case *is* significant. External names may be limited to uniqueness in as few as six characters and it is possible for an implementation to ignore letter case. The C standards will likely be revised in the future to do away with this serious limitation on external names and other archaic practices that linger in some environments.

Here are some valid, unique identifiers for use as internal names:

```
number              Width            error_count
col                 ValidResponse    BufferModified
NumberOfAttempts    __attr__         row
```

The following identifiers satisfy the requirements for external names, such as function names:

```
clrscr       getcol       push
home         page         npages
```

The following function names would be treated as identical on a system that enforces a six-character limit and case insensitivity on external names because they all begin with the same characters in the significant positions:

```
GetWinHeight()      GetWinWidth()      getwinbuffer()
```

Names that begin with a digit or contain any characters other than those specified may produce error messages or unexpected results. Table 3-4 lists some examples of invalid identifiers.

Table 3-4: Invalid Identifiers	
IDENTIFIER	PROBLEM
`amount$`	Contains an illegal character ($)
`31flavors`	Starts with a digit
`max-min`	Not an identifier—subtracts min from max
`float`	C keyword

You could use the identifier `Float` as an internal name in a program because the initial capital F distinguishes the name from the keyword `float`. This practice, however, is discouraged.

Variables

A variable is an object that has a name and an amount of storage that is determined by its data type. The name can be any valid identifier. It is possible to use the same name for different objects as long as no conflict is produced. Conflicts are resolved by scoping rules that we'll discuss later.

Every variable must be declared before being used in a program. A declaration tells the compiler that a variable will be used and what its data type is. You can give a variable an initial value at the time it is declared. The value of a variable is usually subject to change during the running of a program unless it is qualified by the keyword `const`.

Choose the name of each variable with care. A name should be indicative of the purpose of the variable in your program to help you and others who read your programs. An object with a long name is no more space-consuming than one with a short name. The amount of memory used by an object is determined by its type.

Basic Types

C has a small, but comprehensive set of basic types that are closely tied to the dominant machine architectures. The type of an expression determines the meaning of a value that is stored in an object or returned by a function. There are three main categories of types:

- Object types—types that describe objects

- Function types—types that describe functions

- Incomplete types—types that describe objects without providing object size information

We will examine function and incomplete types in later chapters. Among the object types, the bulk are referred to as basic types, and these are the focus of this chapter. Notice that C's typing mechanism is very general, referring not just to data objects, but to functions and expressions as well.

Table 3-5 summarizes the basic types. Other types are derived from these.

Table 3-5: Basic Types

TYPE SPECIFIER	DESCRIPTION
`char`	Plain character
`signed char`	Signed character
`unsigned char`	Nonnegative character
`short int`	Short integer
`int`	Plain integer (usually machine register size)
`long int`	Long integer
`unsigned short int`	Nonnegative short integer
`unsigned int`	Nonnegative integer
`unsigned long int`	Nonnegative long integer
`float`	Single-precision floating point
`double`	Double-precision floating point
`long double`	Extended precision floating point

Now let's examine each of the basic types in detail and see how they are used in C programs.

Character

The `char` type specifies a "plain" character. Whether a plain character is signed or unsigned (more precisely, nonnegative) is implementation-defined. Historically, most implementations have treated the plain character as a signed entity, while others have treated it as unsigned.

A character variable can hold the value of any member of the native character set. In such a case, the value is guaranteed to be positive.

You declare a character object by using the following notation:

```
char c;      /* declare a plain character variable */
```

The keyword `char` establishes the type of the object and the identifier, `c`, provides a convenient name for the object. You can use any valid identifier for the name.

The semicolon following the variable name is a statement terminator, a required component of a declaration statement and most other C language statements. The in-line comment describes the purpose of the statement. Comments are optional, of course, but they are an important part of a program if they are written carefully and kept current as program changes are made.

Once you have declared a suitable variable, you can give it a value. This task is usually accomplished by using an assignment statement. A single equal sign is a C operator that assigns the value of an expression on the right side, into the object on the left side.

The following assignment statement places the value of the character A into the variable `c`.

```
c = 'A';     /* assign the character A to c */
```

The next statement "prints" the value stored in the variable `c` as a character on the standard output, which is usually the user's terminal or a console screen. The term "print" is used loosely to mean *print* on hard-copy devices or *display* on video output devices.

```
putchar(c); /* print the value of c */
```

If you had tried to print the character before assigning a value to it, the output would have been erroneous, an undefined value left over from whatever occupied memory before the variable declaration. A variable declaration doesn't automatically alter the contents of memory except in situations that we'll discuss in later chapters.

Character Constants

The expression 'A' is called a character constant. It yields the internal code (a number) that represents the letter A in the character set.

It is not important for you to know the actual code. Indeed, it may be better that you not know so that you won't be tempted write programs that are not portable. It is sufficient to know that the code for A in the ASCII character set is not the same as the code for A in the EBCDIC character set, for example, and to avoid code that depends on 'A' being a particular value. EBCDIC is the Extended Binary-Coded Interchange Code, an eight-bit code used primarily on IBM mainframe systems.

Don't be confused by differences between numeric values and character values. In ASCII, for example, the numeric value 0 represents the null character (NUL). The ASCII value of the character constant '0' is 48 decimal—a long way from numeric zero.

String Literals

A string literal (or string constant) is a double-quoted sequence of characters. The double quotes delimit the string, but are not part of it. The sequence of characters may be empty.

Here are some examples:

```
"This string is not empty."
""    /* this one is! */
```

A string literal is stored as an array of characters. Once again, an array is a contiguous collection of objects of the same type. The array contains each of the characters in the string literal plus a terminating null character that marks the end.

You can concatenate (join) two or more string literals by simply placing them next to each other. Thus, the adjacent string literals:

```
"Wanna buy " "a used watch?"
```

look the same to a standard C compiler as:

```
"Wanna buy a used watch?"
```

Be careful. String literals and character constants are different. Using double quotes to form a string literal that contains a single character, say "Z", produces an array of two characters (Z and a null character). This is quite different from the character constant 'Z' (single quotes), which is an integer value that represents the letter Z in the machine's character set.

Escape Sequences

Letters, digits, and punctuation characters each have a graphic (visible) representation and can be used directly in character constants and string literals. Several important characters have a formatting effect or other purpose, but have no visible appearance, and some cannot be typed directly. We use escape sequences to give such characters form.

For example, you can use \t to represent a tab character. The backslash (\) introduces an escape sequence. The following character or sequence of characters takes on a special meaning. An escaped letter t symbolizes a tab, whereas the unescaped letter t represents itself. Table 3-6 lists all of the escape sequences.

Table 3-6: Escape Sequences	
ESCAPE SEQUENCE	**DESCRIPTION (ASCII NAME)**
\n	Newline (NL)
\t	Horizontal tabulation (HT)
\v	Vertical tabulation (VT)

Table 3-6: Escape Sequences

ESCAPE SEQUENCE	DESCRIPTION (ASCII NAME)
\b	Backspace (BS)
\r	Carriage return (CR)
\f	Form feed (FF)
\a	Alert/Bell (BEL)
\'	Single quotation mark
\"	Double quotation mark
\?	Question mark
\\	Backslash
\octal digits	Octal integer
\xhex digits	Hexadecimal integer

The most commonly used escape sequence is \n, the new-line character. It appears frequently in `printf()` and `putchar()` statements to force line formatting in text output.

You can use escape sequences in both character constants and string literals. To print a lone new-line character, you can use the statement:

```
putchar('\n');
```

and to print a line of text you can use a statement like:

```
printf("This is a line of text.\n");
```

You can't put a new-line character into a string literal in a source by pressing the Return key because that has the effect of starting a new line in the source file, not in the string literal. You can use escape sequences of octal or hexadecimal digits to create bit patterns. For example, \7 and \x7 are, respectively, octal and hexadecimal escape sequences for the ASCII bell (BEL) character. A portable way of ringing the terminal bell is to use the "alert" escape sequence, \a, which is not tied to any particular character set.

As noted earlier, you can use \0 to represent the null character. Any other code in the character set can also be represented by a backslash and from one to three octal digits. You can also use a hexadecimal escape sequence to represent any character. For example, \xEF represents the ASCII delete (DEL) character.

Integers

The integers are whole number (counting) types that come in both signed and unsigned varieties. The plain integer type is typically the size of the machine's native register or word size. Except for signed char, the keyword signed is assumed, but it can be stated explicitly. Thus signed short int and short int are synonymous.

A short int (or simply short for short) has a range of values that is a subrange of those provided by the int type. The int type has, in turn, a range that is a subrange of the long int (or simply long for short). The same range hierarchy applies to the unsigned integer varieties.

On a given machine, int may have the same size as either a short or a long. For example, on an IBM PC or compatible (16-bit architecture), an int and a short have the same size. On Intel 80286/386-based machines (32-bit architecture), int is the same size as long.

Each of the signed integer types has a corresponding unsigned integer type that has the same size and range, but different maximum and minimum values. The unsigned types hold only nonnegative values.

Printing Integer Data

The program **ints** (the source is in the file **int.c**) shows how to declare integer variables, assign values to them, and print the values of those variables. The variables are declared as plain integers (type int).

```
/*
 * ints.c
 *
 * Print a string that includes variables using a printf().
 */
```

```
#include <stdio.h>
#include <stdlib.h>

main()

{
      /* data declarations */
      int num1, num2;

      /* assign values to variables */
      num1 = 5;
      num2 = 11;

      /* print a description of the numbers */
      printf("Values: num1 = %d and num2 = %d.\n", num1, num2);

      return EXIT_SUCCESS;
}
```

The data declarations of num1 and num2 reserve two plain integer-sized chunks of memory for the variables. The assignment statements provide values for the variables.

The printf() function prints a message that can contain both fixed and variable parts. The printf() function takes at least one argument, a format string that can contain literal text and optional conversion specifiers. Any literal text is printed unchanged. Each conversion specifier determines how a subsequent argument is to be converted.

Integer Conversion Specifiers

The %d character pair used in this example is a conversion specifier. The percent sign is an introducer. It is followed by a conversion character, d, which calls for its companion argument to be printed as a decimal (base 10) number.

In the example program, there are two conversion specifiers. Each requires one additional argument to printf() to provide the value to be converted. Therefore, this function call has a total of three arguments: the format string and two integer values.

Table 3-7 summarizes the basic integer conversion specifiers and their purposes.

CONVERSION CHARACTER	DESCRIPTION
Table 3-7: Integer Conversion Specifiers.	
c	Convert an integer to an unsigned character.
d, i	Convert an integer to a signed decimal.
u	Convert an unsigned integer to unsigned decimal notation.
o	Convert an unsigned integer to octal notation.
x, X	Convert an unsigned integer to hexadecimal notation.

The conversion characters shown in the table can be qualified by prefix characters. The optional prefix h applied to any of the integer conversion characters except c specifies that the conversion specifier applies to a short int or unsigned short int argument. Similarly, the optional prefix l specifies that the conversion specifier applies to long int or unsigned long int argument.

Because % is used as an introducer, we need a way to place a literal percent sign in a format string. Use %% to print a literal percent sign. The pair yields a percent sign as a component of a format string. No conversion takes place and therefore, no companion argument is needed.

Integer Constants

An integer constant has neither fractional part (hence no decimal point) nor exponent. It begins with a digit. Optional prefixes and suffixes specify an integer constants base (the default is 10) and type (the default is int).

The **ints** program contains some examples of integer constants. They are used in the assignment statements that provide values for the num1 and num2 variables. The value 5 in the assignment statement:

```
num1 = 5;
```

is a decimal integer constant.

You can express constant integral values as octal numbers by using a 0 (zero) prefix or as hexadecimal numbers by using a 0x prefix. So you could use 05 or 0x5 in place of the decimal 5 in the assignment.

To specify a long constant, apply an l (or L) suffix to the value. For example, 1000L is the constant value 1000 expressed as a long integer. To specify an unsigned integer constant, apply a u (or U) suffix to the value (Example: 345u). The long and unsigned suffixes can be used together to specify an unsigned long integer constant (example: 4096UL).

Strings

The printf() function accepts the conversion specifier %s in format strings. The %s conversion specifier requests an argument that is a **pointer** to an array of characters. A pointer is the address of an object or function. (See Chapter 7 for a detailed introduction to C pointers.)

The **strings** program (in source file **strings.c**) shows you how to declare, initialize, and print strings.

```
/*
 * strings.c
 *
 * Print character strings. Show how to handle literal
 * strings and strings that contain substitutions.
 */

#include <stdio.h>
#include <stdlib.h>

int
main(void)
{
        static char flower[] = { "rose" };
        static char color[] = { "yellow" };

        printf("1. What's in a name?.\n");
        printf("2. I would like to buy a single %s, please.\n",
```

```
        flower);
    printf("3. I would like to buy a dozen %ss.\n",


        flower);
    printf("4. This flower is a %s %s.\n", color, flower);
    printf("5. A %s by any other name is still a %s.\n",
        flower, flower);

    return EXIT_SUCCESS;
}
```

In the **string** program, two character arrays (`flower` and `color`) are used to hold the two strings. Don't be overly concerned about the declaration and initialization of the variables at this point. We'll examine the use of the `static` storage class keyword, arrays, and braces around the initializer (the string literal in this case) in later chapters. The first declaration:

```
static char flower[] = { "rose" };
```

creates an array of five characters: 'r', 'o', 's', 'e', and '\0'. Similarly, the second declaration creates a seven-character array. These two "strings" are used in all but one of the program's print statements.

The first `printf()` contains a string literal (the format string) and no other arguments. The statement prints literal text with no substitutions because there are no conversion specifiers.

The second `printf()` statement contains a single string substitution that inserts the value of the variable flower into the otherwise fixed text of the format string. The next statement does the same thing with modified text that shows how the `%s` conversion specifier can be tightly embedded in other text without confusing the compiler.

You are not limited to a single string substitution; as you can see in the fourth and fifth `printf()` statements. Multiple string arguments can be mixed any way you like. You can even use the same argument more than once in an argument list.

Floating Types

So far we have dealt only with integral types. Numbers that are encountered often in scientific, engineering, statistical, and other fields are also important. They are real numbers, which are represented in C as floating-point numbers.

The exact internal representation of a floating-point number is not specified by the standard. Each implementation is free to choose its own representation. Many implementations use the IEEE-standard floating-point format, but this is not a universal choice. The IEEE (Institute of Electrical and Electronics Engineers, Inc.) is an international professional organization that, among other things, is involved in creating and promulgating standards.

The floating-point types include `float`, `double`, and `long double`. What varies among these types is the **precision** with which a particular value can be expressed, where precision is a function of the number of significant digits used to represent the value.

The floating-point type hierarchy parallels that of integers. The set of `float` (single precision) values is a subset of `double` (double precision) values, which are, in turn, a subset of `long double` (extended precision) values. In a given implementation, all floating-point types can have the same precision, but `double` cannot have a precision that is less than that of `float` nor greater than that of `long double`.

✍**Programmer's Notebook**

Some existing C programs may contain the obsolete long float type as a synonym for double. Such programs must be rewritten to use double as a type specifier.

Printing Floating-Point Data

To print a floating-point value, you can use `printf()` with a conversion specifier that indicates how the printed value is to be formatted. You have complete control over the printed or displayed presentation of data. For each data item to be printed, provide a conversion specifier and a companion value argument.

The **float** program (the source is in **float.c**) shows how to declare floating-point variables, assign values to them, and print them in various ways. Observe the conversion specifiers in the print statements and then read the details following the source listing.

```
/*
 * float.c
 *
 * Print floating-point (real) data values.
 */

#include <stdio.h>
#include <stdlib.h>

int
main()
{
        /* data declarations */
        float f_var;
        double d_var;

        /* assign values to variables */
        f_var = 106.11;
        d_var = -0.0000654;

        /* print data values in a variety of ways */
        printf("Variable f_var = %.2f\n", f_var);
        printf("Variable d_var = %.10lf\n", d_var);
        printf("Variable f_var = %e\n", f_var);
        printf("Variable d_var = %G\n", d_var);

        return EXIT_SUCCESS;
}
```

This program uses one single-precision variable, f_var, and one double-precision variable, d_var. The conversion specifiers used in the `printf()` statements look a bit more complicated that those we have seen thus far. Let's see what the extra items are and why they are used.

Floating-Point Conversion Specifiers

The general form of a conversion specifier contains two required elements and several optional elements. For now, we are concerned only with the elements of a floating-point conversion specifier.

A conversion specifier has the following form:

`%[flags][width][.precision]type`

The `%` introducer and the `type` are required elements of a conversion specifier. The elements shown inside square brackets are optional. The brackets indicate the optional nature of the enclosed elements, but you don't type the brackets in specifiers.

The `type` element is composed of at least one single letter from Table 3-8 indicating the requested representation. These conversion letters apply to float and double types.

Table 3-8: Type Conversion Letters	
CONVERSION CHARACTER	**DESCRIPTION**
`f`	Generate a signed fractional representation of the value without an exponent. Form: [-]d.dddd
`e (or E)`	Generate a signed fractional representation of the value with an exponent. Form: [-]d.dddde[sign]ddd
`g (or G)`	Generate a signed fractional representation of the value either with or without an exponent.

The g conversion character generates the more compact format (f or e) for a given magnitude and precision. If you use the G conversion character, the specifier generates either an f or an E representation.

If the value argument is a long double type, use the l (or L) type qualifier as a prefix to the conversion character. For example, %LE specifies a long double fractional representation with an exponent.

The optional elements of a conversion specifier give you additional control over the appearance of data items in print statements. The flags element that follow the % consists of zero or more characters. Its characters are listed in Table 3-9.

Table 3-9: Flag Characters

FLAG CHARACTER	DESCRIPTION
- (minus sign)	Left justify the result of a conversion.
+ (plus sign)	Prefix a plus sign for signed values that are positive.
(space)	Prefix a space for signed values that do not carry either a plus sign or a minus sign.
#	Prefix a conversion result with 0 (octal), 0x, or 0X (hexadecimal), or coerce a decimal point in a floating conversion that has no fractional part.
0 (zero digit)	If there is no other padding, pad a conversion with leading zeros following any sign or prefix.

An optional **width** is either a number or an asterisk (*). If it is a number, it specifies the minimum number of characters to generate for a conversion, padding on the left with spaces unless a flag alters this behavior. If an asterisk is used, an integer argument provides the width value and an optional sign.

You can also provide an optional precision (a decimal point followed by a number or an asterisk). If you fail to provide a number or an asterisk, the precision is taken to be zero. If you provide a number, it specifies one of the conversion characters listed in Table 3-10.

Table 3-10: Conversion Characters' Precision Values	
CONVERSION CHARACTER	**PRECISION MEANING**
d, i, etc.	The minimum number of digits to generate.
f, e, or E	The number of fraction digits to generate.
g or G	The maximum number of significant digits to generate.
s	The maximum number of characters to generate for the converted string.

If the precision value is an asterisk, the precision value is provided by an integer argument. If the argument is negative, the precision is taken to be zero.

Storage Requirements and Value Ranges

The **<limits.h>** and **<float.h>** headers document all sizes and limits of a conforming implementation. Integral type values are specified in **<limits.h>** and floating-point type values are specified in **<float.h>**.

These headers contain various symbolic constants that specify such items as the number of bits in a byte, the minimum and maximum values of each type, and so on. You may find it instructive to look at the contents of these headers on your system.

Table 3-11 is an example of the sizes in bytes and the ranges of each of the basic types. The exact numbers may be different on your system. The table is a good reflection of the situations found in most microcomputer C implementations.

Table 3-11: Basic Type Sizes		
TYPE	**BYTES**	**RANGE**
char	1	Either -128 to 127 or 0 to 255 (NOTE 1)
signed char	1	-128 to 127

Table 3-11: Basic Type Sizes

TYPE	BYTES	RANGE
int	(NOTE 2)	
short int	2	-32,768 to 32,767
long int	4	-2,147,482,648 to 2,147,482,647
unsigned char	1	0 to 255
unsigned int	(NOTE 2)	
unsigned short	2	0 to 65,535
unsigned long	4	0 to 4,294,962,295
float	4 (IEEE)	+/- 3.4E-38 to 3.4E+38+/- 1.7E-308 to 1.7E+308 (approx. 7-digit precision)
double	8 (IEEE)	+/- 1.7E-308 to 1.7E+308 (approx. 15-digit precision)
long double	(NOTE 3)	

NOTE 1: The range of the plain `char` type is implementation defined and can be either signed or unsigned. When storing a character of the source character set, the value is guaranteed to be positive.

NOTE 2: The integer types, `int` and unsigned `int`, are implementation-defined. In a typical 16-bit environment, they are equivalent to the `short` and unsigned `short` types. In a 32-bit environment, they are equivalent to the `long` and un-signed `long` types. In no case is `int` smaller than `short` or larger than `long`.

NOTE 3: The extended precision `long double` is a new type that is implementation-defined. Most current C implementations use the `double` semantics, but syntactically `long double` is a distinct type.

Data Input

Most programs, except those that are non-interactive, require some way of getting input from the user. The input routines described in this section

are analogs of the `printf()`, `puts()`, and other output routines described earlier in this chapter.

First, let's take a look at means of reading text strings from the
keyboard. Then we'll see how we can read numbers as well as text.

Reading Text Strings

In Chapter 2, the **greet2** and **greet3** programs read your name from the
keyboard and personalized a message. They used `gets()` to read your
input into a buffer (an array of characters) from which the data can be
read by other routines, such as `printf()`.

The `gets()` macro reads a line of text from its standard input (`stdin`),
which is the user's keyboard unless redirection is used. Under both UNIX
and DOS, you can redirect input by using the < symbol.

A **line** is a sequence of zero or more characters and a new-line character
(\n). After reading the line, `gets()` replaces the new-line character with
a null character (\0), that conveniently creates a string. If you expect
your program to receive a string of up to 20 characters, for example, you
must allocate a character array buffer of at least 21 characters to guarantee that there is enough room to hold the string's characters and the
terminating null character.

Numeric Data as Strings

It may not be immediately apparent, but when you type a number on your
keyboard, you are actually typing a character string. The number 32, for
example, is actually the text characters '3' and '2', followed by the null
character.

You cannot assign the string that represents the number to an integer
variable. The string must first be converted to integer form. This is the
purpose of the `atoi()` library function. This function takes a single
argument, which is a pointer to the string, and returns an integer value.
The name of the character array serves as the needed string pointer (the
address of the array's first element)—a potentially confusing feature of C
that we'll discuss at length in later chapters.

The **readnum** program is a straightforward example of the process of
reading numbers from the keyboard. Two variables are used. The first

variable, `buffer`, is an array of six characters (five for the largest valid
number plus one for the null character). The second variable is `number`,
the integer that receives the converted value from `atoi()`.

Here is the content of the **readnum.c** source file:

```
/*
 * readnum.c
 *
 * Read a number from the keyboard and print
 * it on the screen.
 */

#include <stdio.h>
#include <stdlib.h>

#define NDIGITS 5

main()
{
        /* data declarations */
        char buffer[NDIGITS + 1];
        int number;

        /* prompt the user for a number and read it */
        printf("Enter a whole number and press ENTER: ");
        gets(buffer);
        number = atoi(buffer);

        /* print the number typed by the user */
        printf("\n The number you typed is %d.\n", number);

        return EXIT_SUCCESS;
}
```

Observe the two-step process used in this program to read a single
value: 1) read the string typed by the user and save it in a buffer; 2) convert
the saved string to an integer and store the result in an integer variable.

Numeric Data and scanf()

You can combine the storage and conversion actions into a single action by using the scanf() function, which is the input analog of the printf() output function.

It is a bit dangerous to use scanf() to gather user input because the function was designed to read machine-formatted data. A user can deliberately or unwittingly provide inappropriate inputs that cause your program to act unpredictably. If safety is a concern, you'll want to use better, but decidedly more complicated, input mechanisms that check the input and that provide helpful feedback to the user.

The following program, **get_real**, shows how to use scanf() to read a floating-point number from the standard input. As written, this program will fail ignominiously when challenged by bad input.

```
/*
 *  get_real.c
 *
 *  Prompt the user for a real number and display it
 *  in scientific notation to three decimal places.
 */

#include <stdio.h>
#include <stdlib.h>

main()
{
    float number;

    printf("Real-number input: ");
    scanf("%f", &number);
    printf("\n number = %.3f\n", number);

    return EXIT_SUCCESS;
}
```

The `scanf()` function requires a format string just like `printf()`. It too uses conversion specifiers to identify additional arguments and specify the requested conversions. There is a significant difference, however.

Each of the optional arguments must be a *pointer* to an object that receives the conversion result. In the float program, the object that receives the numeric input is `number` and the pointer to it is obtained by applying the `&` operator to the object's name (`&number`). Accept this at face value for now. We will discuss pointers and indirection in detail in later chapters and show why pointers are required by `scanf()`.

✍**Programmer's Notebook**

If the object used as a buffer is an array, the name of the array is already a pointer to the beginning of the array, so you do not need to use the & operator.

Summary

Types in C apply to objects and expressions, including function returns. A set of basic types mirror the architectures of most modern computer systems. Additional types can be derived from the basic types.

The standard library provides a wealth of input and output routines (both functions and macros). You have been introduced to a small set of standard input/output routines that will serve to get you started. The versatile conversion specifiers give you a great amount of flexibility in data input and output.

We've covered a lot of ground in this chapter, yet there is still much to say about C types and data input and output. In later chapters, you will learn about storage class specifiers and type qualifiers, we will pay more than lip service to the topics of error detection and correction, and we will develop better ways of gathering user input.

Questions and Exercises

1. Identify the three major types of memory and the advantages and disadvantages of each.

2. What is the range of values of an individual bit? What are these values?

3. What is the range of values of two bits? Express these values in decimal form.

4. Convert the following octal values to their decimal counterparts:

   ```
   \0
   01
   06
   10
   12
   ```

5. How are octal numbers distinguished from decimal numbers in C expressions?

6. Convert the following hexadecimal values to their decimal counterparts:

   ```
   0x0
   0X1
   0x6
   0x8
   0XA
   0Xa
   0xC
   0xF
   ```

7. How are hexadecimal numbers distinguished from decimal numbers in C language?

8. What is the equivalent decimal value of this 16–bit word (the most significant bit is on the left)?

   ```
   0010010101000100
   ```

9. What restrictions are placed on C keywords and how can you type them?

10. Which of these identifiers can be used as internal names:

```
junk         yin-yang       sizeof
number       ExtendLine     %seed
4win         Nextpage       CA$H
```

11. Write six identifiers that can be used as external names.

12. Explain what the following C code does in a program:

```
char c;
c = 'D'
putchar(c)
```

13. Why would portability suffer if programs depended on a character constant being a certain number?

14. How are string literals and character constants different? How do you tell them apart?

15. What do escape sequences allow you to do?

16. List the types of integers described in this chapter, and what they are.

17. Why are conversion specifiers used ?

18. What conversion specifier is used in the `printf()` control string to indicate that the argument is to be printed as a string. How does it access the string?

19. What are the three floating-point types? How do they differ?

20. Explain the purpose of the `<limits.h>` and `<float.h>` headers.

21. How many elements must a character array buffer contain in relation to an expected input string?

    a. Two characters more than the maximum expected string size.
    b. The maximum size of the input string, plus one character.
    c. The maximum number of expected input characters.
    d. Size need not be specified.

22. What does the `atoi()` function do?

23. What library function can you use to combine storage and conversion actions into one? Why can use of this function be dangerous?

Additional Exercises

A. Rewrite the **strings.c** program to use three character arrays and additional `printf()` statements. Add comments to describe the operation of the program.

B. Write a program containing a `printf()` statement that involves a mixture of integers, strings, and characters, and which prints them out in some meaningful way. Be sure to use appropriate conversion specifiers in the control string.

C. Rewrite **strings.c** to employ floating-point numbers, using various types and identifiers in the `printf()` statements, as well as character arrays. Be prepared to explain how the program works.

CHAPTER 4

EXPRESSIONS AND STATEMENTS

Having learned about variables and constants, two of the lexical elements of C programs, you will now learn how to combine variables and constants with operators in order to create expressions. You will also learn how to create statements, the stuff of which functions and programs are made.

Introduction

Let's begin with an introduction to operators, expressions, and statements. Following that, we will examine the rich set of C operators and see how they are used to form expressions and statements. Several demonstration programs will show you examples of how the operators are used.

C Operators

C offers an extensive set of operators that you use to assign values, connect and compare objects, access objects indirectly, and do numerous other jobs. We refer to the manipulated objects as **operands**.

The assignment operator is one that we have already used a number of times. It is symbolized by the equal sign (=). The assignment operator takes two operands. Like most other C operators, assignment takes two operands. As we will see shortly, C also has several operators that take only one operand, and one that has three operands.

Expressions

Combinations of operators and operands create **expressions**. An expression performs a calculation and produces a result, or causes some action (called a side effect) to occur. In fact, you can use expressions to specify combinations of these tasks and, in more advanced applications, you can use expressions to designate objects or functions.

In general, the order in which expressions are evaluated is not specified, except as noted below. Therefore, neither is the order in which side effects occur specified. This language design permits compiler writers to take advantage of the behavior of a particular translating or execution environment. It also means that you should write your code in a way that avoids dependence on evaluation order to gain easy portability to a wide range of environments.

Evaluation order is specified by expression syntax (operator precedence) in expressions involving function calls, some logical operators, and the conditional operator. As these topics are covered in the material that follows, evaluation-order details are described.

The behavior of a C program is undefined if the evaluation of an expression produces a mathematically undefined or out-of-range result. The failure to produce a defined, in-range result from an expression evaluation is called an **exception**.

Statements

A statement specifies an action. Statements are generally executed in the order in which they are encountered within a program. However, the order of execution can be altered by statements that transfer control, either to other parts of a program, or outside the program.

A C statement takes one of several forms. The essential C statement is an expression followed by a semicolon and is classified as an expression statement. The semicolon is a statement terminator in C. The following list identifies the syntax of C statements that make up C functions and programs:

- Labelled statement

- Compound statement

- Expression statement

- Selection statement

- Iteration statement

- Jump statement

The expression statement syntax is of primary interest in this chapter. The selection, iteration, jump, and labelled statements are covered in detail in Chapter 5.

A **compound statement**, which is also called a block, is a mechanism that groups a collection of statements into a single syntatic unit. Blocks can be nested and each can contain its own data declarations and initializations in addition to executable statements.

C Operators

As noted earlier, some operators take only a single operand. We call these operators **unary operators**. Most of the C operators take two operands and are, therefore, called **binary operators**. One C operator, the conditional operator, takes three operands and is called a **ternary operator**.

We further classify operators by the types of actions they perform. In the following sections of this chapter, I group operators into the following categories:

- Assignment

- Arithmetic

- sizeof

- Relational

- Logical

- Bitwise

- Increment and decrement

- Shift

- Address and indirection

The descriptions of these categories of operators are illustrated by program fragments and complete sample programs.

Operator Precedence

When an expression involves more than a single operator, the expression is potentially ambiguous, in the order of evaluation result. You can require a particular evaluation order by grouping subexpressions with parentheses. The expression:

```
x + y * z
```

is ambiguous because the result will be different if the compiler does the addition (x + y) first and the multiplication (y * z) second rather than the other way around.

C has a built-in precedence mechanism that makes sense in most situations, eliminating the need for parentheses unless you want something other than the default behavior. Table 4-1 is the C operator precedence chart. You may want to copy the chart onto a sheet of paper and place it near your operating position for ready reference.

Table 4-1: Operator Precedence and Associativity		
OPERATOR	**DESCRIPTION**	**ASSOCIATIVITY**
( ) [ ] -> .	Function call Array index Structure pointer Structure member	Left to right

Table 4-1: Operator Precedence and Associativity

OPERATOR	DESCRIPTION	ASSOCIATIVITY
- + ++ -- ! ~ * & sizeof (type)	Unary minus Unary plus Increment Decrement Logical negation Bitwise complement Indirection Address Object size Type cast (explicit conversion)	Right to left
* / %	Multiplication Division Modulus	Left to right
+ -	Addition Subtraction	Left to right
<< >>	Shift left Shift right	Left to right
< <= > >=	Less than Less than or equal Greater than Greater than or equal	Left to right
== !=	Equal Not equal	Left to right
&	Bitwise AND	Left to right
	Bitwise XOR	Left to right
|	Bitwise OR	Left to right
&&	Logical AND	Left to right
||	Logical OR	Left to right

Table 4-1: Operator Precedence and Associativity		
OPERATOR	**DESCRIPTION**	**ASSOCIATIVITY**
?:	Conditional	Right to left
= += -+ *= /+ %= &= |= ^= <<= >>=	Assignment	Right to left
, (comma)	Sequence	Left to right

Operators that appear near the top of the precedence chart have higher precedence than those nearer the bottom and are said to bind their operands *tightly*. The highest precedence category includes function calls, array indexing, structure member selection, and structure pointer operators.

All operators within the same level in the chart (indicated by a boxed region) have the same precedence. The sequence operator, also known as the comma operator, (',') and most assignment operators rank near the low end of the precedence hierarchy, and therefore, have the lowest precedence and bind least tightly.

If you want to force an expression to be evaluated by the compiler in a certain way, use parentheses to group operands the way you want them. In an unparenthesized expression such as the one shown on page 69, C's precedence mechanism forces the multiplication to be done before the addition, so you would achieve the same effect if you type:

```
a + (b * c) /* do multiplication first */
```

This is an admitted contrived example because the default evaluation is to multiply first, then add. But it doesn't hurt to show exactly what you want, and the parentheses don't slow down the running of your program or affect it in any other way.

If you want the addition to be done first, you must force the compiler to do so by parenthesizing the addition:

```
(a + b) * c /* do the addition first */
```

Use parentheses liberally to show your intentions. You and others who might read or maintain your code in the future will benefit from the extra effort you put into it when you first write it.

The Assignment Operator

The primary C assignment operator is the equal sign ('='). To assign the value 50 into an integer storage location, num, you first declare that num is an integer and then write an assignment statement:

```
int num;
...
num = 50;
```

The assignment operator causes the memory location associated with the variable identifier, num in this example, to contain the assigned value. Here, the value is obtained directly from a literal constant. The value can also be obtained from the evaluation of an expression or from the return value of a function call.

Assignment is low on the precedence hierarchy, so use parentheses if evaluation order is a consideration. Additional assignment operators are covered later in this chapter.

Arithmetic Operators

The arithmetic operators are familiar to anyone who has ever taken a math course or used a calculator. Table 4-2 summarizes the arithmetic operators.

Table 4-2: The Arithmetic Operators	
OPERATOR	DESCRIPTION
+	Addition
-	Subtraction
/	Division
*	Multiplication
-	Unary minus
+	Unary plus
%	Modulus (remainder)

Simple addition adds the values of the two operands, `val1` and `val2`, and produces a sum. You can use the sum in a higher level computation or assign the sum into another variable for later use.

In this example, the arithmetic statement:

```
total = val1 + val2;
```

is instructed to assign the sum into the total variable.

Figure 4-1 shows how objects in memory are manipulated by some of the arithmetic operators. As you can see, the overall effect is to perform the computation represented by the operators in boxes in the figure and store the result in another memory location. It is also often the case that the result is stored back into one of the operands. The accumulator or some other register in the central processor or a temporary memory location is used to perform the computation.

Figure 4-1: Memory Manipulation

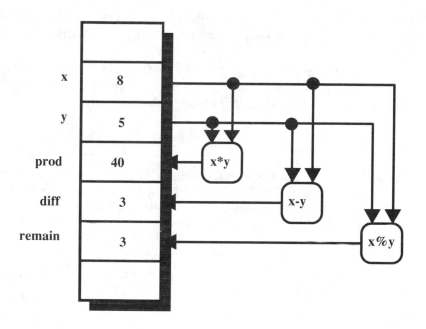

The figure shows the multiplication of two values, which would be coded as:

```
prod = x * y;
```

and the difference of the same two values, coded as:

```
diff = x - y;
```

Three additional arithmetic operators are shown in the table of arithmetic operators. Two of them use symbols that are identical to some we have already seen. What's going on here? The answer is that most arithmetic operators are binary operators, which means they take two operands. Two of the arithmetic operators are unary operators, having only a single operand.

The unary minus (-) operator changes the sign of an object without affecting its magnitude. Thus, given a variable x with a value of 4, -x has a value of -4.

The unary plus (+) operator is a new feature of C. The operator was added to give programmers a way to force a particular order of evaluation. The unary minus operator does not affect order of evaluation.

✍️**Programmer's Notebook**

The unary plus is supported syntactically, but not semantically by many current C compilers. Avoid writing code that depends on unary plus support if portability is a consideration.

The **modulus operator** (%), often called the remainder operator, yields the integer amount that remains following an integer division operation. In Figure 4-1, the statement:

```
remain = x % y;
```

describes the modulus computation. The expression 8 % 5 yields a result of 3 because 5 goes evenly into 8 once, producing a remainder of 3. Note that modulus operations are applicable only to integer operands.

You can use the modulus operator to keep numbers within a specified range of values. Given an unsigned integer, i, the expression:

```
i % 256
```

keeps the value of the expression within the range of 0 to 255, which is a safe range for an unsigned char variable. If you give the divisor a value of 2, the modulus operator tests the number to determine whether it is even or odd. Any number that is divisible evenly by 2 is even, which is indicated by a remainder of zero.

Data Conversions

A C translator must bring operands to a common type before doing a computation. The following list of arithmetic conversions describes the steps taken (order is significant) to obtain the required type before a binary operation is actually performed:

1. Operands of float type are converted to double type.

2. If one operand has long double type, the other operand is converted to long double type.

3. If one operand has double type, the other operand is converted to double type.

4. Any operands of char or short type are converted to int type.

5. Any operands of unsigned char or unsigned short type are converted to unsigned int type.

6. If one operand is of unsigned long type, the other operand is converted to unsigned long type.

7. If one operand is of long type, the other operand is converted to long type.

8. If one of the operands is of unsigned int type, the other operand is converted to unsigned int type.

The **DATACONV** program shows the effects of implicit and explicit data conversions. A set of declarations reserve storage for a character, two integers, and two floating-point variables. The program consists of a series of assignments and print statements. Here is the source:

```
/*
 * dataconv.c
 *
 * This program demonstrates implicit and explicit data
 * conversions in mixed-type expressions.
 */
```

```
#include <stdio.h>
#include <stdlib.h>

int
main(void)
{
        /* data declarations */
        char c;
        int i1, i2;
        float f1, f2;

        /* lost precision */
        i1 = 875;
        c = (char) i1;
        printf("Integer assigned to character: %d -> %d (%c)\n",
                i1, c, c);

        /* integer arithmetic */
        f1 = i1 / 10;
        printf("Integer arithmetic: %d / 10   = %f\n",
                i1, f1);

        /* floating-point arithmetic */
        f1 = i1 / 10.0;
        printf("Floating-point arithmetic: %d / 10.0 = %f\n\n",
                i1, f1);

        /* type promotion */
        f1 = 1.400660e+3;
        f2 = f1 + i1;
        printf("%f = %f + %d\n", f2, f1, i1);

        return EXIT_SUCCESS;
}
```

Using this source listing as a basis, the following observations give insight into how data conversions are done.

Loss of Precision

The statement:

```
c = i1;
```

assigns the value of i1, an integer, to c, a character variable. Precision is lost because i1 is represented by at least two bytes, and often more. The variable c is not that wide—it is represented by only one byte. When the assignment is made, all but the lowest eight bits are effectively thrown away, limiting the stored values to a range of 256 values. The program prints the resulting character value both as a decimal number (the code that represents the character in the character set) and as the character graphic that is printed or displayed.

   Although c is a char, it is implicitly widened to int when used in the printf() statement because the %d format specifier in the control string expects an integer. The compiler does this conversion for you, so you don't need to use a type cast.

Integer Arithmetic

When only integers are involved in an arithmetic calculation, such as shown by the expression f1 = i1 / 10, any fractional part of the result is truncated. The truncation occurs even if the result is assigned to a floating-point variable because the integer computation is performed before the assignment is made.

   To preserve the fractional component of a calculation, you must force one of the computation's operands to type float. You can do this job by casting it to type float or by providing a real number operand. In the example, the value 10.0 is a real number because it contains a decimal point. If the expression consists only of variables, one of them, as a minimum, must be of type float. You can also use a type cast, as in (float)#i1.

Promotion

The last example in the **DATACONV** program demonstrates how a variable might be promoted to another type when it is used in an expression. The C translator must bring values in a computation to a common type before performing the computation, so the integer i1, in the expression:

```
f2 = f2 + i1
```

is promoted to type float by the compiler before being added to f2. Similar conversions take place in expressions involving other related types.

The sizeof Operator

The sizeof operator is the only C operator that is represented by a name. It is neither a function nor a macro. The sizeof operator yields a value that indicates the size in bytes of a specified object.

The general form of a sizeof expression is:

```
sizeof expression
```

where expression is an identifier or a cast of a data type.

The purpose of sizeof is to give you a way of determining the sizes of various objects in a machine-independent way. In later chapters of this book covering arrays and structures, we will use sizeof to determine how large an object is and how many elements an array contains. Given this capability, you can write programs that are portable, barring the use of any other non-portable constructs.

If you want to know how many bytes are used to represent a particular data type, use a cast of the type as the expression, as in the following statements, which determine the size of an integer in the execution environment:

```
size_t bytes;
...
bytes = sizeof (int);
```

The parentheses around the int keyword are required in this case because it is a type cast. If you use sizeof on an ordinary identifier, the parentheses are not needed (although there is no harm in using them).

Relational Operators

Expressions involving the relational operators yield true (non-zero)/false (zero) results after comparing operands. See Table 4-3 for a listing of relational operators.

Table 4-3: The Relational Operators	
OPERATOR	**DESCRIPTION**
<	Less than
<=	Less than or equal
==	Equal
>=	Greater than or equal
>	Greater than
!=	Not equal

For example, if the variables m and n have values of 5 and 11 respectively, the relational expression m < n produces a true result, as do the expressions m <= n, and m != n. Expressions involving the other relational operators yield a false result for the given values.

✍**Programmer's Notebook**

CAUTION: Be sure to note that a double equal sign ("==") tests for equality. In Pascal, BASIC, and other languages, the single equal sign checks for equality. Attempting to use "=" instead of "==" to test for equality is a common C programming error.

Logical Operators

Expressions formed by using the relational operators of the previous section can be linked and modified in various ways in order to model the problem at hand. Compound logical expressions are formed by combining expressions with one or more of the logical operators shown in Table 4-4.

Table 4-4: The Logical Operators	
OPERATOR	**DESCRIPTION**
!	Logical NOT
&&	Logical AND
||	Logical OR

Use the ! operator to negate a logical expression. An expression that yields a true result yields a false result when preceded by the negation operator.

```
x == x       /* yields true result */
!(x == x)    /* yields a false result */
```

The logical connectives && and || are used to piece together compound logical expressions. ANDing two operands produces a true result only when both operands are true. ORing two operands produces a true result if either operand is true or if both operands are true.

Tables 4-5A, 4-5B, and 4-5C show the truth tables for these logical operators. The truth table for logical negation, a unary operator, has a single dimension. Those of the binary logical operators have an additional dimension for the second operand.

Table 4-5A: The Truth Table for Logical Negation		
LOGICAL NEGATION (!)	INITIAL OPERAND VALUE	
	FALSE	TRUE

Table 4-5A: The Truth Table for Logical Negation	
LOGICAL NEGATION	INITIAL OPERAND VALUE
NEGATED VALUE	TRUE FALSE

Table 4-5B: The Truth Table for Logical AND

Logical AND (&&)		RIGHT OPERAND	
		FALSE	TRUE
LEFT OPERAND	FALSE	FALSE	FALSE
	TRUE	FALSE	TRUE

Table 4-5C: The Truth Table for Logical OR

Logical OR (||)		RIGHT OPERAND	
		FALSE	TRUE
LEFT OPERAND	FALSE	FALSE	TRUE
	TRUE	TRUE	TRUE

Here are some examples. The logical connective operators have lower precedence than the relational operators, so the comparisons are performed before the logical connections are made.

```
int m = 20, n = 4;
int x = 2, y = 10;

m && n              /* true */
m > n && x < y      /* true */
m < n || x > y      /* false */
```

The precedence of the `&&` operator is higher than that of the `||` operator. You may need to use parentheses to force the desired order of evaluation in an expression that involves both operators.

The following expression is shown with and without parentheses to demonstrate the effect:

```
With:       (m > n || x > y) && m < x      /* false */
Without:    m > n || x > y && m < x        /* true */
```

Short-circuit Evaluation

In a compound expression containing logical connectives, if the result of the overall expression can be determined before the entire expression is evaluated, the remainder of the expression is not evaluated. Using the same assigned values for the variables as in the previous examples, in the expression:

```
m > n || x < y     /* true */
```

it is not necessary to evaluate $x < y$ because $m > n$ is true. An OR expression yields true if either operand is true, so C saves time by not evaluating the second expression (the right-hand operand of the OR expression) if the first is true. The result of the expression that represents the second operand cannot change the outcome of the logical expression.

Caution: If the unevaluated portions of a logical expression contains side effects, such as function calls or assignments, short-circuit evaluation can provide you with unpleasant surprises. For example, if the expression is:

```
m > n || x < ++y
```

the variable y would not be incremented because the expression:

```
i < ++y
```

is not evaluated (for the given values). If the value of m was less than or equal to n, the increment operation would occur. Portions of your program that depend on the value of y being incremented could be plagued by problems that are a bear to debug. You can easily avoid such problems by not trying to be clever. In addition to operating correctly, clearly written code that doesn't depend on subtle tricks is easy to read and maintain.

Bitwise Operators

C is both cursed and praised for having a low-level, assembly language feel. With the possible exception of pointers, bitwise operators probably contribute more to that attribute of C than any other feature of the language.

The bitwise operators give you access to machine registers and memory words at the bit level. They work with variables of integer data types. The bitwise operators are shown in Table 4-6.

Table 4-6: The Bitwise Operators	
OPERATOR	**DESCRIPTION**
&	Bitwise AND
|	Bitwise OR
	Bitwise exclusive OR
~	Bitwise complement

The result of an expression value depends on whether the values are being ANDed, ORed, exclusive-ORed, or complemented. The values of the operands are compared at the level of individual bits. Table 4-7 shows the relationships between bits for the bitwise exclusive OR. The other bitwise operations follow the pattern of the truth tables shown for logical operators except that we are now dealing with individual bits instead of entire words or bytes.

Table 4-7: The Bitwise Exclusive OR (XOR)			
Bitwise XOR (I)		**SECOND BIT OPERAND**	
		0	1
FIRST BIT OPERAND	0	0	1
	1	1	0

The operand types can differ. Automatic type conversions are done, if necessary, and the resulting type is that of the operand's after conversion. Therefore, bitwise-ANDing a character and an integer produces an integer result so that no bits of the wider object are lost.

In the following example, two values are bitwise-ANDed and -ORed. The comments show the binary equivalents of the hexadecimal values:

```
char result;

char b1 = 0x3C;    /* 00111100 */
char b2 = 0xF0;    /* 11110000 */

result = b1 & b2; /* 00110000 */
result = b1 | b2; /* 11111100 */
```

Because bitwise operators have lower precedence than relational operators, you need to use parentheses in expressions such as this:

```
(b1 & b2)  != b2
```

The bitwise AND operation takes place first, producing a value of 0x30, which is not equal to 0xF0, so the expression yields a true value.

Without the parentheses, the default operand grouping looks like this:

```
b1 &  (b2 != b2)
```

The result of the relational test is false, which is numerically 0. Bitwise ANDing 0 with anything produces 0, which you can think of as the number 0 or as a logically false condition.

The ~ operator is a unary operator that inverts the sense of each bit in its operand. Given the `char` variable b with a binary value of 01010101 (0x55), ~b has a value of 10101010 (0xAA).

The bitwise shift operators also operate at the bit level. The shift operators take two operands: the left operand is the item to be shifted and the right operand is the number of bit positions to shift. Both operands must be integral types. Table 4-8 shows the bitwise operators.

Table 4-8: The Bitwise Shift Operators	
OPERATOR	**DESCRIPTION**
<<	Shift left
>>	Shift right

The left-shift operator shifts bits to the left. Vacated positions on the right are filled with 0s. Bits shifted off the left end of a data item are lost.

✍**Programmer's Notebook**

The original operand is not disturbed by a shift operation unless the result of the shift is assigned back into the operand by some other means.

The right-shift operator (>>) shifts the bits of an object to the right by the specified number of positions. The filling of vacated bit positions on the left is machine-dependent and data-type dependent.

Most machines fill based on the data type of the shifted operand. If the data type is unsigned, for example, zero-fill is done. Signed operands are filled with 1s if the sign bit (the left–most bit) is 1 and with zeros if the sign bit is 0. Machines that use arithmetic shift always fill vacated positions on the left with zeros when data is right-shifted.

The second operand, which is the shift amount, must not be negative because the results are undefined. If you are using a variable as the shift amount, be sure that the value is non-negative and no larger than the size of the object being shifted.

Additional Assignment Operators

We have already used the simple assignment operator (=) in forming expressions. Assignment expressions have the following general form:

expr1 = expr1 op expr2

The expression on the left side of the assign occurs again on the right side. It isn't necessary to type the expression twice. The assignment can be represented in C by a shorter form:

expr1 op = expr2

The advantage of the second form is saved typing and less wasted space on the printed page or terminal screen. Table 4-9 shows a complete summary of the assignment operators.

Table 4-9: The Assignment Operators	
OPERATOR	**DESCRIPTION**
=	Assignment
+=	Addition assignment
-=	Subtraction assignment
*=	Multiplication assignment
/=	Division assignment
%=	Remainder assignment
<<=	Left-shift assignment
>>=	Right-shift assignment
&=	Bitwise-AND assignment
|=	Bitwise-inclusive-OR assignment
	Bitwise-exclusive-OR assignment

The mind-numbing collection of assignment operators may look a bit scary at first, but you will find that the notational convenience they offer outweighs the apparent awkwardness of the syntax. A few examples illustrate the form and utility of the special assignment operators:

```
int n, x = 10;
...
n += 3;      /* equivalent: n = n + 3; */
n *= x;      /* equivalent: n = n * x; */
n <<= 2;     /* equivalent: n = n << 2; */
```

If the participating expressions (n, x, etc.) are more complicated, having to type them only once is a benefit.

Increment and Decrement Operators

The incrementation and decrementation of a variable is a common occurrence in programs. Most machines have built-in instructions that do these operations quickly. C takes advantage of such instructions by providing special increment and decrement operators, which are shown in Table 4-10.

Table 4-10: The Increment and Decrement Operators

OPERATOR	DESCRIPTION
+	Increment
--	Decrement

The effect of the ++ operator is to add one to its operand. You have already seen two other ways to do the same thing. Here are three statements that do the same job:

```
count = count + 1;
count += 1;
++count;
```

They all cause `count` to have a value one greater than before the statement executes. When used in isolated statements as shown above, the operators can be placed before or after the operand to produce the same effect, as in the statement

`count++;`

There are circumstances, however, in which the position of the ++ or -- operator makes a difference.

Prefix and Postfix Notation

When an increment (or decrement) expression is involved in a larger expression context, the behavior is dependent upon the operator position. If the operator is used as a prefix, the value of its operand is incremented (or decremented) before being used in the enclosing expression. If the operator is used in the postfix position, the value of the operand is used as is in the enclosing expression and then the operand is incremented (or decremented).

Don't use the increment and decrement operators indiscriminately. Recall that in logical expressions, short-circuit evaluation might prevent an expression evaluation to be skipped. If the skipped expression involves an increment or decrement expression, you may encounter problems with variables being "off by one" sometimes and not at other times as a function of the logical evaluations. Avoid such tricky programming practices.

Address and Indirection Operators

C is noted for its elegant pointer mechanism. A **pointer** is a variable that contains the address of a variable or function, permitting indirect access to program data and code. In later chapters we will examine the topic of indirection and the use of pointers in detail. This information is provided here for completeness of the discussion of operators. The address and indirection operators are shown in Table 4-11.

Table 4-11: The Address and Indirection Operators	
OPERATOR	**DESCRIPTION**
&	Address of
*	Indirection

The & operator yields the memory address of its operand, producing a pointer to the object represented by the operand. The * operator, which is called the indirection or **dereferencing operator**, provides indirect access to an object through a previously defined pointer to the object. You will need to master the use of pointers if you want to become a capable C programmer.

Sequence Operator

The sequence operator (,) is often called the comma operator. The sequence operator uses the same symbol, but is different from the comma that separates entries in a function parameter list or a series of variables in a declaration or values in an initializer list. We'll see examples of these in later chapters.

The sequence operator is an enforcer. It sets the order of evaluation of expressions and is used in critical situations to guarantee that operations are performed in a specific sequence. The sequence operator has the lowest precedence of all the C operators. Examples of the sequence operator will be presented in example programs involving loops and collections of if statements that must be executed in a specified order.

Questions and Exercises

1. What is the purpose of a C operator?

2. What is an expression? If m and n are declared to be integers, is m – n a valid expression?

3. Give an example of an expression statement in C.

4. Name at least three other types of C statements.

5. Why is it necessary to have a precedence chart for C operators?

6. Write an expression in which operator precedence is ambiguous. Show the default evaluation by using parentheses around the subexpressions.

7. If two or more operators in an expression have the same precedence, what determines the order of evaluation of the expression?

8. In the following code fragment, what data conversions does the translator perform?

```
int offset;
unsigned long base, total;
...
total = base + offset;
```

9. If all of the variables in the following expression are integers, what values are stored in c and d?

```
a = 12;
b = 5;
c = a / b;
d = a % b;
```

10. True or false: sizeof is a C language standard library function.

11. Given the integer variables a equals 9 and b equals 3, indicate whether the following relational expressions are true (non-zero) or false (zero):

```
a   b
a = b
a == b
a != b
```

12. What is the results of the following expressions that involve logical connectives, given the variable declarations shown?

```
int a = 10, b = 3;
int c = 7, d = 20;
int result;
```

```
result = (a >= b) && (c < d);
result = (a < b) || (c <= d);
```

13. What is short-circuit evaluation of a logical expression? Write a statement that in shows how short-circuit evaluation works.

14. What binary bit patterns result from the following bitwise operations on the value bits = 0xF0?

```
bits > 4
bits & 0x2F
~bits
bits | 0x04
```

15. Rewrite the following assignment statement to eliminate the unnecessary duplication of the variable name:

```
count = count + delta;
```

16. In each of the following increment statements, what are the values of n and x after the statements are executed?

```
short n, x;
/* prefix */
n = 5;
x = ++n;
/* postfix */
n = 11;
x = n++;
```

Additional Exercises

A. Parenthesize the following expression to force all additions and subtractions to be done before any multiplications and divisions:

```
int i = 3, j = 5, k = 10;
int x;
x = i * k -j / i + j;
```

What is the value of x after the statement is executed?

B. Given the set of starting values for the participating variables, show the values of each variable following the execution of each statement. NOTE: The results are cumulative, so each statement depends on the results of all previous statement executions.

```
int a = 3, b = 7;
int i = 10, j = 6;
int x;
/* show variable values after statement execution */
x = (a   b--) && (i   j);
x = b == j;
x = (a   b) && (++i = j)
x = i;
```

C. Write a program that prompts the user for an unsigned short integer (0 - 32535). Read the response and show the value in hexadecimal. Swap the high and low bytes by shifting bits and bitwise ORing the shifted values.

CHAPTER 5

PROGRAM FLOW AND CONTROL

All programs, regardless of how simple or complex, exhibit a flow of execution of statements. The simplest programs might entail nothing more than a straight sequential execution of statements. The programs shown in earlier chapters of this book are examples of the simple form.

Programs that do anything more complicated than those shown thus far usually involve alterations to the flow of execution. This chapter describes program flow and shows how you can control it in a disciplined way.

Flow of Control

The straight sequence of program statement execution is broken by either branching forward or backward based on the values of control expressions. Statements that form forward branches are called **selection** (decision-making) statements. Those that branch backward are called **iteration** (looping) statements.

Other statements that alter a program's flow of execution are called **jump** statements. Jump statements, as the name implies, cause program execution to jump abruptly to some statement in the program other than the one that follows in sequence.

Each of the statement categories mentioned contains a set of related statements. Let's look at selection, iteration, and jump statements from a high-level perspective first. Then we will examine each of the control statements in detail and show examples of their uses in working programs.

Selection Statements

A selection statement chooses one of two or more possible paths of program execution. You use selection statements in your programs to make decisions.

In C, the `if` statement is the primary selection statement. As you will see, an `if` statement has several useful variations that give you the flexibility needed to model decision-making logic. The variations involve the use of `else` clauses and the nesting of statements.

In addition, C offers a `switch` statement that provides an efficient and clean way to handle multi-way branching. A `switch` statement uses `case` labels as branching targets and an optional `default` label as a catchall if no other label is matched.

Iteration Statements

The iteration statements give programs a way to execute a statement or group of statements repeatedly. A control expression determines how many iterations are executed.

The `while`, `for`, and `do` statements comprise the set of C iteration statements. These forms have differing attributes that might make one more suited to a particular problem than another. Often, the `for` and `while` forms can be written equivalently.

Jump Statements

You will encounter several uses of jump statements in C programs. The primary jump statement, `goto`, transfers control to a labelled statement somewhere in the same function. Given the good variety of structured control statements, you will rarely, if ever, need to use `goto` statements.

Other C jump statements include `break`, `continue`, and `return`. These statements each have necessary but constrained uses in programs.

Making Decisions with if Statements

We begin our detailed discussions of control statements with the `if` statement. Most programs need to make decisions, and most of the decisions are made by `if` statements.

The primary selection statement in C is the simple `if` statement. The general form of an `if` statement is:

```
if (expression)
     statement
```

The test expression must be contained within parentheses. The parentheses are not optional. This design eliminates the need for a superfluous "then" keyword that is required by many other computer languages.

The indentation of the second line is a convention that we use to show that `statement` is subordinate. Typical indentations are obtained by pressing the tab key (equivalent to eight spaces on most hardware) or by using a few spaces (four spaces is a commonly used amount). Indentation is not required, nor is the use of a separate line, but the conventions serve to make source easily readable.

The flowchart for a simple `if` statement is shown in Figure 5-1. The "bubbles" containing the words "enter" and "exit" mark the points at which execution control enters and exits the selection construct. The bubbles do not represent C statements nor are the words parts of C language.

The flow of program execution is affected by the value of `expression`, which must be a scalar expression. When `expression` is evaluated, it can yield either zero or some nonzero value.

Recall that only scalar (arithmetic or pointer) expressions produce results that can be compared to zero. A zero value as a control expression is logically *false* and any nonzero value is logically *true*.

The simple `if` statement causes the associated statement to be executed if the control expression is true. If the test expression is false, *statement* is bypassed and program execution control passes to the next statement, if any.

Figure 5-1: The Simple if Statement

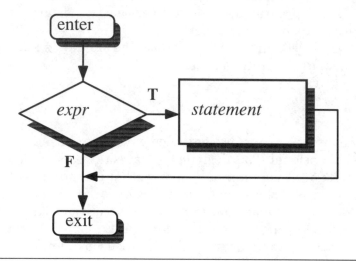

The following code fragment illustrates the use of a simple if statement. The task is to shut off a light if it is on or leave it alone if it is already off. In human language we would say something like "If the light is on, shut it off." In C, given a variable state to represent the state of the light, it might be expressed this way:

```
#define OFF 0
#define ON  1
...
int state;

/* code that determines the state of the light */
...
/* code that conditionally alters the state of the light */
```

```
if (state == ON)
     state = OFF;
```

The #define directives create symbolic names to represent the light-off and light-on conditions. You would need to provide other code that actually determines whether the light is off or on (you might ask the user to tell you, for example).

If, indeed, the light is on, the test expression yields a true logical result and the assignment statement is executed. If the value of state is OFF, the expression is logically false, and the assignment statement is by-passed.

The simple if statement conditionally executes a single program statement. Although this behavior may be adequate in many decision-making circumstances, you will often need to make a choice between two alternatives.

Adding an else Clause

By adding an else clause to the simple if statement, we produce a more general form, as illustrated by Figure 5-2. This form provides a choice between two explicit alternative statements. If the test expression evaluates to a true result, *statement1* is executed. If it evaluates to false, *statement2* is executed. This behavior is sometimes referred to as **alternation**.

This is the general if statement syntax:

```
if (expression)
     statement1
else
     statement2
```

To illustrate, here is a slightly revised version of the program fragment we just examined. The task is modified so that the light state is "toggled," meaning that if is off, turn it on and if it is on, turn it off.

```
#define OFF 0
#define ON  1
. . .
```

```
int state;

/* code that determines the state of the light */
...
/* code that alters the state of the light */
if (state == ON)
     state = OFF;
else
     state = ON;
```

The test expression tests to see whether the light is on. If you prefer, you can test to see whether it is off, but if you do, you will need to reverse the order of the assignment statements to obtain the same program behavior.

Figure 5-2: An if can have an else clause.

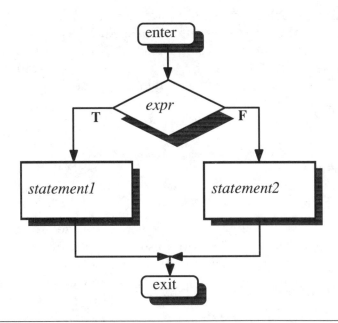

The Conditional Expression

Explicit two-way branches occur frequently in programs. C provides a **conditional operator** that allows you to compactly express such branch statements. The conditional operator is C's only ternary operator—one that takes *three* operands. A conditional expression has the form:

```
expr1 ? expr2 : expr3
```

The value of a conditional expression is the result of evaluating either *expr2* or *expr3*, but how does a program know which to use?

The result of evaluating *expr1*, which must be a scalar type, determines which of the other two expressions is evaluated. If evaluating *expr1* produces a nonzero result, *expr2* is evaluated. Otherwise, *expr3* is evaluated.

Harking back to our "toggle" example, we could use a conditional expression to obtain the same effect as the if statement. Here's how. The expression:

```
state == ON ? OFF : ON
```

yields a result of OFF if *state* has a value of ON or ON if it has a value of OFF. We can assign the evaluated result of the expression to the variable *state*, causing the variable's value to change.

```
/* code that alters the value of the state variable */
state = state == ON ? OFF : ON;
```

In this example, the true and false branches consist of only symbolic constants, but they can be any valid expressions. As we'll see in later chapters, the conditional expression plays an important role in the creation of macros.

Nesting if Statements

Statements are said to be **nested** when one appears within another. With if statements, you can nest them in the true branch, the false branch, or both. Nesting in the true branch looks like this:

```
if (expr1)
    if (expr2)
        statement
```

Nested if statements in the true branch can usually be more compactly and clearly shown as a single if statement with a control expression that involves compound logical expressions formed by using logical operators.

```
if (expr1 && expr2)
    statement
```

These two forms execute *statement* if both *expr1* and *expr2* are true. The second form is easier to read and shows the logic of the problem clearly.

Nesting in the false (else) branch is quite common in C programs. Here's how it looks in a general form:

```
if (expression1)
    statement1
else
    if (expression2)
        statement2
    else
        if (expression3)
            statement3
        else
            statement4
```

This multi-way branching statement can be more compactly and clearly expressed by putting the else and the following if on the same line:

```
if (expression1)
    statement1
else if (expression2)
    statement2
else if (expression3)
    statement3
else
    statement4
```

The else if phrase is simply a realignment of the else and if keywords. The translator sees both of these forms the same way.

The second form has two important attributes. First, it makes the multi-way nature of the construct visually obvious. Second, it prevents deeply–nested statements from disappearing from view off the right side of your screen (or printout). It is otherwise identical to the first form.

The optional else clause is a default branch that is taken if none of the test expressions is true. If there is no default action to perform, no else clause is needed.

As you can see in Figure 5-3, the flow of control cascades through the sequence of test expressions. If one of the expressions is true, its associated statement is executed and control passes to the statement following the if statement.

The **compare** program (in source file **compare.c**) uses a multi-way branch to determine the relationship between two integers provided by the user.

```
/*
 * compare.c
 *
 * Compare two integers and report the relationship to
 * each other (a < b, a == b; a > b) in words.
 */
#include <stdio.h>
#include <stdlib.h>

#define INBUFSIZE 5

int main(void)
{
        int a, b;
        char inbuf1[INBUFSIZE + 1], inbuf2[INBUFSIZE + 1];

        /* get numbers and operator from the user */
        printf("Number a: ");
        gets(inbuf1);
        a = atoi(inbuf1);
```

```
    printf("Number b: ");
    gets(inbuf2);
    b = atoi(inbuf2);

    /* do comparison and print result */
    if (a < b)
        puts("Number a is less than number b.");
    else if (a == b)
        puts("The numbers are equal.");
    else
        puts("Number a is greater than number b.");

    return EXIT_SUCCESS;
}
```

Figure 5-3: Nested if Statements in else Clauses

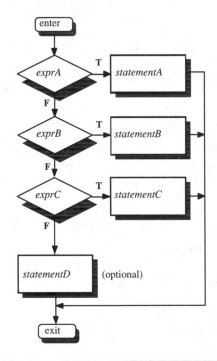

The **compare** program reads user input as strings into two character arrays (buffers) and converts the saved strings to integers (variables a and b) by calling `atoi()`. The buffers accept up to five-digit numbers and each has one additional location to hold the terminating null byte. Be careful not to input numbers that are too large on 16-bit machines (maximum value = 32767). On machines with larger integer sizes, you might want to modify the program to permit more digits for the input values.

The first test checks to see whether the value of a is less than the value of b. If it is, the program prints a message to that effect. Control then passes to the `return` statement, which returns an indication of success to the caller (usually the operating system). If a is not less than b, the program checks to see whether their values are equal, and if so, prints an appropriate message.

If neither of the tested conditions is true, the default message is printed because the value of a must be greater than that of b. Notice that no expression evaluation takes place. None is needed.

Multi-way Branching with switch

C offers yet another way to perform a multi-way branch: the `switch` statement. A `switch` statement uses a single integer expression to calculate where to jump and some number of `case` labels as jump targets. Each `case` label must be a unique integer constant expression.

If none of the `case` labels matches the control expression, control passes either to an optional default label, if one is provided, or to the statement that follows the `switch` statement. Here is the general form of a `switch` statement:

```
switch (expression) {
case label1:
      statement1
case label2:
      statement2
...
default:
      statementN
}
```

Braces delimit the block containing the `case` labels and their associated program statements.

The next program is called four to describe its four-function calculator basis (see source file **four.c**). The program collects three input values as strings from the user: two real numbers and an operator that tells the program what action (addition, subtraction, multiplication, or division) to perform on the two numbers.

```c
/*
 * four.c
 *
 * This program implements a very simple four-function
 * calculator. It uses Reverse Polish Notation (RPN).
 */

#include <stdio.h>
#include <stdlib.h>

#define INBUFSIZE 15

int main(void)
{
        double num1, num2;
        int op;
        char inbuf1[INBUFSIZE + 1], inbuf2[INBUFSIZE + 1];

        /* get numbers and operator from the user */
        printf(" First number: ");
        gets(inbuf1);
        num1 = atof(inbuf1);

        printf("Second number: ");
        gets(inbuf2);
        num2 = atof(inbuf2);

        printf("      Operator: ");
        op = getchar();

        /* do calculation and print result */
```

```
switch (op) {
case '+':
        printf("%lf\n", num1 + num2);
        break;
case '-':
        printf("%lf\n", num1 - num2);
        break;
case '*':
        printf("%lf\n", num1 * num2);
        break;
case '/':
        if (num2 != (float) 0)
                printf("%lf\n", num1 / num2);
        else {
                fprintf(stderr, "Cannot divide by zero\n");
                exit(EXIT_FAILURE);
        }
        break;
default:
        fprintf(stderr, "Unknown operator: %c\n", op);
        exit(EXIT_FAILURE);
}

return EXIT_SUCCESS;
}
```

A **Reverse Polish Notation** (RPN) calculator requires that you input the values first, then issue the command (operator) that tells the calculator what to do with the values.

INBUFSIZE size is set to 15 characters. This number should be big enough to receive a floating point number with all of its significant digits. The `atof()` library function converts a string to its floating-point numeric equivalent.

The `switch` statement is controlled by the value of the `op` variable, which indicates the arithmetic operation requested by the user. A `default` case is used to flag unknown operators if the user presses any key other than the +, -, *, and / keys.

The break Statement

Most of the statement blocks following the `case` labels in the **four** program end with `break` statements. A `break` statement causes control to pass to the statement following the enclosing `switch` or iteration (`while`, `for`, or `do`) statement.

A `break` statement breaks only one level. When it is used inside nested loops or `switch` statements therefore, a `break` statement transfers control to the next outer layer. This mechanism provides the kind of measured control that typifies a structured language.

Unless it is your intent that control pass from the code associated with one `case` block into that of the next `case` (see the section dealing with fall-through), be sure to use a `break`, `return`, or `continue` statement or an `exit()` function call to terminate the statement block associated with the `case` label.

The default Case

A `default` label is equivalent to the else in a multi-way `if` statement. It is effectively a catch-all clause that is used if the control expression of the `switch` statement is not matched by any other label.

You can place the `default` label anywhere in a `switch` statement. It does not have to be placed last, although placing it last is the most common practice and seems the most natural. Be sure to put a `break` or other `jump` statement after the `default` statement block to protect yourself against unwanted fall-through if you add code to the `switch` after the `default` case.

Fall-Through and Multiple Labels

You have wide-ranging flexibility in the way you use `case` labels and statement blocks. As you have already seen, leaving off the termination statement of a block of statements permits control to fall through to the next case. The following source fragment shows the use of fall-through in a `switch` statement:

```
switch (expression) {
...
case label_x:
      statement_x;
      /* falls through to label_y */
case label_y:
      statement_y;
      break;
...
}
```

If the control expression is matched by `label_y`, only `statement_y` is executed before control passes outside the `switch` statement. If the control expression is matched by `label_x`, then both `statement_x` and `statement_y` are executed.

✍**Programmer's Notebook**

If you write a `switch` statement that depends on fall-through behavior, be sure to use comments to clearly identify where and why it is being done. Source code has a propensity to change over time as programs are modified and maintained. It is very likely that someone else will be responsible for changes and they need to know your intent and the details of the design to avoid unwanted changes.

You can lay out a `switch` statement so that two or more `case` labels cause the same code to be executed. This is done by stacking the `case` labels just ahead of the program statement(s). In effect, this is fall-through in which the statement block associated with the first `case` label is empty.

For example, if you want to allow the use of 'a' as a synonym for '+', modify the **four.c** source by adding a `case` label for the 'a' command just before or after the case '+' label, but before any of its associated statements. When the program runs, the '+' command and the 'a' command have the same effect.

```
switch (op) {
...
case '+':
case 'a':
      /* the code for addition goes here */
      ...
      break;
...
}
```

You can also stack the `case` labels horizontally on a single line to save space, but code will be easier to read if you stack them vertically as shown.

The while Loop

In the flow-control statements presented thus far, the transfer of control is always forward (i.e., to a statement that occurs later in the program). It is also possible to transfer control backward to an earlier statement. By doing so, we create iteration statements, more commonly called **loops**.

One of the primary iteration statements is the `while` loop. The purpose of a `while` statement is to execute its statement body as long as the value of the test expression is true. A `while` statement has the following form:

```
while (expression)
      statement
```

A `while` statement tests at the "top" of the loop (see Figure 5-4). That means that if *expression* is evaluated and produces a zero result, the statement body is never executed. If the evaluation of *expression* produces a nonzero result, *statement* is executed. For most looping statements, this is the desired behavior.

```
/*
 * while.c
 *
 * Show the use of a while loop to read a line of text
 * from the keyboard and print it a character at a time.
 */
```

```
#include <stdio.h>
#include <stdlib.h>

int main(void)
{
      int c;

      puts("Type a message (one line) plus RETURN");
      while ((c = getchar()) != '\n')
            putchar(c);       /* print it */

      return EXIT_SUCCESS;
}
```

When you run this program, it prints the simple instruction and waits for your input. As you type characters, they are echoed to the screen and collected in the input buffer. When you press the Return key to end input, the program prints out the text of the line, but not the trailing new-line character. Thus, if you type a lone Return, there is no output at all from the program.

Figure 5-4: A while statement is a primary C loop.

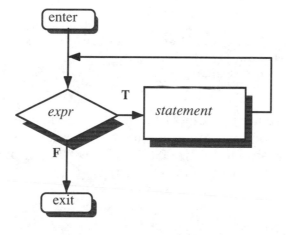

The while loop in the next code fragment prints (displays) a series of new-line characters to put some vertical white space in an output stream. Note the use of an integer variable, n, to control the loop.

```c
int n;
...
n = 5;          /* number of clear lines needed */
while (n > 0) {
      putchar('\n');
      --n;
}
```

We start with the number of new-line characters to print (five in this case). Each time through the loop, the value of the test variable is compared to zero. As long as n is greater than zero, the loop continues to execute. Each time a new-line character is printed, n is decremented (reduced by one). Eventually n is reduced to zero, the test expression becomes false (0), and the loop terminates.

Null Statement

A null statement is a semicolon by itself. Although this may not seem to be a particularly useful construct, it is used occasionally in iteration and selection statements. Here's a simple example:

```c
char c;
...
printf("Press the Return key to continue: ");
while ((c = getchar()) != '\n')
      ;          /* do nothing */
...
```

The print statement prompts the user to press the Return key in order to proceed with the program. The while loop reads the standard input (usually the keyboard unless redirection is in effect), looking for a Return key represented by the new-line character.

✍Programmer's Notebook

When you press the Return key on a typical terminal or console keyboard, two codes are emitted: a carriage return (CR) to get back to the beginning of the current line, and a line-feed character (LF) to get to the next line. In C, which uses a UNIX-style line treatment, the CR/LF pair is translated into a single new-line character (NL). NL and LF have the same code in the ASCII character set. Some character sets, including the minimal C character set, have no line-feed character, but the new-line code suffices.

The effect of the character-reading loop with the null statement body is to read and throw away characters until a new-line character is read. When the new-line character is read, control passes immediately to whatever follows the `while` loop. Normally, the characters being read are echoed to the user's screen, but they are not saved, nor are they used by the program beyond being compared to the new-line character code in order to determine when to stop looping.

The continue Statement

The `continue` statement inside a loop causes the loop to begin its next iteration. Any statements following the `continue` statement are skipped.

The following code fragment reads a line of characters from the standard input stream. Each character (key) is compared to the new-line code (character constant '\n') to determine when to quit processing.

The enclosed `if` statement uses the `isdigit()` routine (a standard library macro or function) to further test the key code. If the code represents any non-digit character, the control expression is true (note the ! used for logical negation) and the `continue` statement is executed, bypassing any other statements in the loop body. If the code represents a digit, the test expression is false, so the digit-processing code is executed. The loop runs until a new-line code is read.

```
int key;
...
while ((key = getchar()) != '\n') {
```

```
if (!isdigit(key))
    continue;
/* digit-processing code */
...
```
}

The continue statement affects only an enclosing while, for, or do statement.

The for Loop

If the statement body of a while loop is large, the control information for the loop can be difficult to relate and understand. Only the loop control expression might be immediately visible to the reader. Initialization of control variables occurs in statements somewhere ahead of the while statement and modifications to those variables are usually hidden somewhere in the loop body. The for statement eliminates that problem by putting all of the loop-control information in one place at the top of the loop statement.

for (*expr1*; *expr2*; *expr3*)
    statement

Figure 5-5 shows a for statement with its three loop-control expressions. The test expression is *expr2*. This is equivalent to the test expression of a while loop. The other two expressions are evaluated only for their side effects, such as assigning a value to a loop-control variable or incrementing that variable.

Upon entering the for loop, *expr1* is evaluated and then control passes to the loop test (*expr2*). If *expr2* is false, we're done. If it is true, *statement* is executed and then *expr3* is evaluated before control returns to the loop test (*expr2* again). Notice that *expr1* is evaluated only once. The other expressions are evaluated each time control passes around the loop.

Figure 5-5: A for loop has three control expressions.

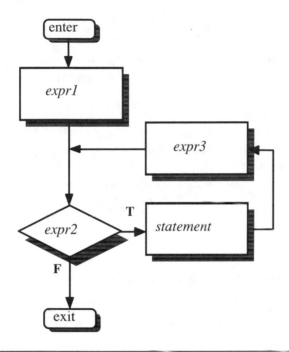

Writing Equivalent while and for Loops

A *for* statement can be expressed as an equivalent while statement, but the control information becomes scattered. Here is the general form of a while statement that is equivalent to the previous for statement:

```
expr1;
...
while (expr2) {
      statement;
      ...
      expr3;
}
```

If only a loop-control test is needed, the `while` statement is a good choice. If the program involves initializing and modifying a control variable in addition to testing it, a `for` statement is usually the best choice.

Infinite Loops

Most loops stop executing after a specified number of iterations or when some condition exists. Sometimes we want a loop that continues executing indefinitely.

A loop that obtains input from the user and interprets the input as commands or text is a good example of an **infinite loop**. Such a loop is at the heart of most text editors and other programs that operate interactively with users.

You can create an infinite loop by writing a loop-control expression that is always true. Any nonzero value will do in a `while` statement.

```
int key;
...
while (1) {
        c = GetKey();        /* read next key */
        switch (key) {
        case K_ESC:
                /* quit command */
                return;
        ...
        default:
                /* text -- just add it to the buffer */
                ...
                break;
        }
...
}
```

The `GetKey()` function is some, as yet undefined function that reads keys from the keyboard as they are pressed rather than waiting for you to press the Return key. We'll see how to do this in both the UNIX and DOS environments in later chapters.

You can also obtain an infinite loop by using a `for` loop with the test expression left empty. Usually, all three expressions are empty, but you must still type the two semicolons.

```
for ( ; ; )
      statement
```

Although this form of an infinite loop statement does not have an explicit nonzero test expression, it is taken to mean "loop forever" by all C compilers.

The do Loop

Unlike the `while` and `for` loops, which execute their statement bodies zero or more times, a `do` loop executes its statement body at least once. The test expression is effectively at the "bottom" of the loop, as shown in Figure 5-6.

This behavior is needed on occasion to guarantee that the statement body is executed immediately even if the test expression is false. When execution control enters the `do` statement, the statement in the loop body is executed and then the test expression is evaluated.

```
do
      statement
while (expression);
```

✍**Programmer's Notebook**

Be sure to place a semicolon after the end of the parenthesized test expression to separate the `do` statement from whatever follows. This can be confusing because you must *not* use a semicolon after the parenthesized test expression of a `while` loop.

This type of loop is used infrequently, but when you need it, you really need it. Here is an example of the `do` statement in action. It is a revision of the **while.c** program source you saw earlier:

Figure 5-6: A do loop tests at the bottom.

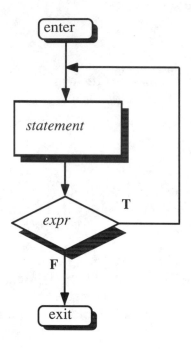

```
/*
 * do_while.c
 *
 * Show the use of a do...while loop to guarantee that
 * a new-line character is printed as part of a string
 * read from the keyboard.
 */

#include <stdio.h>
#include <stdlib.h>

int main(void)
{
```

```
int c;

puts("Type a message (one line) plus RETURN");
do {
        c = getchar();    /* read a character */
        putchar(c);       /* print it */
} while (c != '\n');

return EXIT_SUCCESS;
}
```

When you run this program, it prints the simple instruction and waits for your input. As you type characters, they are echoed to the screen and collected in the input buffer. When you press the Return key to end input, the program prints out the text, *including* the trailing new-line character. Thus, if you type a lone Return, the program prints out a blank line, as it should. Contrast this with the **while.c** program's output. It's a subtle difference, but one worth noting.

An Additional Jump Statement

In addition to break and continue, C offers a goto statement. Unlike BASIC's freewheeling GOTO that can literally jump anywhere, C's goto is restricted to jumps within a single function. A goto statement specifies a target, which is a label, to which control is transferred. Here is the general form of a goto statement:

```
goto label;
...
label: statement
```

In most situations, you will find that there are alternatives to using goto statements. Loops, break and continue statements, and good program design will usually obviate any need for goto statements. In more than a dozen years of writing C programs, I have never had to use one (except in books to describe the goto keyword!).

Sequence, Selection, and Iteration Combined

In modeling the logic of the world around you, it is necessary to apply only a rather limited set of constructs: sequence, selection, and iteration.

It is common to find loops within loops, decision-making hierarchies (nested `if` and `switch` statements), stretches of sequential steps, and myriad combinations of these in real-world problems.

The following program, **calc** (in file **calc.c**), is a revised version of the **four** program shown earlier. Its primary enhancement is the addition of an outer loop that repeatedly runs the data collection/calculation/output sequence. The **four** program does a single run and quits.

Because the loop runs forever, we need to provide a way to quit the program (The 'Q' command). If we don't, the user would have to use a keyboard break command (BREAK or DEL under UNIX; Ctrl+Break under DOS) to exit the program. Using a keyboard break exit is not an elegant way to end a program—somewhat like using the fire escape instead of the front door to leave a building. Save that method for real emergencies.

```
/*
 * calc.c
 *
 * This program implements a very simple calculator that
 * uses Reverse Polish Notation (RPN). It demonstrates
 * sequence, iteration, and selection in an application.
 */

#include <stdio.h>
#include <stdlib.h>
#include <math.h>

#define INBUFSIZE 15

int main(void)
{
        double num1, num2; /* numbers */
        int op;            /* operator */
```

```
int ndp = 2;          /* no. of output decimal places */

/* input buffers */
char inbuf1[INBUFSIZE + 1], inbuf2[INBUFSIZE + 1];

while (1) {
     /* get numbers and operator from the user */
     printf("     First number: ");
     gets(inbuf1);
     num1 = atof(inbuf1);

     printf("     Second number: ");
     gets(inbuf2);
     num2 = atof(inbuf2);

     printf("Operator (q=quit): ");
     op = getchar();    /* get the operator character */
     getchar(); /* throw away the newline */

     /* do calculation and print result */
     switch (op) {
     case 'q':
     case 'Q':
          exit(EXIT_SUCCESS);
     case '+':
          printf("%.*lf\n", ndp, num1 + num2);
          break;
     case '-':
          printf("%.*lf\n", ndp, num1 - num2);
          break;
     case '*':
          printf("%.*lf\n", ndp, num1 * num2);
          break;
     case '/':
          if (num2 != (float) 0)
               printf("%.*lf\n", ndp, num1 / num2);
          else {
               fprintf(stderr,
                    "Cannot divide by zero\n");
```

```
                    exit(EXIT_FAILURE);
            }
            break;
        default:
            fprintf(stderr,
                " Unknown operator: %c\n", op);
            break;
        } /* end switch */

        putchar('\n');  /* put some space between runs */

    } /* end while */

    return EXIT_SUCCESS;
}
```

When you run the program, it works like the original four-function calculator. To quit, give two dummy numbers (just pressing Return twice is ok) and press the Q key followed by a Return. Although not the cleanest way to exit, it will suffice for now. We'll explore simpler ways (from the user's perspective) in later chapters.

Note the use of a "Return eater" in the line:

```
getchar();  /* throw away the newline */
```

This statement is necessary because of the way we are using buffered input, which reads a whole line of input before processing any characters. After learning about "raw" (unbuffered) input in later lessons, we will develop better ways to process user input.

Summary

Although the normal flow of a program is sequential, you can alter the flow by using various selection statements (several variations of the `if` and `switch`) and iteration statements (`while`, `for`, and `do`). Additional control of program flow is obtained by using the `break` and `continue` statements. In limited circumstances, you can use a `goto` statement to make an absolute jump to a labelled statement.

Solutions to real problems usually involve the use of all of these mechanisms in various combinations. Sometimes the relationships are quite complex. The good news is that you can write programs to solve problems of virtually any complexity using this small set of programming constructs.

As you will see in later chapters, the use of functions and macros (collectively called **routines**) allows you to write reusable program modules. Indeed, the standard C library consists of literally hundreds of efficient, speedy, well-debugged routines that are ready for you to use in your programs. Just remember that each routine is built on the constructs you have already learned.

Questions and Exercises

1. What does a simple `if` statement accomplish?

2. How can a simple `if` statement be altered to provide explicit two-way branching with separate statement blocks in each branch?

3. What does the following code fragment do?

   ```
   #define CLOSED 0
   #define OPEN 1

   . . .
   int door = CLOSED;
   door = door == OPEN ? CLOSED : OPEN;
   ```

4. In the program **compare.c**, why is there no testing to see whether the value of `a` is greater than `b`?

5. Describe "fall-through" behavior in a switch statement and explain how to obtain it.

6. List the three types of iteration statements introduced in this chapter, and describe their behaviors.

7. Why are iteration statements used in programs? Give an example and illustrate the use of iteration with a code fragment.

8. How is a null (empty) statement useful in a program?

9. Besides `break` and `continue`, what other jump statement does C offer? Are there any limitations on its use?

Additional Exercises

A. Write a program that reads input from the keyboard until the user ends input (by pressing Ctrl-D under UNIX or Ctrl-Z plus a Return under DOS and OS/2) and prints a message telling how many characters were read.

B. Write a program that prompts the user for a number and then prints a message telling whether the digit is odd or even. What happens to your program if the user types non-digit characters?

C. A collection of numbered "cells" in an N-by-M arrangement can be printed by a program containing two loops, one nested inside the other. Write a program that produces the following 3-by-3 arrangement of cells as output:

```
0-0   0-1   0-2
1-0   1-1   1-2
2-0   2-1   2-2
```

Write the program so that it can be easily modified to use other dimensions without any changes to the main code.

D. To prove that your answer to the previous exercise is written generally, make it print out a 10-by-10 collection of cells by changing only two values (the number of rows and columns) and recompiling.

CHAPTER 6

FUNCTIONS AND PROGRAM ORGANIZATION

The Purpose of Functions

All C programs consist of at least one user-defined function, `main()`, as you have seen numerous times in previous chapters. And virtually all `main()` functions call on other functions to do work. Those functions might be selected from the ones contained in the standard library supplied with your compiler, from specialized third-party libraries, or they might be functions that you write yourself.

As you progress in your development as a C programmer, you will learn to use the standard library effectively, and you will probably develop and maintain your own libraries of functions to support the kinds of work you do.

Functions are the essential building blocks of programs. Programmers use functions analogously to the way engineers use mechanical assemblies and electronic circuits. The concept is to partition a programming task or problem into a set of manageable subproblems and solve them individually.

You will find, as many other programmers already have, that certain programming tasks occur with great frequency. Here are some examples:

- Determining how long a character string is

- Converting a character string to an equivalent number

- Responding to a keyboard interrupt (BREAK)

- Calculating the sine of an angle

- Raising a number to a power

These and many other tasks are candidates for packaging as functions. If a solution is general enough, it can be applied in a wide range of programs. Write a solid, generalized function once and call it any time you need that solution. Indeed, hundreds of common tasks have been "solved" and functions that implement those solutions have been collected together in what has come to be known as the standard library.

Perhaps you need a solution to a special problem that is not handled by a library function. If so, you can write your own function. You can, in fact, create your own libraries of functions using tools available with virtually all C language systems. In C, a function can perform an action, return a value, or both. Functions can optionally have inputs. Using the engineering analogy, a function can be viewed externally as a "black box" that has a known set of input/output characteristics and some internal mechanism that implements a transfer characteristic. That means that the output depends on the values of the inputs in some predictable way.

It is possible to have an output without inputs (the function generates an output based on internal data, such as a pseudo-random number generator might do). A function might also accept inputs and perform an action without producing any output value (for example, move the cursor or mouse pointer to a screen position).

✍Programmer's Notebook

Some computer languages (Pascal, Modula 2, etc.) distinguish between a subprogram that returns a value ("function") and one that does not ("procedure"). C considers all subprograms to be functions regardless of whether they return values or not.

Program Organization and Flow of Control

When you write a program, try to use one function per task to organize your work and to benefit from having reusable modules at your disposal. The one-task-per-function guideline is a good rule that forces you to aim for generality and reusability of code.

Figure 6-1 shows how a program called **boxtext** might be organized. The organization depicted in the figure is a way of doing the job, but is by no means the only way. Each boxed item is the name of a function with `main()` being the starting point for program execution.

Shaded boxes contain the names of standard library functions (or macros, which we'll discuss later). The remaining boxes contain the names of user-defined functions. The figure shows the function-calling hierarchy. For example, `main()` calls `strlen()`, `hborder()`, and `puttext()`. The latter two functions in turn call the `string()` and `putchar()` functions (`putchar()` is often implemented as a macro for speed). In addition, `puttext()` calls the `printf()` standard library function.

In Chapter 5, you learned about program flow of execution and some of the ways to control program flow. In addition to looping and branching statements, program flow is controlled by the function call/return mechanism. This allows a program to save information about its current location and state, and jump to another piece of code. The return address, the state of machine registers and the state of other data is saved on the program stack, a region of memory that serves as an electronic scratchpad.

With the exception of functions that cause program termination, such as `exit()` or `abort()`, a function-call statement eventually returns execution control to the next statement in sequence. In Figure 6-1, for example, you can see that `main()` passes control to `hborder()`, which calls `string()`. The `string()` function uses `putchar()` to print a series of characters and then returns control to `hborder()`, which does some additional work and then returns control to `main()`.

We'll return to the **boxtext** program later in this chapter.

Figure 6-1: A Program's Function-call Hierarchy

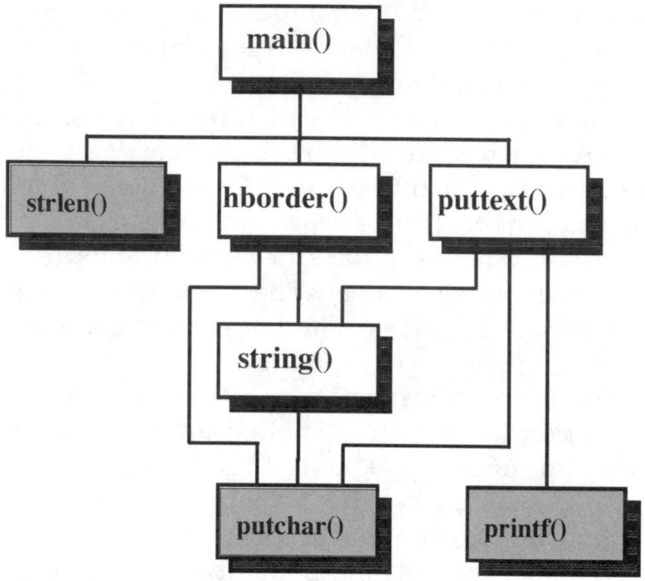

NOTE: Shaded boxes contain the names
of standard library functions and macros.

Information Hiding

Two attributes of functions are that they can be used to maintain data in
a controlled way and can hide details of how a task is carried out. Both
are important attributes of well-designed programs.

Unlike the BASICs of old, which treated all data as global (any part of
a program can read and write it), C lets you manage data as local or global.
Local data is visible, and therefore changeable, only within a function or
other limited scope.

By using local variables in a function to hold important data, you can
provide carefully controlled access to the data, preventing unwanted
access to the data by other parts of a program. This is a particularly

important design consideration in large programs and those that are being worked on by groups of programmers rather than someone working alone.

Hiding the details of a task's implementation is just as important as shielding data from view. One part of a program calls another to do a job and, perhaps, gets back a result. The caller need not be concerned about how the called function does the job.

Say you have a program that collects data on an audio signal input and calculates its average power value. You can package the data collection tasks into one or more functions and the average calculation into another. If you later find a better way to do the average calculation (improved speed or accuracy), you can alter the averaging function without having to make changes to any other functions that call it.

Function Declarations

Now that you have a feel for what functions are and how they are used, let's see how to declare and define them. As with variables, the C translator requires that you provide declarations of functions before you use them in your program. However, certain defaults apply if you do not provide complete declarations.

External Names and Linkages

A C translator, as you know, is responsible for converting source statements into machine instructions and data. It does so on individual **translation units**. In the typical case of a C compiler, the compiler translates a source file and any headers it includes with preprocessor directives.

Recall the discussion in Chapter 1 that shows how a C program can be created from a set of source files. The individual source files are translated into object modules that are linked to produce an executable program file. This method is often called **separate compilation** because each source file is compiled asynchronously with respect to any other source files.

Therein lies a problem. If a function is defined in one source file and called in another, how does the translator know what to do? The answer lies in a design concept called external names and linkages. Although the linker does not need to know any details about C, it needs a list of names that have external linkage.

External names are identifiers that must be unique in the first six characters. Recall that internal names must be unique in the first 31 characters. In addition, letter case can be ignored by the linker. A given implementation can permit longer names and honor letter-case distinctions, but don't count on these enhanced features if portability of your source code is a factor.

Defining Declaration

You must have one defining declaration for each function you use in a program. If you are using standard library functions, the definitions have been prepared for you. When you write your own functions, you create their definitions. A full function definition contains four elements:

- A return type

- A function name

- A parameter list

- A statement body

The first three elements make up the function header. These elements contain all of the information needed to correctly call and use the function, but they don't describe how the function does its job. That is the job of the statement body.

The general form of a function definition is:

```
return_type name (parameter_list)
{
        declaration(s) ...
        statement(s)
        ...
        return_statement
}
```

Let's first look at the function header and learn about its purpose.

Function Header

A function header indicates the type of data being returned, if any. If the function computes a single-precision, floating-point value, for example, the return type and the value used in the return statement in the statement body must be of type `float`.

The return type can be any C type or a derived type. The C data types of `int`, `char`, `float`, and so on, are obviously suitable return types. So is `void`, which actually means that the function returns control, but no data. In addition, you can create your own data types from array, structure, and union types, pointers to objects of a type, and even functions that return data of a particular type. Just be sure the type of the return value agrees or is appropriately cast.

The name of a function is important, too. You can use any name that does not collide with C keywords and standard function names. You should avoid using names that begin with a single underscore because they might duplicate internal names used by the C translator.

The last component of a function header is the parameter list, which is a possibly empty list of parameter types and names inside parentheses. This list shows the number and types of parameters accepted by the function. You'll see more about this topic in the section on function parameters and arguments.

Statement Body

The statement body is where the action takes place. Braces mark the beginning and end of the statement body. When control passes to a called function, it passes to the first executable statement in the function's statement body. Control passes out of a function by control statements such as return, abort, exit, or by just falling off the end (the closing brace).

The parentheses collect the enclosed statements into a block or compound statement, as you saw in the previous chapter. Within the function block, you can have inner blocks. At the top of each block, you can place declaration statements. Such declarations are visible (in scope) only within the enclosing block.

Function Parameters and Arguments

You provide inputs to a function by passing parameters or arguments. Parameter and argument are two different names for the same thing—views from different perspectives.

Looking at it from the view of a function definition, items in the parenthesized list following the function name are called **formal parameters**. From the perspective of a calling function, the values passed to the called function are called **actual arguments**.

The difference between formal parameters and actual arguments is often blurred by writers who freely intermix the terms or favor one over the other. Indeed, the ANSI standard treats the terms "formal parameter" and "formal argument" as synonyms. It also treats "actual argument" and "actual parameter" as synonyms. I prefer to maintain the original distinction to clarify the differences between function definitions and function calls.

Formal Parameters

A parameter is a variable that is created on the program stack when the function is called. The variable serves as a placeholder and its name as a convenient handle for the data being passed.

In the following function definition, the variables n and ch are formal parameters. The function uses a simple count-down loop to print a specified symbol, represented by ch, n times.

```
/* print a specified number of repetitions of a character */
void
string(int n, char ch)
{
      while (n-- > 0)
            putchar(ch);
}
```

The formal parameters provide the translator with data type information for each parameter. If a function accepts no inputs, use the keyword void to tell the translator that the list is, in fact, empty. This distinguishes a truly empty list from one that you may have just left out, affording the translator the opportunity to help you by checking the argument list of a function call against the parameter list of the function definition.

Actual Arguments

Switching to the view of a calling function, a call to the string() function might look like this:

```
string(count, '*');
```

The variable count is an integer that specifies the number of repetitions and the character constant '*' represents the code for the printing symbol. Both count and '*' are called actual arguments because they are the actual values being passed (or something that evaluates to the values).

By putting all this information to work in a complete program, you can see how parameter-passing works. The program **hbars** consists of two functions: the string() function we just wrote, and the mandatory main() entry point. The string() function is called from main() to print lines of varying length on your output device.

Here is the source code for **hbars**:

```
/*
 *  hbars.c
 *
 *  Print a set of horizontal bars of varying length.
 */

#include <stdio.h>
#include <stdlib.h>

#define NLINES   10

/* print a specified number of repetitions of a character */
void
string(int n, char ch)
```

```
{
        while (n-- > 0)
                putchar(ch);
}

int
main(void)
{
        int n;

        for (n = 1; n <= NLINES; ++n) {
                string(n, '*');
                putchar('\n');
        }

        return EXIT_SUCCESS;
}
```

Notice that `string()` is defined in the program before being called by `main()`. Thus, we avoid a potential problem. Had we put `main()` first, `string()` would be called before being defined, so the translator would assume that it returns an integer, which is an error: it doesn't return anything.

This arrangement of functions in the source file might appear to be a handy solution, but it is inconvenient in at least one respect. It is useful to have a program's `main()` function show up first in a source file that contains more than one function because it is usually a kind of blueprint of the program showing the program's organization. If we place it near the beginning of the file, however, we have problems with function return types and other translator assumptions because functions are called before being completely defined.

So how do we get around this problem? The answer is **function prototypes**.

Function Prototypes

A function header has another important purpose beyond its use in a function definition. Used by itself (without an associated statement body), a function header serves as a prototype, which is a forward reference to an as-yet-undefined function.

A function prototype tells the translator what to expect when a function is called, later in a program. It specifies the return type, the function name, and the types of each expected argument. Unless the function accepts a variable number of arguments, the prototype also specifies the number of arguments. All of this information helps the translator check your source code for accurate and consistent use of functions. This avoids troublesome run-time errors that are often hard to find and correct with pre-ANSI translators, most of which don't accept prototypes.

You create a function prototype by appending a semicolon to the function header. In the parameter list, you need only show the data types of the parameters. However, you can put in the parameter names for documentation purposes only. The translator does not do anything with the optional names.

A function prototype for `string()` looks like this:

```
void string(int, char);
```

If you put in the parameter names it would look like this:

```
void string(int n, char ch);
```

The translator ignores the names n and ch, but their use might make your code clearer to someone who reads it if you use descriptive names.

The following program, **tree**, is similar to the **hbars** program. It differs in that `main()` appears before `string()` and by containing a function prototype to tell the translator what to expect when `string()` is defined later in the source file.

```
/*
 *   tree.c
 *
 *   Print set of horizontal bars stacked to form tree-like
 *   display. This program uses the string() function to
 *   print runs of both spaces and tree segment symbols.
 */
```

```
#include <stdio.h>
#include <stdlib.h>

#define NLINES   10

/* function prototype */
void string(int, char);

int
main(void)
{
      int n;

      for (n = 1; n <= NLINES; ++n) {
            /* print the indentation */
            string(NLINES - n, ' ');

            /* print the tree segment */
            string(2 * n - 1, '^');

            /* start a new line */
            putchar('\n');
      }

      return EXIT_SUCCESS;
}


/*  print a specified number of repetitions of a character
*/
void
string(int n, char ch)
{
      while (n-- > 0)
            putchar(ch);
}
```

To make things easier for yourself and anyone else who might use your
functions, you can collect function prototypes into headers for them. In

any program file that uses one of these functions, simply include the header that declares the function.

This method is a real time saver if you create libraries of functions. Indeed, it is the method used in the standard C library. When you include the **stdio.h** header, you are including a large set of function prototypes for standard input and output functions.

A translator creates a symbol table that lists all external names and makes this information available to the linker so that it can resolve external references. The linker may have to get the instructions for printf(), for example, from the standard library to complete a program.

You don't create the printf() object module yourself, of course, but your program references it as an external name and the linker has to know where to get a copy of its instructions. It may be necessary for you to identify the standard C library file explicitly, such as **SLIBCE.LIB** in a LINK command under DOS. Under UNIX, the cc command automatically calls the ld linker with instructions to search **/usr/lib/llibc** and other library files to resolve external references, but you are free to name other libraries, such as **/usr/lib/llibcurses** if your program uses screen-management functions.

If you prepare a program by putting some of your own functions in one file and still other functions in other source files, the linker uses the symbol table information to resolve external references among the files. The same method applies to global data that is stored in external variables.

Call-by-Value Parameter Passing

Unlike BASIC and some other popular programming languages, C uses a technique known as "call-by-value" as its default parameter-passing method. This means that when you call a function that accepts parameters, you provide actual arguments that are copies of the data being passed.

For example, a call out to the string() function passes a copy of count to the function. It does not pass the location of count, so the called function cannot affect what is stored in count.

The alternative technique, used by some languages as a default method, is "call-by-reference," which provides the locations of variables in calling a function (or procedure) as parameters to a called function. The called function is then free, not only to read the values in the variables, but also to change them. C permits both types of parameter passing, but you must use addresses to arrange for call-by-reference, and that requires a knowledge of pointers and indirection. You'll learn about pointers and indirection in the next chapter.

The **boxtext** program ties what you have learned together and emphasizes the organization of a program into functions. The program prints a message inside a box drawn with standard characters. Note the use of function prototypes, call-by-value parameter passing, symbolic names for certain data items, and the inclusion of headers to obtain function prototypes for standard library functions and to obtain additional symbolic constant definitions.

This program is the one you saw described earlier in Figure 6-1 when we briefly examined how a program works:

```
/*
 * boxtext.c
 *
 * Show how functions are used to organize a program into
 * functions that interact to perform a task (print text
 * in a box).
 */

#include <stdio.h>
#include <stdlib.h>
#include <string.h>

/* symbolic constants */
#define BDRWIDTH   3
#define HBAR       '-'
#define VBAR       '|'
#define CORNER     '+'
#define SPACE      ' '

/* function prototypes */
```

```
void string(int, char);
void hborder(int);
void puttext(char []);

int
main(void)
{
        int width;
        static char text[] = {
                "This is a suitably trivial test message"
        };

        /* calculate lengths and positions */
        width = strlen(text) + 2 * BDRWIDTH;

        /* print a top border */
        hborder(width);

        /* print the body text */
        puttext(text);

        /* print a bottom border */
        hborder(width);

        return EXIT_SUCCESS;
}

/* print a specified number of repetitions of a character */
void
string(int n, char ch)
{
        while (n-- > 0)
                putchar(ch);
}

/* print a horizontal border */
void
hborder(int w)
{
```

```
      putchar(CORNER);      /* print the corner */
      string(w - 2, HBAR);  /* print the horiz. line */
      putchar(CORNER);      /* print the corner */
      putchar('\n');        /* print a new line */
}

/*
 * print the message text centered between
 * left and right borders
 */
void
puttext(char mesg[])
{
      /* print left border area */
      putchar(VBAR);
      string(BDRWIDTH - 1, SPACE);

      /* print the centered text */
      printf("%s", mesg);

      /* print right border area */
      string(BDRWIDTH - 1, SPACE);
      putchar(VBAR);
      putchar('\n');
}
```

The program uses symbolic names for the line-drawing characters as a way of permitting changes to be made easily. You can edit the #define directives to use other graphic symbols for the box, such as asterisks or special line-drawing characters, if any are available in the target operating environment. You might even go a step further and put the definitions in a separate header (box.h perhaps) so that you can easily tailor your program to a particular environment simply by changing the header, obviating the need to edit any source files.

Recursion

C supports **recursion**, which is the ability of a function to call itself, either directly or indirectly through other functions. The use of recursion offers benefits in some situations by simplifying the logic of a solution. Recursion has some natural uses in dealing with file system hierarchies and in sorting algorithms, but it has some negative attributes, such as heavy stack use and function-call overhead, that must be accounted for in program design.

The following program, **rfact**, is a recursive implementation of a factorial computation. The factorial of a nonnegative number, n, is symbolized by the expression n!. The value of n! is the product of the consecutive integers between 1 and n. If n is given a value of 4, for example, 4! is computed as 4 * 3 * 2 * 1, which equals 24.

We can show this computation recursively as n * ((n - 1)!) for n greater than 0. Note that 0! is defined as 1:

```c
/*
 * rfact.c
 *
 * Calculate the factorial of a number
 * by using a recursive solution.
 */

#include <stdio.h>
#include <stdlib.h>

#define NDIGITS 10

long factorial(short);

int
main(void)
{
        char input[NDIGITS + 1];        /* input buffer */
        short number;                   /* starting number */
        long result;                    /* factorial result */
```

```
        /* prompt the user for input and read it */
        printf("Type a non-negative integer + RETURN: ");
        gets(input);
        number = (short) atoi(input);

        /* recursively calculate the factorial and print it */
        result = factorial(number);
        printf("The factorial of %hd is %ld\n",
                number, result);

        return EXIT_SUCCESS;
}

long
factorial(short n)   /* recursive version */
{
        if (n <= 1)
                return 1L;
        else
                return (n * factorial(n - 1));
}
```

The `main()` function sets aside a character array as an input buffer. It prompts the user for an input and stores the reply in the buffer. Because the input provided by the user is in character form, the program must convert it to short-integer form before using the value in the computation. The standard library function `atoi()` coverts the string to an integer, which is cast to a `short` integer and saved in the variable `number`. Then the value of `number` is passed to the `factorial()` function as an argument.

The logic of `factorial()` is simple enough. If the value passed as an argument is less than or equal to 1, `factorial()` returns a value of 1L. The suffix L is needed because the function returns a long integer and we must guarantee that all bits are set on machines of any architecture (word size).

If the value of the argument is greater than 1, `factorial()` calls itself with an argument that is one less than the value it received as an argument. The `factorial()` function continues the recursive calls until the passed argument is reduced to 1. Until that happens, no instance of the function returns a value. As soon as the argument value reaches 1 though, a cascade of function returns occurs, ultimately producing the result of the computation as a return to `main()` by the first-called instance of `factorial()`, as shown in Figure 6-2.

Figure 6-2: The rfact Program Involving Recursion

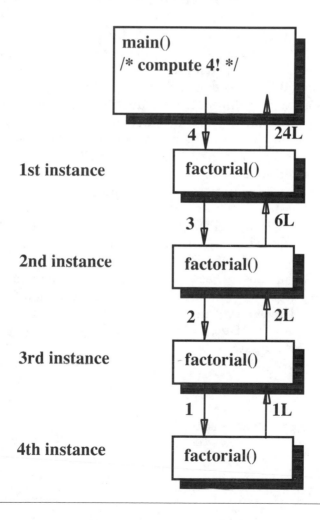

Although recursion can produce easily understood solutions, it is not without problems. Recursion uses the program stack intensively, so you may need to set aside larger allocations of stack space. It also suffers function-call overhead at each level of recursion, possibly slowing program performance if the depth of recursion is great.

Also, be careful to provide a termination condition. Infinite recursion can occur if you don't provide some kind of safety net, such as the test n <= 1 in the **rfact** program. When dealing with a hierarchy of directories in a file system, it may be necessary to set an arbitrary depth or pathname length to prevent infinite recursion. The operating environment often dictates the limits for you, but it will not prevent errors from occurring.

A recursive solution can usually be written as an iterative solution, albeit at some additional code space in many cases. The advantage of an iterative solution is the elimination of function-call overhead beyond that needed for the first call to the computing function. The disadvantage is that the solution might not be as clean looking or obvious.

The **ifact** program (listing `ifact.c`) is an iterative solution to the factorial computation problem. In addition to using iteration in its solution, the program is careful to check the value provided by the user, which the recursive version didn't do. It rejects any negative inputs and any inputs larger than 15 by printing an error message and exiting with an error indication (EXIT_FAILURE) to inform the operating system or other calling program about the error.

The value 15 is chosen because an input of 16 or above causes the program to produce out-of-bounds output. The value of a factorial grows very rapidly as the starting number is incremented. If you want to see what happens, run the **rfact** program on your system and give it a value greater than 15 as input.

```
/*
 * ifact.c
 *
 * Calculate the factorial of a number
 * by using an iterative solution.
 */

#include <stdio.h>
```

```
#include <stdlib.h>

#define NDIGITS 10
#define MAXINPUT 15

long factorial(short);

int
main(void)
{
      char input[NDIGITS + 1];           /* input buffer */
      short number;                      /* starting number */

      /* prompt the user for input and read it */
      printf("Type a non-negative integer + RETURN: ");
      gets(input);
      number = (short) atoi(input);

      /* check the user input for obvious errors */
      if (number < 0 or number > MAXINPUT) {
            fprintf(stderr,
                  "Input must be a small, nonnegative integer");
            exit(EXIT_FAILURE);
      }

      /* iteratively calculate the factorial and print it */
      printf("The factorial of %hd is %ld\n",
            number, factorial(number));

      return EXIT_SUCCESS;
}

long
factorial(short n)   /* iterative version */
{
      long result;

      result = 1L;
      while(n > 1)
```

```
        result *= n--;

    return result;
}
```

The `factorial()` function sets `result` to 1L initially and then computes the final result by looping on the ever-decreasing value of n until n is reduced to 1. Notice that `factorial()` is called only once in this version of the program, reducing function-call overhead.

The C Preprocessor and Macros

The C preprocessor supports a generalized text-replacement facility. You have already used it to create symbolic names for constant values. For example, the directive:

```
#define NDIGITS 10
```

creates the symbolic name NDIGITS for a specific use of the constant 10. Anywhere the name NDIGITS occurs in the translation unit following this directive, the preprocessor replaces it with the text of the definition, in this case, 10 expressed as a string of digits. After preprocessing, the source file appears just as it would if you had typed the number 10 instead of NDIGITS.

The `#define` directive is quite general and not limited to symbolic constants. You use it to create **macros**, which are names that have associated textual definitions. A macro takes one of two forms: an **object-like macro** or a **function-like macro**. Let's look at each of these.

Object-like Macros

An object-like macro is a name that is replaced by its definition text, as shown in the NDIGITS example. You are not limited to simple symbolic constants. The replacement text can be virtually any string of characters.

Here is the general form of an object-like macro:

```
#define name replacement_text
```

The name should not duplicate any of C's reserved words. You should, of course, choose names that are indicative of the purposes of macros. The replacement text is terminated by the new-line character that ends the line. For example, the following macro provides a message text that you can use in print statements:

```
#define ERRMSG_RANGE   "Error: Input out of range"
```

To use this macro in a print statement, simply type its name:

```
if (!inrange(value)) {
     printf("%s\n", ERRMSG_RANGE);
```

Here, `inrange()` is a function that you might write to test the value of data obtained from the keyboard or a file. You would call the function before using the data in your program to guard against honest mistakes or attempts at sabotage by hostile users.

The preprocessor would perform a text replacement operation on the source code before the translator's later passes analyzes the source code and generates executable code for the target processor. The preprocessed source line would become the following after the preprocessor pass runs:

```
if (!inrange(value)) {
     printf("%s\n", "Error: Input out of range");
```

The benefit of using the macro is best seen if there are multiple occurrences of the message text in your source file. If your program source code has, say, 10 occurrences of the message text and you decide to alter the message to "INPUT RANGE ERROR", you need only change it in one place in your source file, not 10 places.

If the entire macro definition cannot fit comfortably on a single line, break it into a sequence of shorter physical lines and "escape" all of the new-line characters, except for the last, with backslashes. The preprocessor and other passes of the translator see the replacement text as a single line, but a reader of the program is treated to shorter, more manageable lines. The PROMPT macro is an example of this technique:

```
#define PROMPT   "To print the report, \
be sure your printer is ready, \
then press the Return key: "
```

Although the prompt message occupies most of three physical lines (shortened for this page presentation), the message prints as a single line on your screen when used in the following print statement:

```
printf("\n%s", PROMPT);
```

The \n places the cursor (or printhead on a hard-copy device) at the beginning of a line before the prompt message is printed.

Function-like Macros

So far, we have dealt only with macros that expand to fixed strings. A more elaborate text-replacement operation is a macro that involves parameters. Such a macro takes on a function-like appearance, hence the name "function-like" macro.

Here is the general form of a function-like macro in C:

```
#define name(identifier_list)   replacement_text
```

The new feature is the `identifier_list` component, which looks and acts like the parameter list of a function. When you define a function-like macro, you provide a formal parameter list. When you call the macro in your source code, you pass it actual arguments, just like functions.

The left parenthesis must not be separated from *name* by white space. The preprocessor looks for white-space characters after the macro name to determine where the replacement text begins. If the preprocessor sees a '(' in the name string without intervening space, it assumes that a parameter list follows and accepts everything up to a closing ')' as part of that list. You can embed white-space characters within the list for clarity.

To see how this works, let's write a macro that determines whether a numeric argument is even or odd. The macro depends on the fact that an even number is evenly divisible by two. Using a conditional expression, the macro EVEN() yields a value of TRUE (1) if its argument is even and

FALSE (0) otherwise. Here are the definitions of the truth constants and the macro:

```
#define FALSE 0
#define TRUE 1
#define EVEN(num)   num % 2 ? FALSE : TRUE
```

You should put parentheses around the num parameter in the definition to guard against unwanted side effects. The program **eventst** (in the file **eventst.c**) shows how this macro can be used in practice.

```
/*
 * eventst.c
 *
 * Test integers to determine whether they are
 * even or odd using a macro.
 */

#include <stdio.h>
#include <stdlib.h>

#define FALSE 0
#define TRUE 1

/* macro to test a number */
#define EVEN(num)   num % 2 ? FALSE : TRUE

int main()
{
    /* hardcoded values for testing */
    int n1 = 33, n2 = 44;

    /* check n1 using if-else */
    if (EVEN(n1))
        printf("%d is even\n", n1);
    else
        printf("%d is odd\n", n1);

    /* check n2 using conditional */
```

```
    printf("%d is %s\n", n2, EVEN(n2) ? "even" : "odd");

    return EXIT_SUCCESS;
}
```

The parameter `num` in the definition specifies that a single value is expected when the macro is called in a program. Notice that the parameter is typeless. You can pass `char`, `short`, `int`, or `long` values to this macro without concern for data type. However, because the modules operator applies only to integral types, you should not pass floating-point data types as arguments to this macro.

The EVEN() macro is called in both the traditional `if-else` decision-making context and in a conditional expression. Although the conditional used to test n2 is more compact than the `if-else` used to test n1, it runs no faster after translation. Most C programmers find the conditional expression harder to understand at first, but when completely familiar with the idiom, tend to use the conditional more frequently.

The output of this program is fixed because the test values are hardcoded.

```
33 is odd
44 is even
```

You can use standard library functions and your own user-defined functions in the replacement text of a macro. The ERR() macro, for example, uses `printf()` to print an error message. Here is the definition:

```
#define ERR(mesg)  printf("ERROR: %s\n", mesg)
```

The macro prints a line of text that consists of a fixed part ("ERROR: ") and a variable part that is supplied by the argument. In the following code fragment, ERR() is called to print a message if a value is bigger than allowed:

```
if (value  MAXVAL)
    ERR("value too large");
```

In some other part of the program, the same macro can be called with a different argument to print an error message with a different text.

Macros and Side Effects

Be careful when defining macros to avoid unwanted side effects. A side effect is an action that occurs as a result of executing a statement. You often write statements for their side effects (clear the screen, store a value, and so on). But sometimes the side effects of a statement execution are not wanted and can produce disastrous results.

Our EVEN() macro is faulty because it will fail to produce the correct result in some circumstances. If we pass it an expression such as a + b instead of a hard-coded number for the `num` parameter, the conditional test expression becomes:

```
a + b % 2
```

instead of the expression:

```
(a + b) % 2
```

that we intended.

If a equals 2 and b equals 4, we have 2 + 4 % 2, which evaluates to 2 + 0, or 2, giving a result of FALSE. The result should be true because 2 + 4 is 6, an even number.

The solution to this problem is to use parentheses liberally in the definition of a macro. This causes the order of evaluation to be what we want. Here is the revised definition of EVEN():

```
#define EVEN(num)  (((num) % 2) ? FALSE : TRUE)
```

Now if you pass it the expression a + b with the values used earlier, the evaluation proceeds as ((2 + 4) % 2), which yields a value of 6 % 2 or 0—the correct result because there is no remainder.

The additional parentheses around the entire replacement text in the macro definition permit the macro to be used conveniently as a component of other expressions.

The Function/Macro Tradeoff

Given that functions and macros can both accept inputs via parameters, which should you use? The answer depends on what you are trying to do and the constraints (speed, size) placed on the program. First, let's look at this issue from the perspective of a program's speed of execution.

The use of a function involves call/return overhead that consumes time because data must be pushed on the stack, control passed to a different place in memory, and then back to the statement following the function call. If a function is called repeatedly inside the body of a loop, for example, the accumulated overhead can become quite costly, slowing the program execution speed.

A macro is expanded to its replacement text each time the macro name is encountered by the preprocessor (except when the name is part of a quoted string). Each expansion of a macro name produces in-line code that executes without the overhead of a function call, saving time. If you are optimizing your program for speed, macros can be an important tool.

Now let's view the issue of functions and macros from the perspective of program size-an important consideration on systems that have limited memory resources.

Because each occurrence of a macro is expanded to its full replacement text, the program size seen by the later passes of the C translator is inflated, and so, too, is the final executable program size. That's a cost of speed.

The benefit of functions is that the executable code produced by the translator appears in the program only once and can be called any number of times without making the program any larger. The cost of this space saving is an attendant speed penalty.

You can use a mixture of functions and macros in your programs to obtain a good balance between speed and program size. I recommend that you write your program initially in terms of functions. Then isolate those parts of the program that slow it down (more easily said than done) and recode them as macros.

Portability

The proposed ANSI C standard has at once solved a serious problem caused by the original design of C and introduced a potential portability problem. Function prototypes are the issue.

Function prototypes are not understood by most pre-ANSI compilers, especially those that run in UNIX and UNIX-like environments. This situation will change, but the problems will continue to exist for many years.

If you are writing a program that must be portable across disparate operating environments, place all function prototypes for functions in a program or library in a header. In the file, use conditional preprocessor directives to include or exclude function prototypes based on whether or not a symbolic name is defined.

Here is an example of the technique. The header shows what you might do for the prototypes used in the **boxtext** program. It is the way I have handled the differences between my DOS and UNIX C compilers.

```
/* boxtext.h */
#define MSDOS

#if defined (MSDOS)
/* DOS function prototypes */
void string(int, char);
void hborder(int);
void puttext(char []);
#endif
#elif defined (UNIX)
/* UNIX function declarations */
void string();
void hborder();
void puttext();
#endif
```

The #define at the top of the file specifies the environment and the #if defined directives conditionally select either full-function prototypes, as supported by most MS-DOS C translators, or earlier function declarations typical of pre-ANSI UNIX system C compilers, which only accept function name and return types in non-defining declarations.

To use this technique, remove the prototypes from the **boxtext.c** file and the following directive:

```
#include <boxtext.h>
```

An empty parameter list poses problems too, because many existing translators do not understand this use of the keyword void. This could be troublesome in the definition of the main() function, which can take arguments. Often, the arguments are ignored in a program. Using void to tell the translator what's going on is a good practice if the translator understands the idiom. Some older translators don't even know what void means in its data type context.

A way around this problem is to define the name VOID for the various operating environments and use the defined name in your program, like so:

Header:

```
#if defined MSDOS
#define VOID void
#elif defined UNIX
#define VOID
#endif
```

Source:

```
int main(VOID)
{
    . . .
}
```

Summary

You have reached the first major plateau along the ascent to C programming expertise. Functions are a key aspect of program design because they help you break a program into a set of tractable subprograms.

Each subprogram can be crafted to do one job well and hide the implementation details from the program at large. You can selectively alter individual functions to improve performance without adverse effects on the rest of the program.

In addition, you can create generalized sets of functions that can be used in the design and implementation of many programs. This technique is the essence of the standard C library. Reusable modules contribute to increased programmer productivity, a reduction in programming errors, and optimization of program performance.

Some problems lend themselves to recursive solutions. You should have recursion in your arsenal of programming weapons, but remember that an iterative solution may provide better performance in many situations.

Another way of coding subprograms is as macros. Macros offer the benefits of improved program speed at the cost of increased program size. A `#define` directive tells the C preprocessor to perform a text-replacement operation, which is the essence of macro creation and application.

Questions and Exercises

1. In your own words, describe the purpose of functions in C programs.

2. Can a program be written entirely in a single function? If so, is this a good programming practice?

3. How is a function called in a C program?

4. What is external linkage? Why is external linkage needed?

5. What is the purpose of a C function prototype?

6. For a function called `Add()`, which takes two integer arguments and returns an integer sum, write two declarations: a) defining declaration, and, b) function prototype.

7. What are the four components of a full-function definition?

8. Explain the difference between formal parameters and actual arguments.

9. True or false: C functions use call-by-reference as the default parameter-passing mechanism.

10. When is it not necessary to provide function prototypes in a C program?

    a) never
    b) when parameter and return types are integers
    c) when function definitions appear before the functions are called
    d) when a function doesn't have a return value

11. What is recursion and why is it useful?

12. What is a more efficient alternative to recursion?

13. Write a C program fragment that shows how to call the `Add()` function described in Question 6.

14. Which of these statements about macros are true?

    a) A macro results in less program code, saving space.
    b) A macro is usually faster than an equivalent functions.
    c) A macro is created by a preprocessor `#define` directive.
    d) Any macro defined in a file of a multi-file program is visible in any other file of the same program.

15. Write a `define` directive for a macro that computes the absolute value of a numeric argument.

Additional Exercises

A. Write the `string()` function as a macro and test its use in the **hbars** program.

B. Write a program that reads a series of four numbers from the keyboard and prints a report of the average value and the minimum and maximum values read. Segregate the tasks of data collection, analysis, and reporting into separate functions.

C. The **tree** program in this chapter produces a tree that has no trunk. Add a function that prints a trunk of two lines centered at the base of the tree. The trunk should consist of an odd or even number of characters depending on the width of the tree.

D. Write a program that prints a box within a box within a box within a box. Each box should be drawn with a different character. Write the program so that simply changing a value determines how many levels of boxes are drawn.

CHAPTER 7

ARRAYS AND POINTERS

In earlier chapters, we have used arrays of characters as input buffers, but you had to accept the concept of an array on faith. The same applies to pointers, which we used in statements involving `gets()`, `atoi()`, and other functions even though you didn't need to know at the time that pointers were involved. Now you need to learn about pointers because much of the power and flexibility of C is due to its elegant pointer mechanism.

A close relationship exists in C between arrays and pointers. This chapter introduces you to these topics, showing you how to create variables of array and pointer types, how to access such variables in your programs, and how to take advantage of the relationship between arrays and pointers.

Array Types

Thus far, we have emphasized scalar data types, such as integers, characters, and floating-point numbers. Much real-world data, however, is more efficiently managed as collections of data items under a common name—an **aggregate**.

An array is a contiguous arrangement of objects that have the same data type. Each object in an array is called an **element** of the array, and the type of an array is derived from the type of its elements. Thus, an array in which each element has type char is called an "array of type char."

In C, the base of an array is the element that has a subscript of 0. If you program in Pascal or other languages that use a base of 1, it may take a while for you to get used to the C approach.

Pay attention to the difference between the size of an array and the offset of its last element. An array of 20 integers has a size of 20. The subscript, or index, of the first element is 0 and the subscript of the last element is 19. If you attempt to access an element with the subscript 20, you are actually accessing whatever is in memory just above the array, not within it.

Declaring Array Variables

As with all variables in a C program, you must declare an array before using it for any purpose. An array declaration tells the C translator what it needs to know about the array, such as its type, name, and size.

This is the general form of an array declaration:

```
type array_name[size];
```

The array_name component is obviously the name by which you access the variable. The size component must be a constant or a constant expression. You cannot use a variable to provide the size of an array. And, of course, type is the data type of the array's elements. The square brackets surrounding the size distinguish an array variable from other types of variables.

Figure 7-1 shows an integer array, bucket, that might be used to keep track of scores in a ratings program. In this figure, an ordinary integer, count, is compared to an array of integers to highlight differences and similarities between a scalar variable and an array derived from the same type.

Declaring an ordinary integer like count creates a variable that occupies some number of bytes in memory, typically two or four bytes. Declaring an array with a size of 10, as shown in the figure, creates a variable consisting of 10 integer elements arranged contiguously in memory. The element with the subscript 0 is at the lowest address of the range and the element with the subscript 9 is at the highest address of the range.

Notice that the value zero is assigned to the variable count and to each element of the bucket array by explicit assignment. You can use explicit assignment statements to assign any valid initial values to the variables, although zero is the most reasonable choice for the variables shown because they are counters.

Figure 7-1: Comparing Integers and Integer Arrays

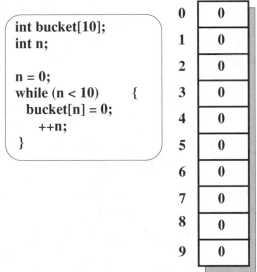

INTEGER VARIABLE:

```
int count;
/* ...*/
count = 0;
```

0

ARRAY OF INTEGERS:

```
int bucket[10];
int n;

n = 0;
while (n < 10)      {
  bucket[n] = 0;
    ++n;
}
```

0	0
1	0
2	0
3	0
4	0
5	0
6	0
7	0
8	0
9	0

Initializing Array Elements

You can provide initializers for array elements in the declaration statement. In the case of an ordinary integer, the initializer is provided by adding an equal sign and a value to the declaration. For example, to give `count` an initial value of 0, you could write the following declaration statement:

```
int count = 0;
```

This combines the earlier variable declaration and separate assignment statement into a single statement.

An array can be initialized in the same way. Instead of declaring the array and then running a loop to provide initial values for the elements, you can provide a set of initializers in the array declaration statement.

```
int bucket[10] = { 0, 0, 0, 0, 0, 0, 0, 0, 0, 0 };
```

The braces surrounding the initializer list are required. Initializers other than 0 are allowed, as long as they are appropriate for the array type, and each can have a different value from the other element values.

You can do a partial initialization by providing less initializers than there are elements. The initializers apply to elements at the start of the array. Do not provide too many initializers because you might overwrite data beyond the end of the array. The values of uninitialized array elements depend on the storage class.

Storage Class

The lifetime, or **storage duration**, of a variable and its "visibility," or **scope**, are specified by its **storage class**.

Storage Duration. Some variables are transient in nature, coming into existence and disappearing as a program runs. Many of the variables we have used in the programs in this book are transient. Other variables have permanent lifetimes, meaning they exist for the duration of the program. These two storage duration categories are called **automatic** and **static**, respectively.

Automatic storage duration is the default. A variable that is declared without the use of the `static` storage-class specifier and that has no linkages, is considered to be automatic. An example of such a variable is a loop counter, call it n, declared within a function. Storage is guaranteed for an instance of the variable n each time the enclosing function is entered and is given up when control passes out of the function.

On the other hand, an object that is declared with linkage, either external or internal, or that is declared with the storage class `static` has static storage duration. A variable with static storage duration has, in effect, a permanent home somewhere in memory. It is initialized once before the program starts running, and it retains the last value stored in it until the program terminates. Examples of permanent variables from our previous work are the text strings stored in `static` arrays.

Scope. The scope of an identifier, which determines where it is visible in a program, falls into one of four categories:

- Function
- File
- Block
- Function Prototype

An identifier used as a label has function scope. A label is used as the target of a `goto` statement. Label names must therefore be unique within a function. The same identifier in a different function is in a different scope, so there is no name conflict.

The position of a declaration statement or type specifier determines the scope of all other identifiers. Identifiers declared outside any block, including the block that forms a function body, has file scope. Such an identifier is, therefore, accessible for reading and writing anywhere in the file, from the declaration to the end of the translation unit.

Most identifiers have block scope, which means they are visible only within the enclosing block, including any inner blocks. An identifier that is declared in the parameter list of a function header is also in scope within the function body.

An identifier declared inside an inner block with the same name as an identifier in an outer block effectively hides the outer declaration while control is in the inner block. In this sample code, the two variables named c are different variables, not separate instances of the same variable:

```
{
    /* outer block */
    char c = 'X';
...
    {
        /* inner block */
        char c = 'Y';
        ...
        putchar(c);  /* prints 'Y' */
    }
    putchar(c);      /* prints 'X' */
}
```

Notice that the variable c in the inner block and operations performed on it, do not affect the value of c in the outer block.

Storage Class Specifiers. The storage class of a variable is indicated by a storage-class specifier in a declaration statement. The primary storage-class specifiers are extern, static, auto, and register. In addition, the keyword typedef is grouped with the storage-class specifiers for convenience, but it is not really a storage-class specifier, as we will see in later chapters.

An identifier having external linkage refers to an identical identifier in some other scope. The identifier must be defined only in one scope, but it can be referred to from elsewhere as long as the keyword extern is applied. Here's how it works:

DEFINING DECLARATION (in one translation unit):

```
int n;
```

REFERENCING DECLARATION (in another translation unit):

```
extern int n;
```

The important difference here is that the defining declaration reserves storage for the variable n. The referencing declaration doesn't. It only tells the translator that the identifier in the referencing declaration refers to the exact same object as the identifier in the defining declaration in the first translation unit. The linker resolves the external reference at link time.

We can also employ internal linkage of identifiers to confine them to a single file. Objects and functions that have file scope and whose declarators contain the static storage-class specifier have internal linkage. Within a translation unit, all instances of an identifier with internal linkage refer to the same object or function. However, there is no linkage to the same identifier outside the translation unit. An identifier with no linkage denotes an entity that is unique, such as a local variable inside a function or other block.

The auto keyword specifies automatic storage, which is transient in nature. If an identifier is declared within a block without the static storage-class specifier, it is auto by default.

Pre-ANSI C translators did not allow you to initialize automatic array variables. It was necessary to apply the static storage-class specifier to an array variable if you wanted to provide a list of initializers. The ANSI standard permits you to initialize any object of automatic duration. In this book, initialized arrays are declared static because most C translators still require it.

If you provide an incomplete list of initializers for a static array, the uninitialized elements are automatically zeroed. Such elements of an automatic array are not set, so they contain meaningless values (the residue of past activity at those memory locations).

Accessing Array Elements

You access array elements by using their subscripts. To print the number stored in bucket element 2, for example, use a statement such as:

```
printf("bucket[n] = %d\n", n, bucket[n]);
```

Be careful to use subscripts in the range of 0 to the array size minus one. There is no element with a subscript equal to the array size, as we have seen, so trying to print the contents of `bucket[10]` would yield an erroneous value.

Let's put our data-collection buckets to work. The **tally** program automates the task of surveying a group. If you were to ask a concert-going audience how they rated the band on a scale of 0 to 9, 9 being the best, **tally** helps you collect the raw data and presents a summary of results. We are most interested in the number of responses in each level of the scale. If buckets in the range of 7 through 9 accumulate high totals and the low numbered buckets don't, it's a good bet that the audience liked the show.

The program prints a brief set of instructions and then prompts you for data. As you enter the data, the program checks it to verify that each value is in range. When you tell it to quit by pressing the Return key by itself, it prints a summary of the collected data and terminates.

Here's the C source code for this handy program:

```
/*
 * tally.c
 *
 * Collect scores from a population of users (music
 * listeners, movie viewers, etc.), analyze the data, and
 * report findings.
 */

#include <stdio.h>
#include <stdlib.h>
#include <ctype.h>

#define RANGE 10
#define NCHARS 20

int
main(void)
{
        int bucket[RANGE] = { 0 };
        char inbuf[NCHARS];
        int count = 0;
        int score;
```

```
    int n;

    /* collect raw data */
    printf("\nTALLY PROGRAM\n");
    printf("Type scores in the range 0 through 9\n");
    printf("Enter each score by pressing Return\n");
    printf("End input by typing no input (just Return)\n");
    while (1) {
            /* prompt for input and read it */
            printf("Score: ");
            if (gets(inbuf) == NULL) {
                    fprintf(stderr, "ERROR: bad read\n");
                    continue;
            }

            /* check for quit command (any nondigit) */
            if (!isdigit(inbuf[0])) {
                    putchar('\n');
                    break;
            }

            /* convert input string to an integer */
            score = atoi(inbuf);

            /* range-check the data; save if good */
            if (score >= 0 && score < RANGE) {
                    ++bucket[score];
                    ++count;
            }
            else {
                    fprintf(stderr,
                        "ERROR: data out of range\n");
                    continue;
            }
    }

    /* report results */
    printf("\nRESULTS:\nScore\tCount\n");
    for (n = 0; n < RANGE; ++n)
```

```
        printf("%d\t%d\n", n, bucket[n]);
    printf("\n%d scores reported\n", count);

    return EXIT_SUCCESS;
}
```

The header **ctype.h** contains a set of macros for categorizing characters. We need to use the isdigit() macro to validate input and check for commands, so we include the header in the program source. The program accepts only whole numbers as data input. Anything below 0 or above 9 is rejected. Any non-digit input, including none at all, is considered a command to quit.

Data is collected in a small input buffer. Remember that input is received in the form of characters typed on the keyboard. If the user types the number 6, for example, the program actually receives the null-terminated string "6", which must be converted to integer form. That job is done by the atoi() function.

A running count of the number of data values collected is maintained in the variable count. Invariably, someone will try to input an out-of-range response or make a typing mistake. It is important to avoid counting bad inputs along with the good inputs, so count is incremented only when a bucket is incremented as a result of good data.

Multidimensional Arrays

An important attribute of any programming language is its ability to model the environment in which it is used. Flexible data types that let you match your program to the problem at hand make your life as a programmer pleasant, or at least bearable.

A common type of data is that of the rectangular array. Think about some board games and most tabular summaries of information as examples of rectangular arrays. A computer spreadsheet or a database is built on this model.

Adding Array Dimensions

Figure 7-2 shows what a two-dimensional array looks like in C. As you can see, it is actually an array of arrays. This array can be viewed as a two-element array (the rows) in which each element is a five-element array (the columns).

All elements of a multidimensional array have the same type, just as with linear arrays. The array still has a name. But now there are two or more subscripts instead of one.

The array in Figure 7-2 has two dimensions, which we can refer to as rows and columns to use a familiar analogy. As you can see from the figure, as we move through the array, the column subscript (right-most) changes faster than the row subscript. If we need a third dimension, we just add another subscript.

Figure 7-2: A Two-dimensional Array

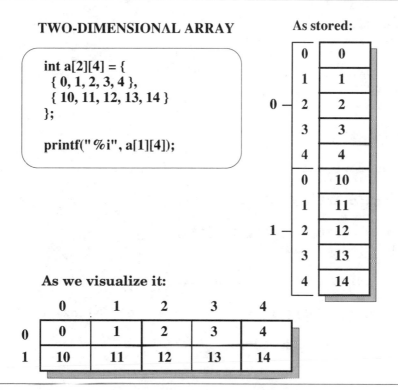

```
int a[2][4] = {
  { 0, 1, 2, 3, 4 },
  { 10, 11, 12, 13, 14 }
};

printf(" %i", a[1][4]);
```

Initializing and Accessing Multidimensional Arrays

As you can see in Figure 7-2, you can initialize a multidimensional array by providing a braced list of initializers. Again, initializers apply to elements at the start of the array. Uninitialized elements are automatically zeroed in static arrays and are undefined in automatic arrays. The same applies to the way external and static scalar variables are treated.

The **array2** program (listing **array2.c**) establishes a two-dimensional array, a, and initializes it. It then prints out the value of an element.

```c
/*
 * array2.c
 *
 * Declare a two-dimensional array with initializers
 * and then print out all of its element values.
 */

#include <stdio.h>
#include <stdlib.h>

#define ROWS    2
#define COLS    5

int
main(void)
{
        int row, col;

        static int a[ROWS][COLS] = {
            {  0,  1,  2,  3,  4 },
            { 10, 11, 12, 13, 14 }
        };

        /* print the value of an array element */
        row = 1, col = 4;
        printf("a[%i][%i] = %i\n", row, col, a[row][col]);

        return EXIT_SUCCESS;
}
```

To get a better feel for how the subscripts work, try modifying the **array2** program so that a table of rows and columns is printed, showing the value of each element of the array. Use the existing `row` and `col` variables to control two loops, one inside the other. Because the column subscript varies faster than the row subscript, it should be the innermost loop.

Pointer Types

A pointer is a variable that contains the address of an object or function. The pointer is another of C's derived types. Although many programming languages implement pointers in some way, the C pointer implementation is one of the most elegant, giving C much of its power.

As you learned in Chapter 4, the address operator, &, yields the address of its operand. Thus, we have a way to find out where an object is located in memory. But how can we preserve and use this information? What we need is a place to store the address information. We get that by declaring a pointer variable.

Declaring Pointer Variables

A pointer declaration incorporates a new element—the indirection operator, `*`. Here is the general form:

```
type *ptr_name;
```

The `type` component specifies the type of data being pointed to and `ptr_name` is the identifier that names the pointer variable.

You can read the declaration most easily by working backwards: "`ptr_name` is a pointer to an object of type `type`." This interpretation of the `*` operator may not seem particularly intuitive at first, but the declaration syntax of a pointer variable is consistent with its use.

Let's use an integer pointer example to examine pointer declarations more closely. Figure 7-3 shows how a pointer is declared and given a value, and how it looks in memory. A plain integer, declared in the following statement, occupies a region of memory, typically two or four bytes, and has a value that is initially undefined.

```
int number;   /* plain integer */
```

You can declare a pointer to an integer by using the following statement:

```
int *p;        /* pointer to integer */
```

This declaration says that p is a pointer to an object of type int, but p also contains an undefined value because nothing has been assigned to it yet. The size of a pointer is implementation-defined, and is typically two or four bytes wide.

Figure 7-3: C has an elegant pointer mechanism.

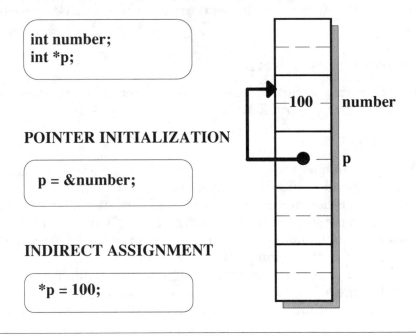

✍**Programmer's Notebook**

Pointer and integer variables often have the same size in a given environment, but they are not interchangeable. Historically, C programmers have blurred the distinction between pointers and integers, but the ANSI standard reasserts the distinction.

Before you can successfully use a pointer, the pointer variable must contain a valid address. Simply declaring a variable to be a pointer to an object of some type does not give the pointer a value. You have to assign one. This is where the & operator comes into play.

The next statement gets the address of the variable number and assigns it to the pointer variable p:

```
p = &number;
```

Because p is a pointer to an object of type int, it must hold the address of an integer. The expression &number yields the address of an integer. Success. After this assignment, p effectively points to number as symbolized by the arrow in Figure 7-3.

Accessing Data Through Pointers

Now you can access the value stored in number either directly by using the variable's name or indirectly by dereferencing the pointer p. The value of number is still not defined because we haven't assigned anything to it yet.

The statement:

```
*p = 100;      /* indirect assignment */
```

assigns the value 100 to number. The statement has the same effect as

```
number = 100;  /* direct assignment */
```

This is true because dereferencing a pointer yields the object being pointed to. Thus *p and number both designate what is stored in the location identified as number.

The program **cptr** shows how to use a pointer with characters. The
process is the same, only the data type changes. In this program, the
variable cp is a pointer to a character and ch is a character. The program
compares direct and indirect assignment of values to the ch variable and
shows how to read the value of ch through the pointer cp.

```c
/*
 * cptr.c
 *
 * This program shows you how to access a character
 * variable directly and indirectly through a pointer.
 */

#include <stdio.h>
#include <stdlib.h>

int
main(void)
{
        char ch;    /* character variable */
        char *cp;   /* pointer to a character */

        /* get the address of ch into cp */
        cp = &ch;

        /* direct assignment */
        ch = 'X';
        printf("DIRECT ASSIGNMENT:   ch = %c\n", ch);

        /* indirect assignment */
        *cp = 'x';
        printf("INDIRECT ASSIGNMENT: ch = %c\n", ch);

        /* print ch indirectly by dereferencing cp */
        printf("INDIRECT ACCESS:     *cp = %c\n", *cp);

        return EXIT_SUCCESS;
}
```

The direct assignment stores the code that represents the letter X in the location associated with the identifier ch and the `printf()` statement shows the result of the assignment. Then the code for lowercase x is stored in the same location via indirection. The expression `*cp`, a dereferenced pointer, designates a character, so it is legal to assign the value of a character to it.

Address Arithmetic

Certain arithmetic operations are permitted on pointer variables. You can use pointers in arithmetic expressions involving the following operations:

- add an integer to a pointer

- subtract an integer from a pointer

- get the difference between two pointers

- compare two pointers for equality

For operations involving printer differences and comparisons, the pointers must point to the same object, such as an array.

No other arithmetic operations are allowed. You cannot add, multiply, divide, or shift pointer variables. And use caution even with allowed operations. You could, for example, attempt to add an amount to a valid pointer that produces an address that is outside the array bounds or that causes segment wrap-around. Such actions would likely produce unpredictable and almost certainly unpleasant results.

The size of a pointer is scaled to the size of the type of the object being pointed to. If you have a pointer to an array of doubles, for example, adding 1 to the pointer means that the pointer points up in memory by the number of bytes needed to address the next array element.

Pointers and Arrays in C

Arrays and pointers work well together. In a C program, you are likely to see pointers to arrays as well as arrays of pointers. Such constructs are easy to create and use. In addition, you will find that arrays and pointers are heavily involved with strings.

C Strings

Unlike most computer languages, C does not have a built-in string data type. Instead, it treats sequences of characters terminated by a null byte (NUL) as a string.

You can create a string by declaring an array of characters and assigning values to the array elements as shown in Figure 7-4. You are responsible for providing the terminating null byte, which is shown as a character constant with a value of ' \0'. If you forget to provide the terminating character, you have a simple array of characters, not a string, and your program will break in ways that are not fun to observe.

Figure 7-4: Character Strings and Pointers

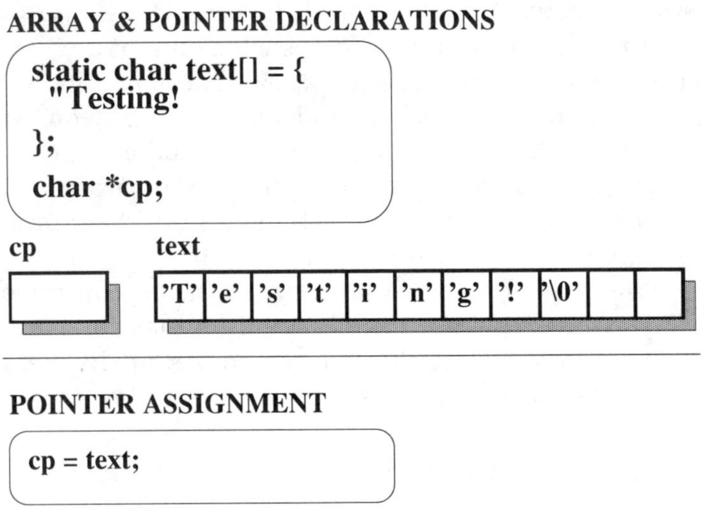

ARRAY & POINTER DECLARATIONS

```
static char text[] = {
   "Testing!
};
char *cp;
```

cp   text

| | | 'T' | 'e' | 's' | 't' | 'i' | 'n' | 'g' | '!' | '\0' | | | |

POINTER ASSIGNMENT

```
cp = text;
```

The **str** program shows you how to create a string and how to access the characters within the string. The program prints the string in two ways. The first way uses an array subscript to retrieve the values stored in successive array elements. The second uses a pointer for element access.

```c
/*
 * str.c
 *
 * Print text strings by using both direct and
 * indirect access methods.
 */

#include <stdio.h>
#include <stdlib.h>
#include <string.h>

int
main(void)
{
    int i;
    char *cp;  /* general character pointer */

    static char str[] = {
        "The quick fox knows something about chickens!\n"
    };

    /* use a subscripted array to print string */
    printf("Direct via putchar(): ");
    for (i = 0; str[i] != '\0'; ++i)
        putchar(str[i]);

    /* use a character pointer to print the string */
    printf("Indirect via a character pointer: ");
    for (cp = str; *cp != '\0'; ++cp)
        putchar(*cp);

    return EXIT_SUCCESS;
}
```

In Chapter 3 we discussed literal strings. Recall that a quoted sequence of characters, such as "The quick fox knows something about chickens!\n", is a literal string. We can use a literal string to initialize an array.

In the array initialization that follows, the literal string completes the incomplete type of the array declaration. No size value was provided (empty brackets), so the translator determines how many characters comprise the array.

```
static char str[] = {
      "The quick fox knows something about chickens!\n"
};
```

There are 47 elements in this array. The \n sequence counts as a single character (a newline) and there is an automatic null byte appended to the string literal that marks the end of the string.

The control variable of the for loop, i, is set to an initial value of 0, which selects the element at the base of the array. The loop continues running as long as the expression str[i] != '\0' is true. This test expression compares the value stored in the ith array element with 0 (expressed as a character constant). Thus, the test expression terminates the loop as soon as the subscript i selects the array element that contains the null byte.

The pointer method of printing out the array's contents also uses a for loop, but a pointer scans the array instead of an array subscript. The initial value of the pointer cp is obtained by assigning the address of the array into the pointer.

In C, the name of an array is a constant pointer to the base of the array, which is the address of the first element. That means we can use the array name as a synonym for a more complicated address expression. The name str, for example, is identical to the expression &str[0]. Thus str, being a constant pointer, can be assigned directly into cp.

The loop-termination test becomes *cp != '\0', which compares the value stored in the location being pointed to by cp against the code for the null byte. As long as the pointer is accessing a non-null character, the loop keeps running.

Note that comparison against zero is automatic in the loop-control expression, so you could use the expression `str[i]` as the loop-control expression. There is no need to do an explicit comparison with the null byte. In the pointer version, you could use `*cp` as the control expression for the same reason.

Subscripted Arrays and Pointer Offsets

As you have seen, you can get at an element of a string or other array by using the familiar array subscript method that is common to many computer languages. But in C you can get at the same element by using a base pointer and an integral offset from the base as shown in Figure 7-5.

Figure 7-5: Using Pointers to Access Array Elements

ARRAY & POINTER DECLARATIONS

```
static char text[] = {
  "Testing!
};
char *cp;
```

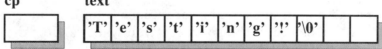

cp   text

| 'T' | 'e' | 's' | 't' | 'i' | 'n' | 'g' | '!' | '\0' | | |

POINTER ASSIGNMENT

```
cp = text;
```

The following code fragments help to clarify what is happening. First we declare and initialize and array with the string `"Testing!"` and establish a pointer, cp, to the base of the array (element 0, or simply the array name as shown):

```
/* test message */
static char text[] = { "Testing!" };
char *cp;   /* character pointer */

/* point to the beginning of the string */
cp = text;
Next we print the character stored in element seven:

/* these statements print the same character */
putchar(str[7]);   /* subscripted array */
putchar(*(cp + 7));      /* dereferenced pointer + offset */
```

The subscripted array example should be obvious to you now, but the pointer method invites discussion.

The expression that yields the character to be printed is `*(cp + 7)`. Because the pointer cp points to the base of the array, adding 7 to it points to an element that is seven elements away from the base of the array. Applying the dereferencing operator, `*`, to the address expression yields what is stored in the addressed element. This element contains the exclamation point.

Note that adding or subtracting an integer from a pointer does not change the value stored in the pointer. If you want to alter the pointer value, you must assign a value to it. For example, the expression cp += 7 would change the pointer value because the expression involves an assignment of a value into the pointer variable (effectively cp = cp + 7).

Arrays of Pointers

The elements of an array don't have to be simple characters or integers. You can declare arrays of pointers or other derived data types, too. But why would you want to?

One purpose for an array of pointers is the creation of irregular or ragged arrays. Figure 7-6 depicts a ragged array that contains the full-text names for the days of the week. If the numeric value of the day, possibly obtained from a calculation based on a date, is used as a subscript to access the array, a program can use the pointer stored in the array to access the full-text name string for that day of the week.

Figure 7-6: Use ragged arrays to save space in memory.

```
static char *dayname[] = {
  "Sunday", "Monday", "Tuesday",
  "Wednesday", "Thursday", "Friday",
  "Saturday"
};
```

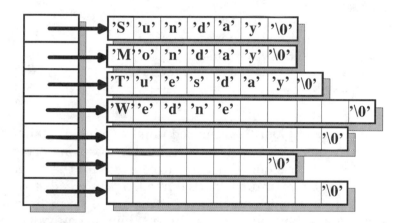

If the day-of-week calculation produces the number 5, for example, the pointer in element 5 of the array points to the start of the string "Friday". Take a close look at the array declaration:

```
static char *dayname[] = {
     "Sunday", "Monday", "Tuesday",
     "Wednesday", "Thursday", "Friday",
     "Saturday"
};
```

The array name is `dayname`. The empty brackets following the array name indicate that it is an array, but no array `size` is specified. The translator knows how to count, so if you provide a full set of initializers, it will compute the value for you.

Each element of the array is a pointer to a character. The literal strings in the initializer list cause strings to be stored somewhere in memory and addresses to be stored in the `dayname` array. Element 0 receives the address of the literal string `"Sunday"`, element 1 receives the address of `"Monday"`, and so on.

Contrast the ragged array just described to a rectangular array, which has dimensions based on the length of the longest string. For the example shown, the array declaration might look like this:

```
#define ROWS 7
#define COLS 10
...
static char dayname[ROWS][COLS] = {
     "Sunday", "Monday", "Tuesday",
     "Wednesday", "Thursday", "Friday",
     "Saturday"
};
```

Instead of occupying just the required number of characters (67), the rectangular array occupies a full 70 character locations. There is an overhead of one pointer element per line to consider for the ragged-array approach, but if the maximum expected line length exceeds the average line length by even a small amount, as it usually does in practice, the ragged-array approach is more space efficient than an equivalent rectangular-array approach.

There are other reasons for using pointers and arrays. In particular, an array of pointers is a convenient way of accessing the arguments typed on the user command line in computing environments that support that feature, such as UNIX and DOS. You'll see examples of command-line argument processing in later chapters.

Pointers and Functions

Another useful pairing is that of pointers and functions. There are three ways to use pointers with functions:

- pointers as function arguments

- function returning a pointer

- pointer to a function

The first two uses are fairly common in C programs. The third is less-frequently encountered, but it provides important capabilities and efficiency gains in some programming situations.

Pointers as Function Arguments

In Chapter 6, you learned that the default parameter-passing method is "call-by-value" and that "call-by-reference" parameter passing is an alternative that depends on the use of pointers. Using pointer variables as function arguments gives you a way to "return" multiple values to a calling function where only a single return value is permitted by the return statement of a function. It also permits a called function to affect the values of variables in the calling function, which is not possible when "call-by-value" methods are used.

Here is an example of a function definition that uses a pointer as a formal parameter:

```
int
StringLength(char *str)
{
    char *cp;

    /* point to start of string */
    cp = str;

    /* find the terminating null byte */
    while (*cp != '\0')
        ++cp;
```

```
      /* compute string length */
      return cp - str;
}
```

This function, as its name implies, computes the length of a string. It receives the address of the string to be measured, sets a temporary character pointer (cp) to the beginning of the string, scans the string looking for the null byte, and then returns the difference between the position of the null byte and the beginning of the string. The return value, a result of address arithmetic, is the string length.

The standard library provides a wealth of often-used routines. Among them are many string-handling functions, including one called strlen(), which does the same job as our StringLength(). It is useful to develop such functions to see how they work, but in programs you should use the available library functions to obtain the greatest portability to other C-supporting environments and to minimize your own programming effort. Concentrate on the things that are unique to your program and build as much as possible on the work of others.

Functions Returning Pointers

In programs presented thus far in the book, functions have either returned nothing (void), or have returned numeric values, such as 0 to indicate success or some other number to indicate failure. In the cas eof StringLength(), the return value is an integer.

Functions that return pointers are particularly useful in performing string manipulations, managing databases, searching and sorting text, and many other common tasks. Here, for example, is a function that returns a pointer to a character. The function is called StringCopy because its job is to copy one string, str2, to another, str1. You must ensure that str1 is large enough to receive str2 including its terminating null byte. If the destination string is not large enough, you will overwrite some other region of memory.

```
char *
StringCopy(char *str1, char *str2)
```

```
{
        char *p, *q;

        /* set up temporary pointers */
        p = str1;
        q = str2;

        /* copy str2 onto str1 */
        while (*q != '\0') {
                *p = *q;
                ++p;
                ++q;
        }

        /* terminate destination string */
        *p = '\0';

        /* point to start of destination string */
        return str1;
}
```

The function does its job by establishing two temporary pointers, p and q, to the two input pointers. While the source pointer, q, points to a valid character (non-null), the loop runs, copying characters from the source string to the destination string. When the loop terminates, the destination string is terminated by a null byte. Then a pointer to the start of the destination string is returned. Notice that the return type of StringC-opy() is char *, a pointer to a character.

Although it is not necessary to return a pointer to the start of the destination string, doing so adds greatly to the utility of the function. Having the pointer available as a result of the function call lets you use embedded assignment and provides a natural means of expressing common actions, such as printing the result of a string copy.

The following main() function serves to test the preceding string functions. It calls StringLength() and StringCopy() embedded in the argument lists of printf() statements. This method precludes the need for temporary variables to hold return values--the length, for example.

The following program consists of function prototypes and a `main()` function that exercises the string functions we just created.

```c
/*
 * strtest.c
 *
 * Test various string functions.
 */

#include <stdio.h>
#include <stdlib.h>

/* function prototypes */
int StringLength(char *);
char *StringCopy(char *, char *);

int
main()
{
        /* messages and buffers */
        static char mesg[] = { "This is a test!" };
        static char buffer[] = {
                "BUFFER BUFFER BUFFER BUFFER"
        };

        puts("\nStringLength() test:");
        printf("String contents = %s\n", mesg);
        printf("Number of characters = %d\n",
                StringLength(mesg));

        puts("\nStringCopy() test:");
        printf("Buffer before copying = %s\n", buffer);
        printf("Buffer after copying =  %s\n",
                StringCopy(buffer, mesg));

        return EXIT_SUCCESS;
}
```

To prepare the executable **strtest** program, you can either combine the `main()` and string functions in a single module or separately translate the three functions and link the separate modules. Either way, the function prototypes in `main()` provide the needed forward references for the string functions. The output produced by **strtest** looks like this:

```
StringLength() test:
String contents = This is a test!
Number of characters = 15

StringCopy() test:
Buffer before copying = BUFFER BUFFER BUFFER BUFFER
Buffer after copying =  This is a test!
```

Notice how the `buffer` array is initialized. The string with a repeated text message ("BUFFER") effectively reserves memory and puts a recognizable pattern in that memory. This lets you see the effect of overwriting the buffer with the text in the `mesg` array and it helps you diagnose problems in the `StringCopy()` function.

For example, if you forgot to terminate the destination string by leaving the line

```
*str1 = '\0';
```

out of the `StringCopy()` function, the output would show residue of the initial string because `printf()` would not stop printing until it finds the original terminate null byte. Try modifying the program to introduce the error and test it.

Pointers to Functions

A pointer to a function is quite different from a function that returns a pointer, and their declarations are necessarily different. Although a function in C is not a variable, it is possible to take the address of a function and use the address in various ways, just as you can use any other pointer.

The declaration of a pointer to a function may look a bit bizarre at first glance. Study it until it feels right. Here is the general form of such a declaration:

```
type (*fptr)();
```

The essential attribute of this kind of declaration is the use of parentheses to force the correct binding. The parentheses around the expression *fptr are needed because the default binding associates the name func with the set of matching parentheses that follow it. Without the extra parentheses, the declaration becomes

```
type *fptr();    /* function return pointer */
```

This declares a function that returns a pointer to an object of the specified type—not what we need. With all parentheses in place, read the declaration as "func is a pointer to a function returning type."

The following declaration is for a variable, f, that is a pointer, denoted by the *, to a function, shown by the parentheses, that returns an integer (int):

```
int (*f)();
```

The **qsrtdemo** program shows off the standard library qsort() and the use of a pointer to a function that returns an integer. The function is icompare(), which takes two pointer-to-integer arguments and returns an integer value.

```
/*
 * qsrtdemo.c
 *
 * Sort an array of numbers quickly by using the
 * qsort() library routine.
 */

#include <stdio.h>
#include <stdlib.h>

/* function prototype */
```

```
int icompare(int *, int *);

int
main(void)
{
        int n, *ptr;   /* loop counter and pointer */
        int size;      /* array size in elements */

        /* unsorted array of integers */
        static int num[] = {
                400, 1, 230, -16, 81, 120, 33, -54, 60
        };

        /* calculate the array size */
        size = sizeof num / sizeof (int);

        /* display contents of the unsorted array */
        puts("\nUnsorted Array:");
        for (n = size, ptr = num; n-- > 0; ++ptr)
                printf("%5d  ", *ptr);
        putchar('\n');

        /* use qsort() to sort the array */
        qsort((void *) num, (size_t) size,
                sizeof (int), icompare);

        /* display the sorted array */
        puts("\nSorted Array:");
        for (n = size, ptr = num; n-- > 0; ++ptr)
                printf("%5d  ", *ptr);
        putchar('\n');

        return EXIT_SUCCESS;
}

int
icompare(int *n1, int *n2 )
{
        if (*n1 > *n2)
```

```
        return 1;
    else if (*n1 < *n2)
        return -1;
    else
        return 0;
}
```

The **qsrtdemo** program uses a built-in array of numbers. It sorts the array by calling on `qsort()`. The last argument to `qsort()` is a pointer to a data comparison function that returns an integer. The value of the return from the comparison function indicates whether the two values passed as arguments to it are equal (0) or unequal. Values of -1 or +1 indicate that the first argument value is less than or greater than the value of the second argument.

The function prototype for `qsort()` is obtained from the <stdlib.h> header. It looks like this in most current C implementations:

```
void qsort(void *base, size_t nmemb, size_t size,
    int (*compar)(const void *, const void *));
```

The function does not return a value, so it is declared void. We call `qsort()` only for its side effect, which is to quickly sort an array of elements.

The base parameter is a pointer to the start of the array being sorted. The `void *` type specifier is new. In pre-ANSI C translators, the "generic" pointer type was `char *`. Now `void *` is the generic pointer type. It has the same alignment requirements as `char *`.

The `nmemb` parameter specifies the number of elements in the range being sorted and the `size` parameter specifies the uniform size of each element. Both `nmemb` and `size` have type `size_t`, which is the unsigned integral type of the result of the sizeof operator. This type is defined in **<stddef.h>** and other headers, including **<stdio.h>**.

The `compar` parameter is a pointer to the comparison function. The declaration says that `compar` is a pointer to a function that returns and integer. The `compar` declaration also says that the comparison function has two pointer parameters, each of type `const void *`. The `const` type qualifier used in a parameter list indicates that the value of the parameter is not changed by the call to the function. In the qsrtdemo program, the call to qsort() uses the function name icompare as an argument because the unadorned name of a function is a pointer to the function's code, just as the unadorned name of an array is a pointer to its first element.

Portability

Most portability issues related to arrays and pointers relate to differences between computer architectures that affect sizes and ranges.

The maximum array size is a function of the addressing range of a computer and the way a given C implementation chooses to deal with the problem. For example, the segmented architecture of an Intel 8086 (and 80286) processor imposes a limiting size of any object to one 64 kilobyte segment. Most C translators in that operate in a PC environment provide a huge keyword that gets around this limitation, but portability to other environments is diminished.

In segmented environments, pointer sizes vary with the memory model being used. You have to deal with small, medium, and large models as a minimum. In addition, some translators offer tiny and compact models, and the extended keywords `near` and `far`, which permit "mixed-model" programming. If you must use extended features in one environment, try to put all system-specific code and data in a single file or a small set of files. These can be modified for other environments, but the bulk of your program will not require changes.

Summary

This chapter has introduced the topics of arrays and pointers in C. Both are derived types, which are created by applying the [ ] and * operators to basic types.

Arrays can be either internal (declared inside a function) or external. The static keyword applied to an internal array makes it permanent so that its values are maintained across function calls. You can initialize both automatic and static arrays, although pre-ANSI compilers only allow initialization of the latter type.

Applying the static keyword to an external array declaration makes the array private from the point of declaration to the end of the file in which it is declared. Otherwise, the array is globally visible.

You can create the effect of a multidimensional array by declaring an array within which each element is itself an array. Each dimension requires an additional bracketed size specifier. Elements are accessed by application of bracketed subscripts, one for each dimension.

Closely related to arrays, but not identical to them, are pointers. The pointer mechanism supported by C is extremely flexible and natural. The pointer dereferencing operator * accesses the object or function pointed to by the pointer variable. Use the & operator to obtain the address of an object. An array name is a constant pointer to the base of the array and a function name is a constant pointer to its code. You do not use & with array and function names.

A literal string is a sequence of characters terminated with a null byte. You can store a string in a character array provided that the array is large enough to hold all of the strings characters including the null byte.

The declaration syntax of arrays and pointers is consistent with their uses. Thus, a declaration such as char *cp says that cp is a pointer to a character (char *), and *cp is a character.

The array/pointer relationship in C is a close one. Given an array and a pointer to it, you can access any element via a subscript or the pointer and an integral offset. The later method is an example of pointer arithmetic, which permits you to perform many other useful operations, such as computing a length and comparing pointers for equality or inequality.

Questions and Exercises

1. An array in C has which of the following properties:

   a) All elements have a common type
   b) The array base (starting element) has a subscript of 1
   c) Elements are be arranged contiguously
   d) All of the above

2. True or false: An automatic array cannot be initialized in a declaration statement.

2. True or false: An automatic array cannot be initialized in a declaration statement.

3. Explain what the keyword `static` is used for in an internal array declaration, such as:

```
static char mesg[] = { "ERROR: input out of range" };
```

4. Describe how C, which does not have a true multidimensional array type, obtains the effect anyway.

5. Given the following array declaration, write a statement that loops through the array, adding 1 to each element that contains an odd value.

```
int a[20];
```

6. What is a pointer?

7. Write declarations of a plain integer, `i`, and a pointer ,`ip`, to an integer. Also write a statement that makes the pointer point to `i`.

8. Study the following statements and briefly describe what each does. Fill in the missing statement (indicated by the underline) so that the assignment through the pointer variable makes sense.

```
char ch, *cp;
_____
*cp = 'Q';
putchar(ch);
```

9. Which of the following arithmetic operations are permitted on pointers (in situations involving two pointers, both point to the same object)?

a) Subtract one pointer from the other
b) Add the two pointers together
c) Add or subtract a pointer and an integer
d) All of the above
e) None of the above

10. Write a loop statement that converts each capital letter in the following array to its lowercase equivalent. HINT: Use the `tolower()` macro provided by your C translator standard library to do the conversion.

```
static char text[] = { "MACROS.C" };
```

Additional Exercises

A. Write a program that prompts the user for a line of text (up to 65 characters), reads it, and reports the following:

   a) The number of letters (use `isalpha()`)
   b) The number of digits (use `isdigit()`)
   c) The number of all other characters
   d) The total number of characters in the input line

B. Write a program that creates the table of decimal and equivalent hexadecimal values shown below. Use a static array of values as a decimal-to-hex conversion table.

0	0
1	1
2	2
3	3
4	4
. . .	
10	A
11	B
12	C
13	D
14	E
15	F

C. Write a program that collects student test grades and produces a summary of the test results. Report the average grade and the number of students with grades in the following ranges:

   90 and above (A)
   80 to 89 (B)
   70 to 79 (C)
   60 to 69 (D)
   Below 60 (F)

D. Modify the **qsrtdemo** program so that it sorts an array of doubles. (You need to makes changes in `main()` and provide a different comparison function.)

CHAPTER 8

STRUCTURES

C provides a comprehensive set of basic data types and several ways to derive higher-level data types from the basic types. This chapter describes structures and structure-like features called unions and bit fields.

In addition, this chapter introduces you to enumerations and to a way of creating new data type names.

Introduction to Structures

A structure provides a convenient means of handling collections of variables of the same or differing types. You can group data items that are related to each other in some way under a common name and access the items through that name and a technique called member selection. A C structure is an aggregate that is analogous to a Pascal record. Some recent BASIC implementations offer similar record-like features.

Records in databases from simple card files to sophisticated personnel and payroll systems are examples of structures. In such databases, a record or structure typically contains account numbers, names, addresses, phone numbers, and other information about each contact or employee.

Structure Declarations

A structure declaration in C has the following general form:

```
struct tag {
     type varname;
     ...
};
```

The keyword `struct` identifies this as a structure declaration. The optional `tag` gives a unique name to a particular structure. The list of variable declarations specifies the members of the structure. The result of such a declaration is the creation of a structure **template** that you can use as a type specifier.

Here is a structure declaration that creates a template for a structure used to maintain information about the months of the year:

```
struct month_st {
     char name[10];
     char abbrev[4];
     short days;
};
```

The structure template created by this declaration specifies the form of any variable that is declared to have type `struct month_st`. The suffix "_st" is a convention I use to indicate that the name carrying the suffix is a structure tag. You will find many derived types in the standard C library that carry a "_t" suffix for the same purpose. The type `size_t` is an example of this practice.

Figure 8-1 shows the declaration of a variable called `month` that has the type `struct month_st`. The two character arrays occupy fixed amounts of space in memory because the structure declaration is designed to hold a month name plus a terminating null byte in the `name` member and a three-letter abbreviation plus its null byte in the `abbrev` member. The `days` member is a short integer, which occupies two bytes.

Because the `name` and `abbrev` members are arrays, the members occupy the same amount of space regardless of what `month` data is stored in them.

Figure 8-1: Declaring Structure Template and Variables

STRUCTURE TEMPLATE

```
struct month_st {
    char name[10];
    char abbrev[4];
    short days;
};
```

VARIABLE DECLARATION

```
struct month_st month;
```

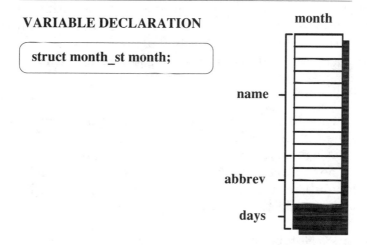

Using Structures

Once you have declared a structure variable, what can you do with it? First, you can assign or copy values to its members. To assign the number of days in January to the month variable, for example, use this statement:

```
month.days = 31;
```

The dot ('.') is called the structure member operator. The precedence of this operator is very high—right at the top of the table along with functions (parentheses), arrays (square brackets), and the odd-looking

"->", which we'll examine shortly. To access a member of a structure variable, apply the dot operator:

varname.member

The `varname` component of the expression identifies the structure variable and the member component identifies the member of interest. The type of the member-selection expression is that of the member itself. In the case of the `days` member, the type is `short int`.

As you probably know by now (or will find out if you try it), you cannot simply assign a string literal to an array variable because an array name is not a modifiable value. Attempting to assign the string "January" to the `name` member of `month` fails. You have to copy each character from the string to the variable individually. This is most easily accomplished by using the `strcpy()` function from the standard library, like so:

```
strcpy(month.name, "January");
```

The arguments to `strcpy()` are the destination and the source—in that order. The expression `month.name` selects the `name` member of the structure. This is an array name, which is a constant pointer to the start of the array. The characters of the string constant are copied by `strcpy()` and a proper null termination is applied as long as you have allowed enough room in the destination array.

✍Programmer's Notebook
___

If the destination array is too short for what is being copied into it, something following it in memory is likely to be overwritten. Be sure to allow enough room for the largest expected string in the destination array.

By the same technique, this next statement copies the abbreviation of the month name into the `abbrev` member of the structure:

```
strcpy(month.abbrev, "Jan");
```

If you have two or more structures of the same type, the ANSI standard allows you to assign one of the structures into another. Thus, if `s1` and `s2` both have type `struct month_st`, it is permissible to write statements like this one:

```
s1 = s2;
```

Before this addition to C, you would have had to copy or assign each of the members individually. Structure assignment was supported by a few pre-ANSI C translators, but most still do not allow it.

Structures Containing Pointers

The `month` structure declared with array members is inefficient in its use of memory. For a single variable, a few unused bytes, such as when you store the data for May, is no big deal. Consider an array of variables of this type, or worse, a large array of structure variables designed to hold lines of text.

A more efficient way of storing data is to use pointers as structure members and point them to efficiently stored strings (no wasted character positions). We can easily modify the earlier declaration of the `month` structure to use pointer members. Here's the new declaration of the structure template:

```
struct month_st {
      char *name;
      char *abbrev;
      short days;
};
```

The two character arrays are replaced by character pointers, each occupying the space needed for a pointer. The `days` member is unchanged. An array of variables of this type, one for each month of the year, makes a nice lookup table. Now we have to get values into the table.

To provide initial values for structure variables, add a list of initializers to the declaration statement. Figure 8-2 shows how this is done. The declaration defines the structure template, allocates storage for an array of variables of this type, and initializes the members of all elements of the array.

Figure 8-2: Initializing an Array of Structures

DECLARATION & INITIALIZATION

```
struct month_st {
    char *name;
    char *abbrev;
    short days;
} month[] = {
    "BAD", "BAD", 0,
    "January", "Jan", 31,
    ...
};
```

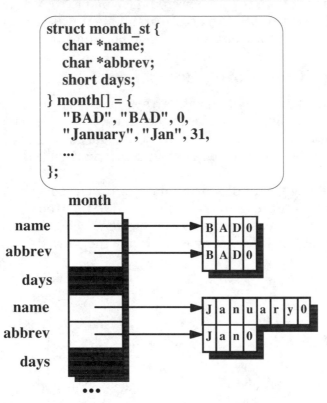

The first variable in the array has a subscript of 0. If we want to have the months numbered 1 through 12, we need to do something special for element 0. The initializer list shown in the figure arranges for the two character pointers in element 0 to point to the special string "BAD" and assigns a value of 0 to the `days` member. Each of these values is a clear indication that the data in this array element is bogus.

The initialization of element 1 is typical of the rest. The `name` member of element 1 (`month[1].name`) is initialized to the string "January" and the `abbrev` member (`month[1].abbrev`) is initialized to "Jan". The `days` member of this array element is assigned a value of 31, which is the number of days in the month.

Structures and Functions

Although structures are typically more complicated than ordinary variables, they can still be treated in much the same way as, say, an integer. You can pass a structure as a function parameter and a function can return a structure to its caller.

Passing Structures as Parameters

If a function is defined to take a structure as a parameter, you can call the function with a structure as an actual argument. By passing a structure to a function as an argument, you make available a copy of each of the structure variable's elements. This means that the value of each member can be used in the function, but the function cannot affect the values of the variable's members (call-by-value, remember?).

The program **date** consists of a few functions that access the data stored in structures. The program source code is contained in the file **date.c**. A separate header, **date.h**, contains data declarations and some initializations. Let's examine the header first.

```
/* date.h */

/* structure template */
struct date_st {
      int day;
      int month;
      int year;
};
```

```
/* global structure variable declaration */
struct month_st {
      char *name;
      char *abbrev;
      int days;
} month[] = {
      "BAD",        "BAD", 0,
      "January",    "Jan", 31,
      "February",   "Feb", 28,
      "March",      "Mar", 31,
      "April",      "Apr", 30,
      "May",        "May", 31,
      "June",       "Jun", 30,
      "July",       "Jul", 31,
      "August",     "Aug", 31,
      "September",  "Sep", 30,
      "October",    "Oct", 31,
      "November",   "Nov", 30,
      "December",   "Dec", 31
};
```

The header contains two structure declarations. The first defines a template for a structure that maintains a date. No variables of this type are declared in the header. The data type `struct date_st` is used, however, in the program source file.

The second declaration creates the `struct month_st` data type we discussed earlier, but this time with its full text. In addition, it declares an array variable called `month`, and initializes it with the name, abbreviation, and number of days for each month of the year. This array forms a table of values that plays a role in the **date** program.

Because the `month` array is declared outside any function, it is global. It is, therefore, available to any part of the program for reading or writing.

The **date** program consists of some declarations and directives, a `main()` function and three supporting functions. Here are the declarations, directives, and the code for `main()`:

```
/*
 * date.c
 *
 * This program exercises some date functions.
 */

#include <stdio.h>
#include <stdlib.h>
#include "date.h"

#define NCHARS 5

/* function prototypes */
int days(struct date_st);
int leapyear(struct date_st);
char *monthname(struct date_st);

int
main(void)
{
        struct date_st date;
        char input[NCHARS];

        /* get date values from the user */
        printf("Enter the month (1=January, etc.): ");
        gets(input);
        date.month = atoi(input);
        printf("Enter the year (nnnn): ");
        gets(input);
        date.year = atoi(input);

        printf("The year %d %s a leap year.\n",
               date.year, leapyear(date) ? "is" : "is not");
        printf("The month of %s has %d days.\n",
               monthname(date), days(date));

        return EXIT_SUCCESS;
}
```

In the function prototypes, the formal parameter of each supporting function has type `struct date_st`. Each function receives a copy of a variable of this type.

Both `days()` and `monthname()` need access to the `month` array as well, but it is not passed as a parameter because it was declared globally. This program uses global data to show how it's done, but it is not meant to encourage the widespread use of global data. Indeed, my advice is to use as little global data as possible to reduce the potential for errors caused by unwanted access to data.

The data upon which this program acts is obtained from the user. The data is stored in the `date` variable, which has type `struct date_st`. It contains, therefore, `day`, `month`, and `year` members.

The character array, `input`, serves as an input buffer. As the program user types his or her input, it is captured in character form by `gets()` and saved in the input buffer. Then `atoi()` converts the string in the buffer to its numeric equivalent, which is assigned to the appropriate element of the `date` variable. Only the `year` and `month` elements are used in this program.

Two print statements produce the program's output. The first of these states whether or not the year given by the user is a leap year. The copy of the `date` variable passed as an argument is examined only for the value of its `year` member.

A standard formula is applied to the value to determine whether the year is a leap year or an ordinary year. Any year that is evenly divisible by 4 and not by 100, or that is evenly divisible by 400 is a leap year. In such cases `leapyear()` returns a value of 1. Otherwise it returns 0.

Here is the code for `leapyear()`:

```
int
leapyear(struct date_st date)
{
        if ((date.year % 4 == 0 &&
            date.year % 100 != 0) ||
            date.year % 400 == 0)
              return 1;
        return 0;
}
```

The call to monthname() in the second output print statement also takes the date variable as an argument and uses the value of the month member of the date structure as a subscript for the month array. The return value of monthname() is a pointer to the location of the name string for the specified month.

```
char *
monthname(struct date_st date)
{
        return month[date.month].name;
}
```

The last support function in the **date** program is days(), which returns the number of days in the specified month. This is a simple lookup task, complicated only by the fact that February usually has 28 days, but has 29 days in a leap year. Thus, days() calls leapyear() if the month is February. Most of the time, it doesn't need to make the call because the first test fails, obviating the need to test the year.

Here is the code for days():

```
int
days(struct date_st date)
{
        if (date.month == 2 && leapyear(date))
                return 29;
        return month[date.month].days;
}
```

Returning Structure

You can also write functions that return structures. The defined structure template is specified as the function return type. For example, a function called future_date() might receive a date structure and a number of days as input and return a filled-in date structure that contains the future date.

Here is a prototype for this useful function:

```
struct date_st future_date(struct date_st, days);
```

The function would have to accommodate such details as changes from one month to the next and from one year to the next while computing the future date.

Pointers and Structures

Earlier in this chapter, you saw pointers as structure members. Pointers and structures work closely in other ways, too. Structures have addresses, so it should not be a surprise that you can point to them.

To establish a pointer to a structure, declare a pointer to an object of the same type as the structure and assign the address of the structure to the pointer. One of the more common occurrences is a pointer to an array of structures. The pointer points to a particular element of the array and is used to access members of the structure.

The **resistor** program demonstrates this use of a pointer to an array of structures to handle an electronic components problem. The program is a simplified, but functional one that reads a set of color codes from the standard input and converts them to a resistor value in Ohms. The program consists of several functions, which we'll examine individually. Here is the source for `main()`, the associated function prototypes, data declarations, and other trimmings:

```
/*
 * resistor.c
 *
 * Convert a resistor color code into the resistor
 * value. This program takes a three-color band list
 * and prints the value in Ohms. It does not do anything
 * with the tolerance band.
 *
 * Example: red violet orange -> 27000-Ohms
 */

#include <stdio.h>
#include <stdlib.h>
#include <math.h>
#include <string.h>
```

```c
#define MAXNAME 7

/* lookup table */
struct resistor_st {
      char *color;
      int digit;
      double mult;
} resistor[] = {
      "black",   0,   1.0,
      "brown",   1,   10.0,
      "red",     2,   100.0,
      "orange",  3,   1000.0,
      "yellow",  4,   10000.0,
      "green",   5,   100000.0,
      "blue",    6,   1000000.0,
      "violet",  7,   10000000.0,
      "grey",    8,   0.01,
      "white",   9,   0.1,
      NULL,     -1,  -1.0
};

/* function prototypes */
int color_to_digit(char *);
double color_to_mult(char *);
void error(char *);

int
main(void)
{
      double ohms;
      int digit1, digit2;
      double mult;
      char band1[MAXNAME], band2[MAXNAME], band3[MAXNAME];

      /* get the color code */
      puts("Type colors (Ex: brown black red) + Return:");
      scanf("%s %s %s", band1, band2, band3);
```

```
/* convert the code to a value */
if ((digit1 = color_to_digit(band1)) == -1)
        error(band1);
if ((digit2 = color_to_digit(band2)) == -1)
        error(band2);
if ((mult = color_to_mult(band3)) == -1.0)
        error(band3);
ohms = (10 * digit1 + digit2) * mult;
printf("Value = %.2lf Ohms\n", ohms);

return EXIT_SUCCESS;
}
```

The `struct resistor_st` data type defines the form of entries in a table that relates the colors of bands on a resistor to the significant digits and the multiplier that specify the component's value. A value of 470 Ohms is represented by the colors yellow, violet, and brown, which is evaluated as 47 times 10.0.

The resistor table is an array of structures, each of which contains three members. The first member is the color of the band. The second member contains the integer value that the color represents when used to specify one of the two significant digits of a value. The third is a floating-point number that specifies the value of the color when used as the third band, which is the multiplier.

The **resistor** program uses three character arrays as input buffers and collects values from the standard input by calling `scanf()`. The program user is instructed to type in a list of three colors and press Return.

✎**Programmer's Notebook**

Using `scanf()` is not the best way to gather user input because it is so easy to make a mistake or a deliberate error that confounds the function. It was designed for reading carefully formatted input from files and is unforgiving of input errors.

The computation of the resistor value is straightforward. The first significant digit is multiplied by 10 and added to the second significant digit. That sum is multiplied by the multiplier value, producing the value of the resistor in Ohms. Each converted color value is error-checked to guard against the user who decides that pink is one of the standard colors (it isn't—check the table).

A trio of supporting functions handles data conversion and error tasks. The function `color_to_digit()` converts a color value presented as a string argument to a significant digit (0 through 9). The function is called twice, once for each of the significant digits that contribute to a resistor's value.

Notice the variable p, which is declared to be a pointer to an object of type `struct resistor_st`. The initial address assigned to p is the base of the `resistor` array (element 0). All access to members of array elements is handled via the pointer.

Take a look at the code first. Then we'll examine the member-selection notation used for pointers to arrays.

```
int
color_to_digit(char *color)
{
        struct resistor_st *p;

        /* look for the code in the resistor table */
        p = resistor;
        while (p->color != NULL) {
                if (strcmp(p->color, color) == 0)
                        break;
                ++p;
        }

        return p->digit;
}
```

Given a color argument of, say, "orange", `color_to_digit()` loops through the array comparing the specified color to each color entry in the global array. As you can see from the declaration of the resistor table, the sequence of colors is "black" (0), "brown" (1), "red" (2), "orange" (3), and so on. The parenthesized numbers are the equivalent values for the first two color bands.

The pointer method of selecting a structure member can be represented in two ways: standard notation using structure name and the dot operator; and using the structure pointer ("-"). Here are the declarations for a typical situation:

```
struct tag {
      type m;
      . . .
};
struct tag s, *p; /* structure and pointer */
p = &s;                    /* p now points to s */
```

Without using a pointer, you access the member m by applying the dot operator:

```
s.m
```

When using the previously-established pointer, p, the expression *p is the structure (the same as using s directly). The expression:

```
(*p).m
```

yields the member m. The parentheses are needed here because the dot operator binds more tightly than the dereferencing operator (*).

Selection of a structure member through a pointer occurs often in C programs. Because of this and the fact that an expression like (*p).m is somewhat obtuse, a convenient shorthand is offered: p->m.

The operator is a minus sign followed by a greater-than symbol with no intervening white space. Its application quickly becomes second nature because it is visually symbolic of the pointing operation.

The expression p->color != NULL controls the processing loop in color_to_digit() and the statement ++p; in the loop body advances the pointer. If the color specified by the user is not found in the table, the last array element contains sentinel values that mark the end of the table. If the NULL pointer is matched, a negative value is returned to indicate the failure to match the color name. If the color matches an entry in the table, the corresponding value is returned to the caller.

A companion function called color_to_mult() converts a band color to its double-precision floating-point value. The function works just like color_to_digit() except that it gets the value from the mult member of the resistor variable and returns a double.

```
double
color_to_mult(char *color)
{
        struct resistor_st *p;

        /* look for the code in the resistor table */
        p = resistor;
        while (p->color != NULL) {
                if (strcmp(p->color, color) == 0)
                        break;
                ++p;
        }

        return p->mult;
}
```

The last function in the resistor is error(), which prints an error message and exits with an error indication. The text argument is the user-specified color that failed to produce a match.

```
void
error(char *text)
{
        fprintf(stderr, "Bad color spec: %s\n", text);
        exit(EXIT_FAILURE);
}
```

EXIT_FAILURE is a symbolic constant defined in the <stdlib.h> header. It tells the operating system or other calling program that the program did not run successfully. DOS ignores this information, but UNIX saves it and lets the user decide what to do if the program fails.

User-Defined Types and typedef

You have seen how to build aggregate data types of your own design by using structures, arrays, and pointers in various combinations. You don't create new basic types, but you do build higher level types from the basic types (char, int, float, and so on) and derived types (arrays and pointers) offered by the C language.

Derived data types often have ungainly type names, making for lots of typing in source files, and generally reducing the readability of a program. For example, the following declaration generates the type name struct cell_st:

```
struct cell_st {
      unsigned char ch;
      unsigned char attrib;
};
```

To declare a variable of this type, you would type lines such as these:

```
struct cell_st screen[SCRNSIZE];
struct cell_st *loc;
```

The first declaration reserves storage for an array of character and attribute cells and the second reserves storage for a pointer to an object of this type. Although these are not too difficult to type a few times, you would probably tire of typing such type specifiers, or more complex ones, frequently in a program.

The typedef keyword helps solve this problem. The general form of a typedef statement is:

```
typedef type_name alternate_name;
```

In your program, a statement of this form lets you use alternate_name anywhere you would use type_name. In its simplest form, typedef provides an alias for a standard type name, as in:

```
typedef int COUNT;
```

which establishes the name COUNT as an alias for `int`. You can then declare integer variables of this type:

```
COUNT c1, c2, c3, total;
```

This statement has the same effect as:

```
int c1, c2, c3, total;
```

but the type COUNT has a connotation that the ordinary `int` type might not. In any event, the counters work the same way regardless of which declaration is used.

The earlier structure declaration for character/attribute cells can be rewritten this way:

```
typedef struct cell_st {
     unsigned char ch;
     unsigned char attrib;
} CELL;
```

Following this declaration, which creates the structure template, you can declare variables of the type CELL, as shown in Figure 8-3.

```
CELL screen[SCRNSIZE];
CELL *loc;
```

Because the name CELL is created by the `typedef` statement, you can leave out the structure tag from the declaration as shown in the figure. However, you will have to use CELL as the type name because the keyword `struct` without an associated tag cannot be used as a type specifier.

Enumerations

Many C translators have supported an enumeration type for many years, but this was not a standard feature of C until it was added to the ANSI standard. The usual way of handling such situations as Boolean values

(True or False) has been to use the integral value 0 as False and any other value, typically 1, as True.

Figure 8-3: Using a Pointer to a Structure

DECLARATIONS

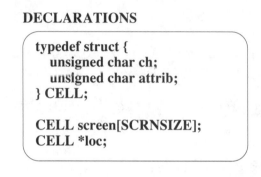

```
typedef struct {
    unsigned char ch;
    unsigned char attrib;
} CELL;

CELL screen[SCRNSIZE];
CELL *loc;
```

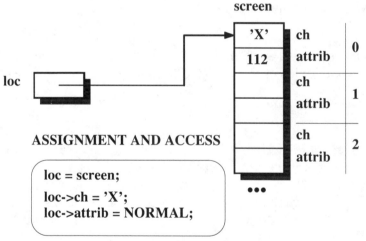

ASSIGNMENT AND ACCESS

```
loc = screen;
loc->ch = 'X';
loc->attrib = NORMAL;
```

Using the `enum` keyword, you can associate a name with a set of enumeration constants. You might, for example, write:

```
enum boolean { FALSE, TRUE };
```

to declare a Boolean data type, `enum boolean`, with two integer values. FALSE is automatically given a value of 0, and TRUE is given a value of 1. You can then declare variables of this type and functions returning this type (`enum boolean`):

```
enum boolean door_open;
enum boolean button_down(int);
```

The variable `door_open` can be assigned values of FALSE (0) or TRUE (1). Similarly, the function `button_down()` can return either of the same two values.

By combining `enum` and `typedef`, you can create enumeration types with more manageable names:

```
num { FALSE, TRUE } BOOL;
```

Following this definition, you declare variables and functions with statements like these:

```
BOOL door_open;
BOOL button_down(int);
```

The members of the list of enumeration constants take on sequential integer values starting with 0. You can, however, specify values for any of the constants, even negative values. Any unspecified values in the list follow the incremental sequence from the last-specified value. Thus, you can write enumerations such as these:

```
typedef enum { BELOW = -1, EQUAL, ABOVE } COMPARE
typedef enum { ZERO = '0', ONE, TWO, ... NINE } DIGITS;
```

Because all enumerations share a common name space, member names in different enumerations must be distinct. However, in an enumeration, values need not be unique.

Unions

A union is a C type that provides a common region of storage for one of several different object types. The C union is analogous to the Pascal variant record type.

Declaring a Union

The appearance of a union declaration is similar to that of a structure declaration. There is, however, a significant difference between the two. A structure is an aggregate type, bringing objects of possibly differing types together under a common name. A union is scalar, having a single element that can have at any time only one of the specified types.

Figure 8-4 shows how unions are declared and used. The declaration of the variable input is typical of union declarations. The union template specifies that variable and functions of this type can be of type char, short, or long.

The illustration shows a four-byte region of memory reserved for the input variable, enough to hold the largest of the specified types. Storage of any type allowed by the union declaration starts at the lowest address, which is at the top of the illustration because we are using the convention of addressing increasing as we move down the page.

When used to store a character, input actively uses only the first byte. When storing a short integer, two bytes are used. All four bytes are occupied by a long integer.

Using Union Variables

The figure shows two examples of access to the input variable. The first example shows how to store and print a character. Only the c member of the union participates in this activity. The second part of the example shows how to store and print a long integer. The entire union, designated by the member l (letter "ell") participates in this activity.

Be careful when using unions. You are responsible for knowing what type of data is stored in the union at any time. Attempting to store data as one type and read it as another produces unpredictable results.

Figure 8-4: Using a Union Variable for Mixed Types

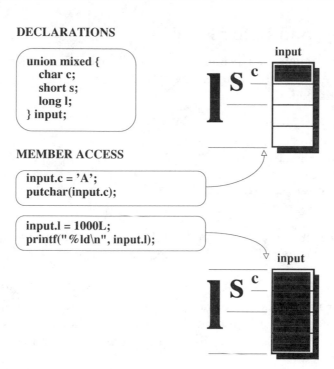

DECLARATIONS

```
union mixed {
    char c;
    short s;
    long l;
} input;
```

MEMBER ACCESS

```
input.c = 'A';
putchar(input.c);
```

```
input.l = 1000L;
printf(" %ld\n", input.l);
```

Bit Fields

Bit fields, or simply fields, are a means of providing compact storage in C. This topic is at once one that endears C to many former assembly-language programmers and brings tears to the eyes of most former BASIC programmers.

The concept of fields is a simple one: a region of memory is chopped up into a collection of smaller subregions that have integral ranges of values of limited extent. For example, if you need to do a count from 0 to 15, all you need is four bits. Why waste 12 bits in a 16-bit word (or 28 bits in a 32-bit word) to count to 15? Another example is maintaining a set of flags that need to have values of either 0 or 1. You can pack 16 of these flags in a single 16-bit word, saving considerable space compared to using a full word for each flag.

Declaring and Using Fields

Structures are used as the basis of fields. Figure 8-5 shows how to declare and access a bit-field variable. The type `struct point_st` is defined by the following code:

```
struct point_st {
      unsigned int row : 5;
      unsigned int col : 7;
      unsigned int visible : 1;
      unsigned int colortab : 3;
};
```

This definition creates a template that you can use to declare variables of this type. Declare fields only as explicitly signed or unsigned integer types.

Although the `unsigned int` type specifier appears four times in the bit-field definition, variables of the type `struct point_st` do not occupy four integer locations in memory. Only the number of bits specified and possibly some bits used for padding are actually reserved for each variable or array element.

The width of each field is specified by a number separated from the field name by a colon. The `row` field, for example, is five bits wide. The template created by the declaration also contains a seven-bit field for the `col` member, a one-bit flag called `visible`, and a three-bit index into a color table (`colortab`). Although the figure shows the fields stored from right to left, they would be stored from left to right on some machines.

To declare a bit-field variable, do what you always do to declare a variable—provide a type specifier and a name:

```
struct point_st point;
```

After declaring the variable `point`, you can access the fields by using the same notation as you do for accessing structure members. The dot operator selects a field, so the statement:

```
point.row = 12;
```

assigns the value 12 into the row field.

As shown in the figure, you can pass a bit-field variable as a function parameter. You can also declare a pointer to a bit-field variable and select members using the "->" notation. Note, however, that individual fields do not have addresses.

Figure 8-5: Bit Fields Provide Compact Storage

```
struct point_st {
    unsigned int row : 5;
    unsigned int col : 7;
    unsigned int visible : 1;
    unsigned int colortab : 3;
} point;
```

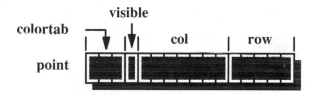

MEMBER ACCESS

```
point.row = 12;
point.col = 40;
point.visible = 1;
point.colortab = STANDARD;

...
movepoint(point);
```

Portability

The primary portability issues regarding structures and structure-like objects are object size and member alignment.

The sizes of structure members may differ from one environment to another. Members of type `int` can be equivalent to `short` on one machine and `long` on another, resulting in different ranges in the two environments. Avoid hard-coding size information in your programs. Use `sizeof` to compute array and structure sizes.

Alignment of members differs among implementations. Holes may appear in structures due to alignment requirements placed on members by the implementation. Avoid writing code that "knows" where structure members are located.

Of course, you could use knowledge of alignment details in a given environment to hide data or to implement copy protection schemes. In such situations portability doesn't matter at all.

The bit-field feature of C is a highly implementation-dependent one. Code that uses fields is not portable because the arrangement of fields varies among implementations. If you write code that involves fields, put it in separate modules that can be easily replaced in different environments.

Summary

The C language structure provides a means of managing collections of related but distinct variables under a common name. Structures can be assigned, passed as function arguments, and returned from functions. Structure members are accessed by either direct selection with the dot operator or indirectly through a structure pointer.

A union, based on the syntax of the structure, is a region of storage that can have, at any time, one of several specified data types. You are responsible for knowing what type of data is stored and accessing it correctly.

A bit-field variable, also based on structure syntax, provides what are, in effect, small integers. Fields are typically used for data compaction and low-level system access.

You can use the `typedef` keyword to create new data type names. The purpose is to create names that are more meaningful and easier to use than their raw equivalents, which typically involve `struct`, `union`, and `enum` keywords and tag names.

The `enum` keyword lets you create enumeration variables, which have restricted sets of values and symbolic names. The effect is the same as defining a collection of symbolic constants by using preprocessor directives, but enumerations are easier to use and visually more appealing.

Questions and Exercises

1. The aggregate data types in C include which of the following?

   a) arrays
   b) unsigned long
   c) structures
   d) unions

2. Describe what a structure is and give an example of how one could be applied to something taken from your own experience.

3. True or false: A structure declaration must always include a tag in addition to the keyword `struct`.

4. Given this structure declaration, how much storage is reserved?

   ```
   struct time_st {
     int hour;
     int minute;
     int second;
   };
   ```

5. Declare a variable called now with the type created in Question 4 and assign the time 14:18:00 to the variable.

6. What is the advantage of using character pointers rather than character arrays as structure members when dealing with strings?

7. Describe what is wrong with the following code and modify the code to correct the problem.

```
struct person_st {
  char first_name[10];
  char last_name[15];
  /* lots of other data here */
} person[100];
person[22].first_name = "Fran";
```

8. The following statements declare a pointer to an object of the type created in Question 7 and assign the pointer to the base of the person array:

```
struct person_st *p;
p = person;
```

Using pointer notation, write a statement that assigns the name "Jones" to the last_name member of array element 0.

9. Do the same thing as in the previous exercise, but without altering the position of the pointer assign the name "Williams" to the last_name member of array element 3.

10. Given an array of structures called dates and a pointer dp to the array's base, which of the following is equivalent to the expression dp->year:

a) *dp.year
b) dates[0].year
c) (*dp).year
d) *(dp.year)

11. True or false: A typedef statement creates a new data type.

12. Given the following typedef statement, how would you declare an array of ten objects of this type and a pointer to the array? Call the array cards and the pointer cardptr.

```
typedef struct cdfile_st {
  char *first_name;
  char *last_name;
  /* ... */
} CARD;
```

13. Write an enumeration declaration for a type that can have only the values READING, WRITING, PROCESSING, and IDLE. Declare a variable called `state` to have this type and assign it the "idle" condition.

14. Which of the following statements about unions are true?

    a) A union is an aggregate that can contain variables of different types at the same time.
    b) The union is based on the syntax of the C struct.
    c) The members of a union can be accessed by the dot (.) operator.
    d) Members of a union must always be integer types.

15. Declare a `union` variable that has members of type `char`, type `long`, and type `float`, and then assign the value 326.19 to the variable's `float` member.

16. In the following bit-field variable declaration, what is the range of values for each of the fields?

    ```
    struct bit_st {
      unsigned int a : 3;
      unsigned int b : 5;
      unsigned int c : 2;
      unsigned int d : 6;
    } bits;
    ```

17. In the bit-field declaration from the previous question, the statement:

    ```
    bits.d = 57;
    ```

    assigns a value to the d field. Write a statement that assigns half the value of field d into the b field. Then write a statement that prints the value in the b field. What value will be printed?

Additional Exercises

A. Write a program that prompts the user for a date as a series of three numbers (month, day, year) and prints the date in the traditional U.S. long-hand format (e.g., January 8, 1990).

B. Users don't always provide good data. Add code to the program you wrote in A to make sure the day is valid for the month and year and report any input errors.

C. In the section called **Returning a Structure**, mention was made of a function `future_date()` that has the following properties:

- It takes two arguments: a date structure filled in with a valid date, and an integral number of days.

- It returns a date structure filled in with the "future" date.

Write the function and test it in the date program presented in the preceding section. Be sure to account for possible month and year changes, leap year compensation, and so.

D. Add code to the resistor program to accept a fourth color band that specifies the resistor tolerance. The tolerance is specified as a percentage of the resistor value. It indicates how much variation in the value is allowed. Concern yourself only with the following tolerance values:

Color	Tolerance
(None)	20%
Silver	10%
Gold	5%

NOTE: You'll need to interpret an empty string ("") as none for the 20% value and invent a way to flag silver and gold for any of the first three bands as bad input.

CHAPTER 9

INPUT, OUTPUT, AND FILES

Programs usually need to read data from external devices and write data to other external devices. Up to this point in the book, we have written programs that read input from the keyboard, write output to the user's display screen, or both. Such input and output is transient in nature, disappearing almost as quickly as it appears.

A degree of data permanence is obtained by using magnetic media or other forms of storage that retain data for long periods of time. A typical personal computer is equipped with diskette and hard-disk drives. Larger computer systems often have high-speed magnetic tape drives in addition to disks of various types. Data stored on such devices is organized into files.

This chapter examines input and output aspects of C programs, including the use of files. Emphasis is placed on the use of basic input/output functions provided in the standard subroutine library provided with virtually all C translators.

Input and Output

As noted in earlier chapters, the C standard does not define input and output operations as part of the language. There are many differences among operating environments (machines and system software), particularly with regard to the ways in which support for input and output is provided, making it difficult or impossible to provide universal I/O features in the language.

The solution adopted by the developers of C is the use of externally-defined library subroutines (functions and macros) that handle all I/O operations. The C subroutine library contains numerous functions and several macros that handle I/O operations at two levels:

- Stream (high-level) I/O

- System (low-level) I/O

Of these, stream I/O is the more portable across operating environments, providing a uniform concept of streams that transcends and hides the details of underlying physical devices. Details such as input and output buffering for efficiency and data translation to accommodate differences among systems and internal processing models are handled automatically.

System I/O, on the other hand, is intimately involved with the details of a particular implementation. When you use low-level I/O, you are responsible for all buffering and data translations.

Standard Streams

Data input and output devices have many forms. Among the more common physical devices are keyboards, screens in display devices, disk drives, and magnetic tape drives. Some devices store and retrieve data sequentially as a series of bytes, while other devices organize data into blocks. Access to the data is sequential or random depending on the device and the mode of access.

The standardized input and output functions are based on a stream model, which provides a uniform logical view of I/O without concern for the medium involved. The stream model is derived from the UNIX operating system environment. In a concession to existing operating environments that make a distinction between text and binary streams, the C standard recognizes both types of streams. However, no distinction between text and binary data is required. We'll examine this issue and its ramifications in later sections of this chapter.

Figure 9-1 shows the UNIX model of standard streams. The three standard streams are called standard input (stdin), standard output (stdout), and standard error (stderr). The figure shows the default "connections" that are established for these standard streams and indicates their relationships to a running program (a process).

Figure 9-1: The UNIX Standard Streams Model

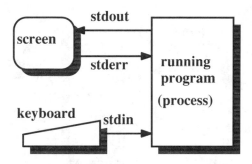

The process' stdin stream is connected by default to the user's keyboard. This stream is buffered into lines, which means that the process doesn't receive any input until the user presses the Return key.

Output from a running program goes to the standard output stream, stdout, which is connected by default to the user's screen. This stream is also buffered for performance reasons, so output is collected into lines.

The third standard stream in this model is the standard error stream, stderr, which is also connected by default to the user's terminal or console screen. It is, however, unbuffered to prevent error messages from being held up in a buffer out of the user's view. Thus, error messages and error alerts (the bell) go to the error output device without delay.

The DOS standard streams model is shown in Figure 9-2. In nearly all respects it is the same as the UNIX model. The primary difference is that DOS supports two additional standard streams. The stdprn stream is directed to the default printer port and the stdaux stream goes to the default serial communications port.

When a program starts running (becomes a process), all of the standard files supported by the environment are opened automatically. Therefore, the user's keyboard and screen are immediately available in both UNIX and DOS environments. In addition, DOS processes have access to the default printer and serial communication line if appropriate devices are installed and operational.

Figure 9-2: The MS-DOS Standard Streams Model

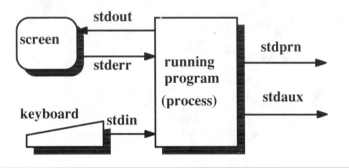

Files

A file is a named sequence of bytes. Files are typically stored on some physical device, such as a disk or tape drive. Files provide both long-term storage of data and easy access to it.

You will most likely deal with disk files, particularly hard disks, which provide quick access to large quantities of data. Such devices are available in nearly all operating environments because the cost of hard disks has dropped significantly in recent years and because the size of today's programs demands large storage capacities.

Text files stored in the UNIX and DOS environments differ in two primary ways. A text file is a file that contains only "printing" characters and a limited number of control codes (horizontal tab and line-termination characters).

In the UNIX environment, the line-termination character is called a **newline** (NL). In a DOS environment, each text line is terminated by a **carriage return** (CR) and a **linefeed** (LF). Either the CR/LF convention or the NL convention is allowed by the ASCII rules The ASCII rules is the character set upon which UNIX and C were originally based. When disk files are read by a C program, CR/LF pairs are converted to a single NL code. On output, the NL code is converted to CR/LF.

This end-of-line (EOL) treatment, as it is called, is depicted in Figure 9-3. As you can see, UNIX saves one character per line compared to DOS and other systems that use the CR/LF convention.

By the way, the legend on the Enter key of IBM and compatible personal computers symbolizes the CR and LF behavior that ensues from pressing the key (except that the actions are reversed in the key legend).

Figure 9-3: UNIX and DOS End-of-line Treatments Differ

END-OF-LINE TREATMENT:

The DOS model	The UNIX model
CR LF	NL

NOTE: The Enter key on an IBM PC or compatible microcomputer uses the following keycap symbol. The order of operations indicated is reversed.

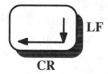

Another difference between UNIX and DOS text files is the end-of-file (EOF) treatment. Early versions of DOS used a Ctrl-Z code in the file to indicate where the end of the text was. DOS versions beginning with 3.0 use the UNIX method, which is to maintain an accurate file size in the file's directory entry and to indicate the EOF condition when an attempt is made to read or write beyond the end of the file. There is no code in the file.

C translators that run in a DOS environment understand these conventions and do needed translations so that the internal representation of a file is correct. You can see the difference between supposedly identical DOS and UNIX text files by looking at their file sizes. The DOS file has one additional character per line and possibly one additional character for the Ctrl-Z character. In some other environments, such as CP/M, you may also find that the last line contains a string of null bytes that pad the file out to the next 128-byte boundary.

Redirection

The uniformity afforded by the streams concept makes it possible to shuffle data around without concern for the source and destination device types. Programs can interact with terminal devices, data in disk files, communication ports, and other devices with no need for special conversions or access methods.

A comprehensive and consistent set of stream I/O subroutines has been developed over a period of nearly two decades. These subroutines have been documented in the Library portion of the ANSI C standard, providing a basis for portable input and output operations across a wide range of operating environments.

Many, but not all operating environments support input and output redirection. Input redirection means that the standard input to a process obtains data from a source other than the keyboard. It is usually symbolized by the less-than sign (<). An example of input redirection under both UNIX and DOS (version 2.0 or later) is the command:

```
more   filename
```

which reads data from `filename` and displays it in screen-sized chunks, pausing at the end of each screen "page" until the user presses a key to continue the paging process.

Output redirection means that the standard output of a process is diverted from the screen to a different output device. Output redirection is usually symbolized by the greater-than sign (>). An example of output redirection under UNIX is the command:

```
cat   filename
```

which causes the output of the **cat** program to be saved in `filename`.

The user types input as lines of text and terminates input by typing an end-of-file code on a line by itself. Under UNIX, the end of file condition is obtained by pressing Ctrl+D.

DOS doesn't have a direct equivalent to the **cat** command, but the same effect can be obtained without redirection by using the command:

```
COPY CON FILENAME
```

which copies console input (from the keyboard) to `FILENAME`. End input by moving to a new line, pressing Ctrl+Z, and then pressing Ctrl+Break (or Ctrl+C).

As an extension of I/O redirection, a program can have its output feed as input to another program. When you connect processes this way, you establish a pipe, which is usually symbolized by the vertical bar (|).

UNIX, which is a multitasking operating system, implements piping by the use of in-memory buffers. DOS, which is really a file manager and monitor and not a true operating system, can run only one process at a time. To effect the behavior of a pipe, DOS uses temporary disk files. It redirects the output of a program to a temporary file and then reads the temporary file into the next program in the pipeline by input redirection. This method works, but it isn't as fast as the in-memory method used by UNIX systems, especially on systems that use floppy diskette storage systems.

The creation of a pipeline is depicted in Figure 9-4. Something, often the user's keyboard, serves as the source which shoves data into the pipeline at the left. Program one does its job, producing output that becomes the input to program two. The output of program two is then sent to the **sink**, or pipeline terminus, which is usually the user's screen.

Each program in the pipeline must be a filter, which reads from its standard input stream, performs some processing operation on the received data, and delivers output to the standard output stream. Programs like **more** and **sort** are filters.

Figure 9-4: Pipelines Connect Programs Together

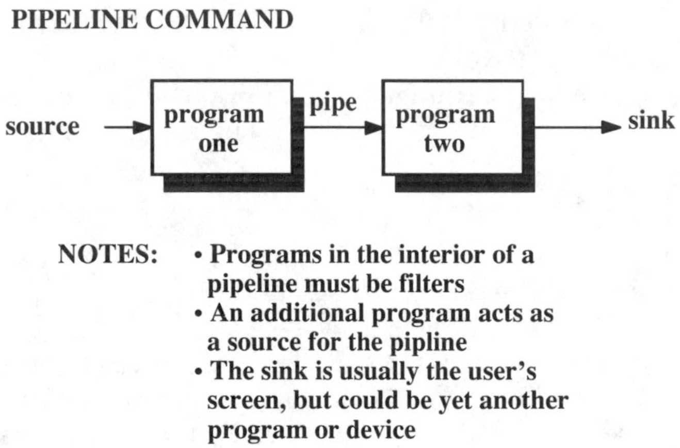

PIPELINE COMMAND

NOTES: • Programs in the interior of a
          pipeline must be filters
          • An additional program acts as
          a source for the pipline
          • The sink is usually the user's
          screen, but could be yet another
          program or device

File Input/Output

File I/O is an important aspect of most functional computer programs. Database management systems, spreadsheet and financial analysis programs, wordprocessors, computer programming language translators, and many other classes of programs consume and generate large quantities of data that are usually maintained in external files on secondary storage devices.

In order to use an external file in a C program, you need to associate a stream with the file. This task involves declaring a variable called a file pointer and giving it a value. The value is obtained from a call to a function that attempts to open a specified file. From the user's perspective, a file has a name and possibly some contents. From the program's perspective, with just a few exceptions, a file is a stream of bytes that is accessed through the file pointer.

All operations that access the contents of the file or that perform certain operations on the file are controlled through the file pointer. A few operations on files use the filename and don't need a file pointer.

So what is a file pointer? Short question—long answer.

File Pointer

As its name suggests, a file pointer is a pointer. A valid file pointer points to a data structure that has the type name FILE, which is created by a typedef statement in the **<stdio.h>** header. A variable of type FILE (our file pointer being an example of such a variable) contains members that record all pertinent data needed to control a stream.

A declaration of a variable fp that is a file pointer looks like this:

```
FILE *fp;
```

The declaration follows the pattern of others you have seen. Reading backwards in the declaration, the identifier fp is the variable name, which is a pointer (*) to an object of type FILE.

In case you're feeling a bit uneasy about this mysterious type FILE, here is what its defining declaration looks like in at least one (unnamed) C implementation:

```
typedef struct _iobuf {
      int _cnt;
      unsigned char *_ptr;
      unsigned char *_base;
      char _flag;
      char _file;
} FILE;
```

In the declaration, the member _base points to the start of the buffer, if any, for the stream. The _ptr member points to the location in the buffer where the next access operation takes place, and `_flag` is a byte that maintains end-of-file and error indicator flag bits. A given implementation can declare additional structure members for other purposes related to managing a stream.

File Access

Having declared a file pointer variable, `fp`, we are only halfway to having a stream that we can play with. The next step is to open a file for access. The function `fopen()` attempts to open a named file and associate it with a stream designated by the pointer variable. This function is declared in `<stdio.h>` and has the following general form:

```
FILE *fopen(const char *filename, const char *mode);
```

Recall that the `const` type qualifier in this context means that the function does not attempt to change the values passed to it as arguments.

The `filename` argument is a string that contains the name of the file to be opened. You can hard-code a name in a literal string, but a more likely scenario is that the filename is provided by pointing to a buffer that contains a name obtained from the operating system shell, a command-line argument, or direct user input.

The `mode` argument is a string that begins with the character sequences shown in Table 9-1, which lists the `mode` argument codes and briefly describes what the codes mean. Additional characters are allowed in the `mode` argument string following the initial sequences shown.

Table 9-1: Mode Argument Codes	
MODE STRING	**DESCRIPTION**
r	Open text file for reading
w	Truncate to zero length or create text file for writing
a	Append; open or create text file for writing at end
rb	Open binary file for reading

Table 9-1: Mode Argument Codes	
MODE STRING	**DESCRIPTION**
wb	Truncate to zero length or create binary file for writing
ab	Append; open or create text file for writing at end
r+	Open text file for update (reading and writing)
w+	Truncate to zero length or create text file for update
a+	Append; open or create text file for update, writing at end
r+b (or rb+)	Open binary file for update (reading and writing)
w+b (or wb+)	Truncate to zero length or create binary file for update
a+b (or ab+)	Append; open or create binary file for writing at end

The mode strings with the letter b in them specify binary file treatment. In binary access mode, all bits of each byte are significant, and no translations are done on the file contents on input and output.

Modes that contain a+ in the second or third character position are called "update" modes. Update mode means that the file can be both read and written as long as a file-positioning function call intervenes. The file-positioning functions are `fseek()`, `fsetpos()`, and `rewind()`. In addition, input can follow output if there is a call to `fflush()` between the operations.

The normal return from a call to `fopen()` is a valid file pointer that can be assigned into a pointer variable. If the specified file cannot be opened, `fopen()` produces an error return of NULL to flag the error. Do not ignore error returns because they are important indicators of possible trouble. For example, attempting to read characters from a file that could not be opened is an error. So is writing to a file that could not be opened.

Considering these points, here is a program that opens a file for reading and displays its contents. The **listfile** program is a highly simplified version of the UNIX **cat** program.

```
/*
 * listfile.c
 *
 * List the contents of a file to the standard output.
 */

#include <stdio.h>
#include <stdlib.h>

#if defined(MSDOS)
      #define MAXPATH 64
#else
      #define MAXPATH 128
#endif

int
main(void)
{
      int ch;
      char name[MAXPATH];
      FILE *fp;

      /* get the filename from the user */
      printf("File to list: ");
      gets(name);

      /* check the name and attempt to open the file */
      if (name[0] == '\0') {
            fprintf(stderr, "No filename typed\n");
            exit(EXIT_SUCCESS);
      }
      fp = fopen(name, "r");
      if (fp == NULL) {
            fprintf(stderr, "Cannot open %s\n", name);
            exit(EXIT_FAILURE);
      }

      /* list the contents of the file */
      while ((ch = fgetc(fp)) != EOF)
```

```
        putchar(ch);

    return EXIT_SUCCESS;
}
```

The **listfile** program is rather simple. It declares a file pointer, prompts the user for a filename, and attempts to open the file. If it can, it reads characters from the specified file and prints them on the standard output stream. If it cannot open the file, it prints an error message and quits with an error indication (an exit code other than zero).

The program tests the filename by looking at its first character. If it is a null byte, the user pressed Return without typing a name, so `listfile` prints a message and exits. The exit code does not indicate an error condition because no error occurred.

The attempt to open the file in read mode (`"r"`) is straightforward. The `filename` argument is provided by the string stored in the name array. The return value of the call to `fopen()` is saved in `fp`, which is checked in the following `if` statement. If it is NULL, the open failed. Otherwise, `fp` is a valid file pointer.

You will often see the code for opening a file and testing the file pointer collapsed into a nested form:

```
if ((fp = fopen(name, "r")) == NULL) {
    fprintf(stderr, "Cannot open %s\n", name);
    exit(EXIT_FAILURE);
}
```

Note the use of parentheses around the assignment expression. These are needed to force the assignment to occur before the test against NULL.

The `while` loop statement that reads characters from the file and prints them on the standard output stream calls `fgetc()` to read characters:

```
while ((ch = fgetc(fp)) != EOF)
    putchar(ch);
```

This function takes a single parameter that specifies the stream from which to read. It returns an integer so it can deliver valid character codes or the end-of-file indicator. We'll look at this and other character-oriented functions and macros later in this chapter.

One of the details that is missing from **listfile** is an explicit closing of the file. In this program, it doesn't matter because the file is closed automatically when the program exits. However, in most circumstances, you should call `fclose()` to close the external file and disassociate the stream from the file.

For now, you can simply add the statement:

```
fclose(fp);
```

before the return statement.

You should note that `fclose()` returns a value of zero to indicate success in closing the stream or EOF if errors occurred. If an error occurs during a file-close operation, there may be a problem with the disk or other storage that will prevent the directory or the file contents from being updated correctly, leading to future problems.

You should check for such error indications and at least inform the user that something is possibly amiss in the event of an error. The topic of error handling is covered in detail in the next section.

The `freopen()` function is an interesting adaptation of the primary file-opening function. It has the following prototype:

```
FILE *freopen(const char *filename,
      const char *mode, FILE *stream);
```

The purpose of this function is to open the file specified by the `filename` parameter, and associate it with the stream specified by the `stream` parameter. The `mode` parameter specifies the requested file-access mode.

The `freopen()` function is most frequently used to associate a file with one of the standard streams (`stdin`, `stdout`, or `stderr`). It might seem that simply assigning the return value from an `fopen()` call to, say, `stdout`, would do the job, but this fails because `stdout` is a constant pointer to a file-control structure, not a variable.

A potential problem that arises from using buffered output is occasionally having output remain in a buffer where it cannot be seen by the user.

The `fflush()` function takes a stream parameter and flushes (empties) the buffer associated with the specified stream. The special stream pointer of NULL means flush all open streams.

To control buffering of a stream, a program can call `setvbuf()` after the stream is associated with an open file and before any other operations occur on the stream.

Here is the prototype:

```
int setvbuf(FILE *stream, char *buf,
    int mode, size_t size);
```

The `stream` parameter specifies the open stream. The `buf` parameter can be NULL, which tells `setvbuf()` to allocate its own buffer, but it can specify an array to be used as the buffer.

The `mode` parameter specifies input/output buffering. The three kinds of input and output buffering are the following:

- full (_IOFBF)

- line (_IOLBF)

- none (_IONBF)

Full buffering collects characters into a block of some predetermined size before delivering them to their destination. Line buffering gathers characters into a block of variable size that is transmitted when a new-line character is received. Unbuffered streams should be transmitted as soon as possible.

The `size` parameter specifies the size of the array being used as a buffer. If the mode is specified as unbuffered, both `buf` and `size` are ignored. An integer return value of zero indicates success and any nonzero value flags an error.

To change buffering of the stream designated by `fp` to unbuffered, for example, use the following statement:

```
setvbuf(fp, NULL, _IONBF, 0);
```

Going the other way, you can set up your own buffer and enable full buffering with the following statements:

```
char mybuf[BUFSIZ];
...
setvbuf(fp, mybuf, _IOFBF, sizeof mybuf);
```

The `setbuf()` function is a version of `setvbuf()` that takes only stream and buffer parameters. If the buffer parameter is NULL, buffering is turned off. Otherwise, full buffering is enabled using the specified buffer. Although less flexible than `setvbuf()`, `setbuf()` is easier to use in many common circumstances.

The following statement turns off buffering on the specified stream:

```
setbuf(fp, NULL);
```

Formatted Input and Output

Many of the programs in this book use `printf()` for formatted output and a few use `scanf()` for formatted input. Refer to the description of `printf()` and `scanf()` in Chapter 3 for details about control strings and format specifiers and the use of these functions.

The `printf()` family of functions includes several useful variations on the basic function. The `fprintf()` function, as you have seen, prints to a specified output stream rather than to the standard output stream that is specified by its first parameter.

The function `sprintf()` formats data and "prints" it to a string rather than to a stream. The input analog of this function is `sscanf()`, which gathers its input from a string rather than from a stream.

Character-Oriented Input and Output

Several functions and macros handle character-oriented read and write operations.

For reading individual characters, you can use the `getc()` macro, the `fgetc()` function, or the `getchar()` function (some C translator libraries implement `getchar()` as a macro). The **listfile** program earlier in this chapter used `fgetc()` to read input from a file. The function takes a single parameter that specifies which stream to read from.

The getc() macro does the same job as fgetc() and operates with greater efficiency at a cost of more in-line code in your program. A negative aspect of using the macro is that of having to rescan the stream if the macro is used in an expression that has side effects. Either avoid such situations or use fgetc() and suffer the function-call overhead.

You can output characters by using the putc() macro, the fputc() function, and putchar(), which can also be implemented as a macro. Several of the programs in this book have used putchar() to write to the standard output stream. In fact, putchar() is equivalent to putc (stdin). If you need to write to a specific stream, use putc() or fputc().

The **wrtfile** program uses getchar() to read input from the standard input and the putc() macro to write output to a file, effectively copying the file's contents to the output device. This program is nearly identical to the **listfile** program except for the fact that the copying process has the opposite sense:

```c
/*
 * wrtfile.c
 *
 * Save text from the standard input in a named file.
 */

#include <stdio.h>
#include <stdlib.h>

#if defined(MSDOS)
        #define MAXPATH 64
#else
        #define MAXPATH 128
#endif

int
main(void)
{
        int ch;
        char name[MAXPATH];
        FILE *fp;
```

```
/* get the filename from the user */
printf("Save file: ");
gets(name);

/* check the name and attempt to open the file */
if (name[0] == '\0') {
      fprintf(stderr, "No filename typed\n");
      exit(EXIT_SUCCESS);
}
fp = fopen(name, "w");
if (fp == NULL) {
      fprintf(stderr, "Cannot open %s\n", name);
      exit(EXIT_FAILURE);
}

/* write input to the file */
while ((ch = getchar()) != EOF)
      putc(ch, fp);

/* close the "save" file */
fclose(fp);

return EXIT_SUCCESS;
}
```

The **wrtfile** program also shows the use of `fclose()` to explicitly close the file rather than depending on the default behavior when the process terminates. It's good to get into the habit of explicitly closing files so that you don't forget when it matters. Operating systems impose limits on the number of files each user can have open at one time and on the total number of open files on the system. This is because each open file requires buffering resources and table entries. Each of these resources is finite and allocated from your system's memory.

It may be more convenient to read and write text as lines rather than as individual characters. The `gets()` and `fgets()` functions read lines. The `puts()` and `fputs()` functions write lines. Their function prototypes are in the **<stdio.h>** header, as is the case for all of the other standard I/O functions and macros.

```
char *gets(char *string);
char *fgets(char *string, int n, FILE *stream);
int puts(const char *string);
int fputs(const char *string, FILE *stream);
```

Both of the string input functions read characters up to EOF or until a new-line character is read. Both copy what they read into a specified buffer pointed to by the string parameter.

An immediately obvious difference between gets() and fgets() is that fgets() takes a size parameter, n, and a stream parameter that specifies the source of its input. The gets() function is similar to fgets(), except that it reads from stdin and has no buffer-size parameter. There is one subtle, but important difference between the behaviors of these functions. The gets() function discards any new-line characters it reads, but fgets() retains them.

Similarly, there is a difference between puts() and fputs(). A new-line character is appended to the string printed by puts(). The fputs() function does not append a newline. Both functions print all characters in the string up to, but not including, the terminating null byte.

To use the string functions in the **listfile** program, create a line buffer and change the loop as shown by these statements:

```
char line[MAXLINE];
...
while (fgets(line, sizeof line, fp) != NULL)
    fputs(line, stdout)
```

The maximum buffer dimension needed for the fgets() call is determined by the sizeof operator. It is best to pair fgets() and fputs() or gets() and puts(). That way you won't end up with double-spaced output, or worse yet, output with no line breaks.

Error Handling

If our systems were perfect and we were too, we could ignore the possibility of errors. Sadly, neither of these conditions holds, so errors are a fact of life that we must be prepared to handle.

Functions that read or write return values can and should be used for error detection and recovery. Some of these returns are ambiguous. The return from `getc()`, for example, is EOF to indicate either an error or that the end of the file has been reached. It is inappropriate to simply assume that the input was read correctly.

The standard library provides some useful macros and functions that resolve ambiguous returns from I/O function calls. The macros `ferror()` and `feof()` handle the ambiguous EOF return. Here are their prototypes:

```
int ferror(FILE *stream);
int feof(FILE *stream);
```

The `ferror()` macro tests the specified stream and returns a nonzero value if the error flag is set. The `feof()` macro returns nonzero if the stream's EOF flag is set. To check for errors in the **wrtfile** program, you could add the following code just after the character-processing loop:

```
if (ferror(fp) != 0) {
    fprintf(stderr, "Error writing to file\n");
    exit(EXIT_FAILURE);
}
```

Exiting closes the file, which leaves the possibly erroneous data in the file, but at least the program has warned the user of a potential problem. The explicit test against 0 is not needed, but it helps to put it in the test expression to show your intent.

The program **lwc** reads a text file and reports on the number of lines, words, and characters in the file (like the UNIX **wc** program). It combines many of the functions presented in this chapter.

```
/*
 * lwc.c
 *
 * Read the contents of a specified file and report
 * the number of lines, words, and characters to the
 * standard output.
 */
```

```c
#include <stdio.h>
#include <stdlib.h>

#if defined(MSDOS)
      #define MAXPATH 64
#else
      #define MAXPATH 128
#endif

typedef enum { FALSE, TRUE } BOOL;

int
main(void)
{
      BOOL inword;
      long l_count, w_count, c_count;
      int ch;
      char name[MAXPATH];
      FILE *fp;

      /* get the filename from the user */
      printf("File to list: ");
      gets(name);

      /* check the name and attempt to open the file */
      if (name[0] == '\0') {
            fprintf(stderr, "No filename typed\n");
            exit(EXIT_SUCCESS);
      }
      fp = fopen(name, "r");
      if (fp == NULL) {
            fprintf(stderr, "Cannot open %s\n", name);
            exit(EXIT_FAILURE);
      }

      /* analyze the contents of the file */
      l_count = w_count = c_count = 0;
      inword = FALSE;
```

```
while ((ch = fgetc(fp)) != EOF) {
        ++c_count;
        if (ch == ' ' || ch == '\t' || ch == '\n')
                inword = FALSE;
        else if (inword == FALSE) {
                ++w_count;
                inword = TRUE;
        }
        if (ch == '\n')
                ++l_count;
}
if (ferror(fp) != 0) {
        fprintf(stderr, "READ ERROR: %s\n", name);
        exit(EXIT_FAILURE);
}

/* report results of the anaylsis */
printf("%s: %ld %ld %ld\n",
        name, l_count, w_count, c_count);

return EXIT_SUCCESS;
}
```

File Operations

Here are several functions that operate on files as units rather than on their contents. We won't go into them in detail here, but you may want to investigate the remove() and rename() functions. The first of these removes a file from a directory of file entries. The second changes the name of a file without changing any other information about the file. If the old and new names have different leading pathnames, the file is effectively moved between directories. In some environments, DOS among them, it is necessary to copy the file to its destination directory and then remove the original file.

The tmpnam() and tmpfile() functions are used to create temporary names and binary files. These functions provide support for programs that need to use temporary files while they are running. It is critical that a temporary file not overwrite or remove valid data in existing files, so `tmpname()` creates names that don't duplicate any names already in use.

Summary

This chapter introduced you to some of the many input and output functions that are available to you in the standard library. After you feel reasonably comfortable with these, venture into the standard library documentation provided with your system or C translator and learn about other macros and functions that are used for I/O operations and other purposes.

If you come away from this discussion with the attitude that error handling is an important consideration in program design and coding, you will be way ahead of many of your peers. Too many programmers, regardless of the language they are using, are simply too lazy or uncaring to do the whole job. Error-handling is one area that is often left for "later," which usually translates into "never" or into "panic" when the customer complains about mysterious errors. Don't get caught in this trap.

Questions and Exercises

1. What are streams and why are they important?

2. Why is buffering used on most I/O streams?

3. Why is the standard error stream unbuffered?

4. Write a command line that shows how you can redirect the output of a program called **random**, which normally writes to the screen, to a file called **numbers**.

5. What is a pipeline command? Show an example of one.

6. Why are text-file translations needed during read and write operations in some operating environments?

7. The following command is intended to "page" text from the named file onto the user's screen. What is wrong with the command and what actually happens?

    ```
    more > myfile.txt
    ```

8. Briefly describe the type FILE and its purpose.

9. Write statements that declare a file pointer called f_in and show how to open the files for reading.

10. What is the meaning of the keyword const when used in the parameter list of a function?

11. Describe the behavior requested by the mode "rb" in an fopen() statement.

12. What does the use of a plus sign (+) in the second or third position of a mode specifier mean?

13. What does a return value of NULL from a call to fopen() mean? What conditions might cause this to happen?

14. True or false: All open files are automatically closed when a process terminates, so it is never necessary to close file explicitly.

15. Given a file pointer fp and an array called buf, what is achieved by the following statement?

    ```
    setvbuf(fp, buf, _IOLBF, sizeof buf);
    ```

16. If the function getc() reads a character, why do we need fgetc()?

17. Write a code fragment that reads a string from the standard input stream into an array called line by calling fgets(). Will the resulting string have a newline character in it or not?

18. What is the purpose of the feof() macro? Show an example of its use in a code fragment being careful to get the sense of the test correct.

Additional Exercises

A. Write a program that prompts for a source filename and a destination filename (full pathnames allowed) and then copies the source to the destination without regard for the presence or absence of the destination file.

B. Add code to the program in Exercise A that guards against accidentally overwriting an existing destination file. The code should ask the user to accept or reject the overwrite by typing a Y or N followed by a Return.

There is no reason to ask the user anything if the destination file does not exist. A way of determining whether the destination file exists is to try opening it for reading and checking the return from `fopen()`. Don't forget to close the file if the open succeeds.

C. Write a program that reads a text file named by the user and converts all uppercase letters to lowercase, sending its output to the standard output stream. Use the `tolower()` macro for the conversion (prototype in the **<ctype.h>** header). Be sure to detect and report all error conditions.

D. Write a program that reads a text file and reports the length of the longest and shortest words and the longest and shortest lines in the file.

E. Write a program that reads a text file and creates an output on `stdout` that consists of one word per line.

CHAPTER 10

THE PROGRAM DEVELOPMENT PROCESS

This chapter approaches the program development process without regard to the language you use for program coding. The goal is to suggest a workable strategy for developing programs. To that end, the topics covered here are the following:

- Problem Analysis

- Program Design

- Coding

- Testing

- Maintenance

An approach to program development that works for one programmer might not be the best one for you. Take this information as it is intended—simply as a model that you can mold to your own purposes.

Problem Analysis

A lot of the problems you will encounter, but by no means all, already have known solutions and require little more than expressing the solutions in some programming language or using someone else's prepackaged solutions.

If you take this approach, try to understand why and how the solution works and determine what its limitations are. Using strlen() in a C program to find the length of a character array will probably lead to trouble because the array might not have a terminating null byte. String functions should only be applied to null-terminated strings, and if you don't know that you can have serious trouble.

The other problems, those that are unstructured and unsolved, pose the kind of challenges that make occupations such as systems analyst and programmer interesting and rewarding. The satisfaction you can derive from making a box full of silicon chips and a myriad of other electronic and mechanical parts do your bidding is hard to describe, but it sure feels good.

So how do you go about analyzing a problem?

The simple answer is that you think a lot about the problem. Flip as that answer is, thinking really is the key to understanding the nature of a problem and to getting a good description of it down on paper or keyed into a computer. If you attempt to apply canned solutions to a poorly described problem, you will usually produce a program that doesn't run at all or one that works poorly.

Try to break a problem down into a set of smaller, more easily managed subproblems. Let's say, for example, that you need to install a TV antenna to get a better picture and that giving up TV viewing, though probably a good idea, is not an acceptable option for you. Here are some questions you might ask yourself:

- Does it have to be outside or can it go in the attic?

- How big is the antenna?

- Do I have to be able to rotate it?

- Will the antenna have a clear shot at the transmitting antennas?

- Are there any ordinances preventing outdoor antenna installations?

- What kind of mounting system can I use?

- How far away from the receiver is the proposed antenna location?

- Are there any power lines or interfering structures near the site?

- What tools do I need to do the installation?

- How much is this going to cost?

You can probably come up with a lot more relevant questions. Probably a few that are not so relevant, too. The answers to some of the questions might affect your responses to the other questions. The outcome of a session like this should be a better, more detailed, description of the task at hand. The data obtained through an inquiry process can influence "go/no go" decisions and can help you put realistic bounds on the problem and its solutions.

What works for TV antenna installations works well for programming projects, too. Think, for example, about how the **lwc** program (see Chapter 9) counts characters, words, and lines.

Counting characters is easy enough. Just start a counter at zero and increment the counter each time a character is read. Counting lines is just as easy. Simply count the number of newlines read.

✍**Programmer's Notebook**

Some editor programs allow the last line of a file to end without a newline character, and whether this is allowed is implementation-defined. The lwc program doesn't take this into account.

Counting words is a bit more complicated. You have to decide what a word is. In the **lwc** program, the simplistic notion of a word is a sequence of displayable characters separated from other such sequences by spaces, tabs, or newlines.

Program Design

Program design is often a straightforward, rote process. At other times, especially when dealing with interfaces to hardware and humans, it is anything but routine.

Program design involves designing the right data structures to represent the data items of a program, and choosing or designing appropriate algorithms. Getting the right data structures is, perhaps, the most important aspect of program design. Successful programmers put a lot of effort on the data-design part of each programming project before proceeding with the rest of the work. It usually pays off.

In designing a program, the use of brainstorming techniques with a group of designers can be very helpful. An important aspect of this design technique is to capture ideas as they surface and make them accessible. Try not to criticize any ideas brought out during this activity because that serves only to discourage participation and tends to block the free flow of ideas. You have plenty of opportunity to analyze each suggestion later.

Designers and programmers have tried many techniques to capture design ideas in a way that is understandable and accessible. The goal is to describe a programming solution to a problem in a computer language-independent way, preferably in English or your native tongue. The solution can then be coded by you, or as is often the case, by someone else, in any suitable computer language.

Flowcharts, Varnier-Orr diagrams, data-low diagrams, and numerous other techniques attempt to capture the design of a program in a visual presentation. Each has strengths and weaknesses in a given situation.

One of the design aids that I prefer is the use of **pseudocode**, which is a description in a language that, in my case, has elements of English and C or Pascal. Pseudcoode shows the structure of a program, is easy to read, and is easy to convert to a real computer language. Its primary benefit is that pseudocode can be created and maintained by the use of outliner programs such a Ready!, Think Tank, or the one built into Microsoft Word. Such programs permit you to expand and collapse outlines, move whole sections up and down in a hierarchy, and reorganize sections of the outline with ease.

Returning to the word-counting problem, we can write a pseudocode description of the counting logic. We have to think of a way to determine when the code that processes the input is in a word and when it's not. Just as a TV antenna installation might involve the use of some temporary facilities, such as a ladder and rope, a program often requires temporary elements, such as a variable to track the state of being in or out of a word (inword).

Here is the pseudocode description I wrote for the character-processing loop of the **lwc** program before coding it in C:

set all counters to zero
clear the inword flag
while characters remain read the next character
        increment the character counter
        if the character is a space, tab, or newline
                set the inword flag
        else if the inword flag is cleared
                increment the word counter
                set the inword flag
        if the character is a newline
                increment the line counter

This computer language-independent description of the program's main processing loop shows what has to be done to analyze the incoming stream of characters without being specific about what code to write.

Coding

The first part of this book teaches the C language, one of a large and growing field of computer programming languages. Most programmers learn several languages during their careers, and assembly language programmers might have to learn a new language each time a new microprocessor is introduced and endure the agony of converting their existing programs to the new programming environment.

Choosing a language in which to code a program is often a matter of prior experience. Sometimes the choice has been made for you by someone who is paying the bills. And at times you may choose to use a language as a way of forcing yourself to learn it.

If you or someone else has written a good design document, coding should be a relatively simple matter if you already know the target language. Converting pseudocode to source code may require some interpretation, but both the functional arrangement of the program and the logic should be well defined before coding starts.

While coding, use descriptive names for symbolic constants, variables, and functions. Don't skimp on comments. If written well, they will be important to you and anyone else who has to deal with your code in the future.

During this phase, you or someone working closely with you should prepare program documentation. If you wait until later to do the documentation, it will never get written, or it will be slapped together in a hurry when the customer complains. At that point, it's usually too late to do it right.

Testing

This is a critical, but often overlooked aspect of program development. Today's programs are often incredibly complex. Assuming that they have been written correctly is dangerous. Don't assume anything at all or assume the worst. Even the best programmers make mistakes and someone has to find and fix them.

Here are some guidelines for testing programs:

- Use a test plan. The plan can often be written during the analysis and design phases when program behavior and performance is being specified.

- Test for correct responses to expected inputs to be sure that the program does what it was designed to do.

- Test also to see that the program doesn't do anything it shouldn't do. This means that you should insert errors into the input data and check the program's ability to detect and correct or report the errors. You should also check responses to unexpected commands.

- Observe behavior at the boundaries. Write test cases that force the program to deal with data that falls just below, at, and just above natural boundaries, such as printed page breaks and video display screen dimensions.

- Test performance of your program against specifications for accuracy, speed, apparent responsiveness to user commands, and so on.

- Check to see that the interaction with the user is natural and unambiguous. The user interface is the part of a program that influences a user's impression of a program more than any other.

When you're satisfied that the program is working correctly and performing well, find out what other user's think. Invariably, they have different expectations and different experiences than you and will point out problems that you will never see.

Maintenance

A program is rarely a static entity. If a program is not useful to anyone, it languishes and dies after a while. However, a program that is useful tends to stick around for a long time and will usually change for a variety of reasons as time passes:

- Bug fixes. All programs have bugs (sometimes called undocumented features) that need to be found and purged.

- Revisions to add features. Users put tremendous pressure on developers to add "just one more feature." Software companies often add features for marketing reasons rather than technical or operational reasons.

- Multiple versions. Software companies are finding that programs running on multiple platforms (primarily UNIX, DOS, OS/2, and Macintosh) sell better than those that are geared to a single operating environment.

- Improvements in performance and appearance. With the rapid move toward windowing and menu-driven interfaces, developers are scrambling to make programs run faster and look better.

All of these reasons for change have one thing in common. They require a way to keep track of versions of programs. Many users will resist upgrades for a while, except possibly for bug fixes, so a developer has to maintain multiple versions of a program and accompanying documents.

Release control software such as SCCS or RCS under UNIX is extremely important to maintaining not only the program and document source and object files, but also the developer's sanity. Similar programs are available for DOS and other microcomputer operating systems.

Questions and Exercises

1. Describe the tasks you perform from the time you awaken until you get to work, school, the shopping mall, your exercise class, or whatever you do on a typical day.

2. Write a description in a human language or pseudocode for a function that converts all lowercase letters in a string to uppercase letters and returns a pointer to the start of the converted string.

3. Write the pseudocode description for a program that checks a string typed by the user to see whether it is a palindrome (a word or number that reads the same in either direction, like LIL, OTTO, and 1881). Letter case differences are ignored.

4. Write a pseudocode description for a program that filters a stream, converting all tab characters into some visible representation (such as "->").

Additional Exercises

A. Write a program called dummy that loops indefinitely admonishing the user ("Don't press the Return key) and waiting for the user to type something. The program ignores all input except a Return. It then prints "I told you not to do that!" and continues with the next iteration of the loop.

B. Because the **lwc** program in Chapter 9 doesn't account for an unterminated last line, its count of lines might be off by one. Devise a way to account for an unterminated last line in the source file and revise the code accordingly.

CHAPTER 11

STACKS AND QUEUES

Equipped with a basic knowledge of C language and some techniques for program development, you should now be able to take on some significant programming challenges. But don't try to do everything from scratch. Learn to build on the work of others who have created solutions to many common programming problems.

This chapter investigates some important data structures and related processing algorithms that you will encounter frequently in programs that you read. Soon you will be using them in your own programs.

Stacks

The stack is a widely used mechanism for buffering data. Stacks find broad application in managing priorities, performing arithmetic operations, and numerous other tasks.

The Stack Data Type

A stack is a linear data type that behaves as a last-in, first-out (LIFO) storage mechanism. The most commonly used analogy for a stack in the workaday world is the stack of plates found in most cafeterias. The last plate put on the top of the stack is the first one taken off the stack.

Virtually all modern computers are stack-oriented machines. Stacks are used for many purposes, such as saving the machine state, while interrupt-service routines respond to higher-priority tasks, passing parameters to functions, keeping track of overlapping windows in display system software, and so on.

A stack has the attributes of a data type. It can be implemented in several ways. The simplest implementation of a stack is an array and supporting pointers or subscripts to show where data is to be written or read. You can also implement stacks by using linked data structures (see Chapter 12).

Because the name of an array is a constant pointer to the start of the array, a convenient "base" pointer is always readily available. Establishing a pointer to an object of the type of the array elements and initially assigning it the value of the array base, gives you a convenient way of showing where the "top" of the array is. The top is the location at which the next `write` operation takes place.

Figure 11-1 graphically portrays a five-position stack (an array of five elements). The array is initially empty, so top equals base. Whether the top and base components are pointers or array subscripts doesn't really matter except to the code that manages the contents of the stack.

The code that manages the stack in the simplest cases involves only two functions: `push()` to write data onto the stack, and `pop()` to read data from the stack. The act of pushing an item onto a stack that is not full has the side effect of incrementing the top pointer or subscript. And, of course, popping an item off a stack that isn't empty decrements the pointer or subscript.

In the figure, the stack is initially empty. Pushing a number on the stack fills in element 0 with the pushed value and increments the `top` index. Pushing a second value fills in the stack element designated by `top` and increments `top` again.

If the program controlling the stack has a multiply instruction, it pops the two elements off the stack, multiplies them, and pushes the result back onto the stack, producing the situation shown in the right column of the figure. Each of the `pop()` operations retrieves the value designated by the value of the `top` index and decrements `top`.

Figure 11-1: An Array Implementation of a Stack

STACK (last in, first out)

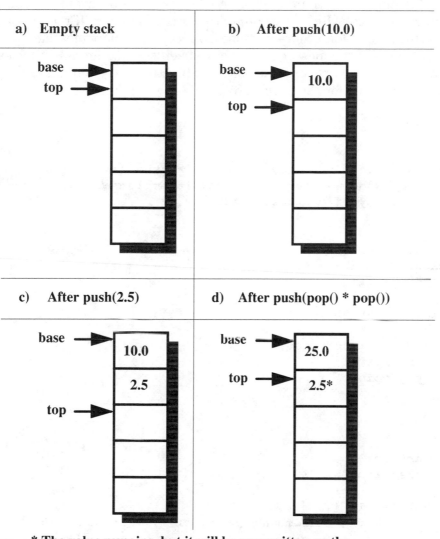

a)   **Empty stack**

base

top

b)   **After push(10.0)**

base   10.0

top

c)   **After push(2.5)**

base   10.0

2.5

top

d)   **After push(pop() * pop())**

base   25.0

top   2.5*

* The value remains, but it will be overwritten on the
next call to the push() function.

The stack Demonstration Program

The **stack** program demonstrates the use of a stack to manage a set of messages. The program prompts you to press a letter to specify a command. Issuing a 'w' command (write) causes the program to prompt you for a message, which it attempts to store in memory. If the message stack is full, the **stack** program refuses to accept any more messages until you read some of the messages that have been stacked for you. You read messages in the reverse order of that in which they were collected.

Here is the code for the **stack** program's main() function:

```
/*
 * stack.c
 *
 * Demonstrate a stack by using one as the basis
 * of a message manager. The stack is implemented
 * as an array of character pointers.
 */

#include <stdio.h>
#include <stdlib.h>
#include <string.h>

#define NBYTES 80

/* function prototypes */
int push(char *);
char *pop(void);

int
main(void)
{
      int ch;
      char line[NBYTES + 1];

      while (1) {
            printf("Command (w, r, or q) + Return: ");
            gets(line);
            switch (line[0]) {
```

```
        case 'w':
        case 'W':
                /* write (push) a new message */
                printf("Message: ");
                gets(line);
                if (push(line) != 0)
                        printf("Stack full\n");
                break;
        case 'r':
        case 'R':
                /* read (pop) a message */
                printf("%s\n", pop());
                break;
        case 'q':
        case 'Q':
                exit(EXIT_SUCCESS);
        }
    }

    return EXIT_SUCCESS;
}
```

The code in `main()` consists of a "forever" loop in which the major attractions are a string reading a set of statements and a switch statement that extracts command codes and processes them. The character array, `line`, is a general-purpose input buffer that is used to read user commands and data (message) inputs.

The call to `gets()` reads a string from the keyboard. Recall that `gets()` replaces the newline character with a null byte. The only character in the received string that is of interest is contained in element 0. Everything else in the string is ignored, so the user can type "`write`" instead of "`w`" to invoke the write command. In fact, any string that is smaller than or equal to the line-buffer size starts with a letter `'w'` will do the job. Similarly, any command string that starts with the letter `'r'` invokes the `read` command and a command that starts with `'q'` terminates the program. Multiple case labels are used to make the command-processing code insensitive to letter case.

The same `line` array acts as an input buffer to read the message typed by the user in response to a `write` command. The text of the line is passed as a parameter to `push()`, which attempts to push the message onto the stack. If there is room on the stack, the push operation succeeds, `push()` increments the stack index, and returns a 0. If the stack is full, `push()` simply returns a nonzero code to flag the problem, which causes a "*Stack full*" diagnostic message to be printed.

A `read` command calls `pop()` to attempt to pop the message off the top of the stack. If the stack is empty, `pop()` returns the diagnostic message "*Stack empty*" to notify the user of the condition; otherwise, it retrieves the message at the top of the stack and decrements the stack index.

The code for the `push()` and `pop()` functions is also part of the **stack.c** source file. Notice the stack variables, `stack` and `index`, are both declared `static`. They are visible to the companion `push()` and `pop()` functions that interact with the stack, but are not visible to other parts of the program. The stack has ten elements, determined by the STACKSIZE constant, with each element being an array of characters that is large enough to hold a message of NBYTES, which has been arbitrarily set to 80 bytes. The extra byte in each stack element is there, of course, to allow space for the terminating null byte.

```
#define STACKSIZE 10

/* message stack */
static char stack[STACKSIZE][NBYTES + 1];
static int index = 0;


/*
 * push()
 *
 * Push an item (message text) onto the stack unless
 * the stack is full. Report an error if it is full.
 */

int
push(char *mesg)
```

```
{
        int rc = 0;

        if (index < STACKSIZE)
                strcpy(stack[index++], mesg);
        else
                ++rc;

        return rc;
}


/*
 * pop()
 *
 * Pop an item off the top of the stack and return
 * a pointer to it. If the stack is empty, return
 * an error message.
 */

char *
pop(void)
{
        if (index > 0)
                return stack[--index];
        else
                return "Stack empty";
}
```

In each of these functions, a check against the relevant stack boundary is made before anything is written or read. In the case of the push() function, the bounds check of index against the STACKSIZE constant must be made to prevent writing a message to a full stack. Similarly, pop() must be sure that index is greater than 0 to verify that there is a message to be popped.

Here is the display for a sample session, showing the user's input in italics and the **stack** program output in bold type:

```
$ stack
Command (w, r, or q): w
line 1
Command (w, r, or q): w
line 2
Command (w, r, or q): r
line 2
Command (w, r, or q): w
another line
Command (w, r, or q): r
another line
Command (w, r, or q): r
line 1
Command (w, r, or q): r
Stack empty
Command (w, r, or q): q
$ _
```

The message stack shown in this demonstration program can be used in a larger program context to manage a message line for an interactive display. Let's say you have a single line at the bottom of the screen reserved for messages. If a process generates several messages as it runs, each message would overwrite the previous message, perhaps before the user could read the earlier messages. By setting up a reasonably deep stack and giving the user some commands to pop messages off the stack on demand, you prevent loss of important information.

Queues

In the design of the **stack** program, messages are read in the reverse order of their arrivals, which might be disconcerting to the user. If we use a queue instead of a stack, the messages can be read in the order in which they are received, which seems the more natural way of presenting them. The buffers that allow devices with widely divergent data transmission rates, such as CPUs and disk drives, are usually implemented as queues.

This section describes queues and shows you how to use them in programs.

The Queue Data Type

The queue is a first-in, first-out (FIFO) data storage type mechanism The first item queued is the first item retrieved. We can use an array implementation of a queue just as we did for the stack.

Figure 11-2 depicts a linear queue containing only five elements. It is implemented as an array of characters. Initially, the head and tail indexes are equal, both designating element 0 of the queue. The head index indicates where the next `write` operation takes place and the tail index indicates where the next `read` operation occurs.

We use the function `enqueue()` to write an item to the queue and `dequeue()` to read an item from the queue. When you attempt to write an item to the queue, the head index is first checked. If it is not already beyond the end of the queue, the item is written to the location designated by the head index, then `head` is incremented. If `head` is already off the end of the queue, nothing can be written.

The item read from the queue is designated by the tail index. If tail equals head, the queue is empty and nothing remains to be read. Otherwise, the `read` operation occurs and the tail index is incremented.

Figure 11-2: An Array Implementation of a Queue

QUEUE (first in, first out)

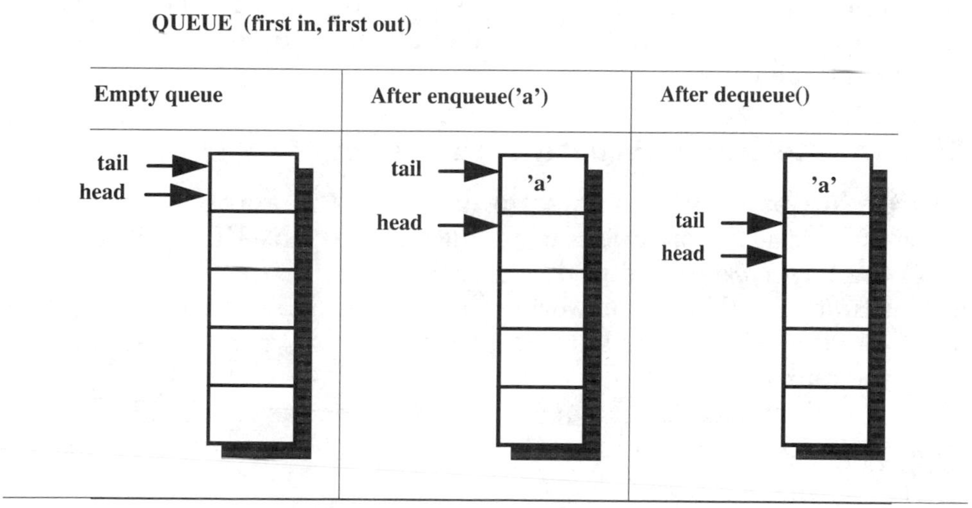

The Circular Queue

Linear queues are limited by the length of the queue. Because of this, they are not often used. However, a variation of the linear queue called the circular queue, is frequently used, especially in buffering data transfers. A circular queue is also a stretch of memory locations, but the access methods effectively wrap back to the beginning when the end of the queue is reached.

A good example of a circular queue is the keyboard buffer of a typical personal computer. The keyboard buffer receives characters as quickly as you type them and delivers them to a process on demand. If the process is busy doing something else, such as reformatting text (word processing) or translating a statement (language compiler), the buffers lets you continue typing without dropping any of your input.

The keyboard buffer in an IBM PC has only 16 positions, so if you type fast enough, you can sometimes fill the buffer. When this happens, the machine beeps at you, telling you it can't accept any more input. One way to solve this problem is to create a separate, larger buffer and use it to feed the program. A queue of 128 bytes is a popular size.

Going to a circular queue poses a problem. If the tail and the head indexes are equal, is the queue full or empty? You can't tell. We have to devise a way of differentiating the two conditions. The problem is solved by sacrificing one position in the queue. The tail index is started one behind the head index and is not allowed to catch up to it. Let's see how this technique works.

The queue Demonstration Program

The **queue** program is similar in design to the **stack** program. The difference is the use of a queue to handle messages in a FIFO order, rather than the LIFO order produced by a stack.

The functions that do the work in this program are enqueue(), which writes an item to the circular queue, and dequeue() which reads an item from the queue.

The main() function for a queue looks the same as the one in the **stack** program, except for the names of the queueing functions.

```
/*
 * queue.c
 *
 * Demonstrate a circular queue by using one as the
 * basis of a message manager. The queue is
 * implemented as an array of character pointers.
 */

#include <stdio.h>
#include <stdlib.h>
#include <string.h>

#define NBYTES 80

/* function prototypes */
int enqueue(char *);
char *dequeue(void);

int
main(void)
{
      int ch;
      char line[NBYTES + 1];


      while (1) {
            printf("Command (w=write r=read q=quit) + Return: ");
            gets(line);
            switch (line[0]) {
            case 'w':
            case 'W':
                  /* write (enqueue) a new message */
                  printf("Message: ");
                  gets(line);
                  if (enqueue(line) != 0)
                        printf("Queue full\n");
                  break;
            case 'r':
            case 'R':
```

```
                        /* read (dequeue) a message */
                        printf("%s\n", dequeue());
                        break;
                case 'q':
                case 'Q':
                        exit(EXIT_SUCCESS);
                }
        }

        return EXIT_SUCCESS;
}
```

In the following code, the head and tail indexes are called `write` and `read` respectively. Note that the queue and the indexes are `static` and, therefore, are visible only to the queueing functions.

```
#define QSIZE 10

/* message queue */
static char queue[QSIZE][NBYTES + 1];
static int write = 0;
static int read = QSIZE - 1;


/*
 * enqueue()
 *
 * Add an item (message text) to the queue unless
 * the queue is full. Report an error if it is full.
 */

int
enqueue(char *mesg)
{
        int rc = 0;

        if (write != read) {
                strcpy(queue[write++], mesg);
                if (write == QSIZE)
```

```
                write = 0;
    }
    else
            /* queue full */
            ++rc;

    return rc;
}


/*
 * dequeue()
 *
 * Take an item off the queue and return a pointer
 * to it. If the queue is empty, return an error message.
 */

char *
dequeue(void)
{
    if ((read + 1) % QSIZE != write) {
            if (++read == QSIZE)
                    read = 0;
            return queue[read];
    }
    else
            return "Queue empty";
}
```

The enqueue() function first determines the status of the queue. If the write index has caught up with the read index, the queue is full and the function simply returns an error flag. If there is room in the queue, the message passed as an argument is added to the queue and the write pointer is incremented. Notice how the write pointer is wrapped back to the beginning of the queue if it exceeds the queue's upper bound.

The code for dequeue() involves a new wrinkle. It uses the modulus operator to keep the value of the read index in range in the expression:

```
(read + 1) % DSIZE != write
```

Using this expression to control the `if` statement avoids having to write a more complex check that compares the indexes two ways: one for the normal cases (read less than write) and one for the case in which the write index has wrapped back to the beginning of the queue and the read index has not. If the queue is not empty, the read index is incremented, taking wrapping into account, and message is returned to the caller.

Compare the following output from a sample run of the **queue** program with that of the **stack** program. Again, user input is shown in italics and the **queue** program output is shown in bold type.

```
$ queue
Command (w, r, or q): w
line 1
Command (w, r, or q): w
line 2
Command (w, r, or q): r
line 1
Command (w, r, or q): w
another line
Command (w, r, or q): r
line 2
Command (w, r, or q): r
another line
Command (w, r, or q): r
Queue empty
Command (w, r, or q): q
$ _
```

Try running the program yourself and attempt to key in more messages than the queue can hold. How many messages do you think it can hold when it is full?

Summary

Stacks and queues are important data types. They are handy for controlling priorities and for buffering data transfers, especially between devices that operate at different speeds,

The stack is a last-in, first-out memory object. A queue, on the other hand, is a first-in, first-out memory object. The circular queue is especially useful for data buffering applications because there is little need to be concerned about queue size—as there would be with a linear queue as long as the queue is made large enough to avoid overflow.

Questions and Exercises

1. What are the primary properties of a stack?

2. Describe a stack from your own non-programming experience.

3. What condition of the index of an array-type stack indicates that the stack is empty?

4. Figure 11-1 shows how a multiplication is performed. Write out the sequences of `push` and `pop` operations needed to implement the remaining operations of a four-function postfix (RPN) type calculator. This type of calculator takes the numeric values first and then the operator that says what to do with the numbers.

5. What is the purpose of a queue?

6. Given write and read indexes to a circular queue, what condition indicates that the queue is full?

7. Given write and read indexes to a circular queue, what condition indicates that the queue is empty?

8. What limitation of a linear queue makes it unsuitable for use as a data buffering mechanism?

9. For a circular queue with an array size of 20 elements, how many queued items can it hold when full?

Additional Exercises

A. Write a function that would allow you to peek at the value on the top of a stack without actually popping it. Call the function `peek()` and have it return a pointer to a character that designates the message.

B. It is sometimes necessary to know whether a stack is empty without altering it. Write a function called `empty()` that returns a Boolean (TRUE or FALSE) value to its caller.

C. Write a function that would allow you to examine the value at the head of a queue without actually removing it. Call the function `qhead()` and have it return a pointer to a character that designates the message at the head of the queue.

D. Write a function that examines a queue and reports whether it is empty or not without actually attempting to read or write anything. Call the function `qempty()` and have it return a Boolean (TRUE or FALSE) value to its caller.

CHAPTER 12

LINKED DATA STRUCTURES

The previous chapter described contiguous allocations of memory for stacks and queues. These constructs are very useful, but they have limitations.

First, they require allocation of a fixed amount of memory regardless of the amount actually used by a program. You might set aside a stack of, say, two kilobytes to be sure you have enough room for the worst case and then use only a few hundred bytes of it. Second, elements of a stack or queue are adjacent to each other. It is often more convenient to allow items to be arranged in seemingly arbitrary ways and thread them together rather than enforce a linear arrangement.

In earlier chapters you were introduced to structures, pointers, and combinations of these. Pointers to structures provide a convenient way to access structure members. If a structure member is a pointer to an object of the same type, we have a simple way of stringing objects together in various ways.

A structure that contains a pointer to an object of its own type is called a self-referential data structure, which is the basis of linked lists, various tree-like data structures, as well as dynamically modifiable stacks and queues. This chapter introduces self-referential data structures and their application to linked lists. In addition, it introduces memory management functions that provide ways of dynamically allocating and deallocating regions of memory.

Singly-Linked Lists

A singly-linked list is a collection of nodes connected by pointers in one direction. Each node is a structure variable that contains a forward pointer member. A list can contain a varying number of nodes, which is one of the primary virtues of linked lists. If you only need three nodes to manage your list data, then that's how many you use. There is no need to waste space on unneeded nodes.

Figure 12-1 shows how the components of a linked list are declared. The top half of the figure relates the data declarations to the objects for which memory is reserved. A single node, `listhead`, and two pointer variables, `head` and `current`, are created by the declarations.

The bottom half of the figure depicts the first three nodes of a singly-linked list of some unspecified size. The `listhead` node is a "helper" node called the **prefirst node**. It simplifies the code for list operations, as we'll see in the next few sections of this chapter. The prefirst node, sometimes called a "dummy" node, is usually a structure of the same type as the rest of the nodes. In most cases, only its pointer member is used. Some list-management schemes use other members of the prefirst node to store special information about the list, such as the number of nodes.

Just as we have used character pointers to mark a position in a string, we can use a pointer to mark the current position in the list. The current pointer is just that—a pointer, so its size is that of a pointer variable, not that of a structure. The same is true for the `head` pointer, which marks the position of the `listhead` node.

The `typedef` statement creates the type name SNODE, which you can use as a synonym for `struct node_st` in declaration statement for list nodes and pointers, and type casts. A singly-linked list has a pointer per node for a forward link. The forward pointer has the same type as the list nodes themselves. Other members of the node structure can hold data and pointers to other memory objects that hold data outside the list node.

Figure 12-1: A Singly-linked List of Data Structures

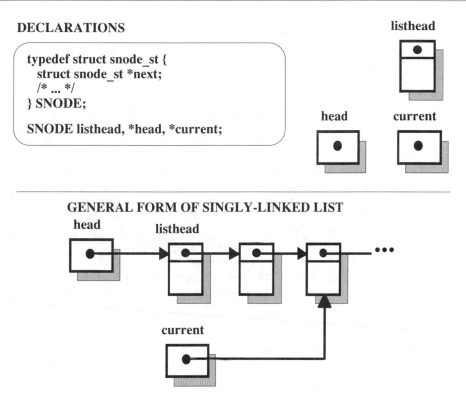

DECLARATIONS

```
typedef struct snode_st {
  struct snode_st *next;
  /* ... */
} SNODE;

SNODE listhead, *head, *current;
```

GENERAL FORM OF SINGLY-LINKED LIST

Operations on a List

The node pointed to by the current pointer is used by list management functions as a reference point for insertions, deletions, and other operations. So how do we establish a list of nodes such as the one shown in the figure? Obviously we need a way to create the nodes themselves and some way to hook up the forward pointers to form a chain of nodes (the list).

The advantage of a prefirst node at the head of a list can be seen in the descriptions of list operations. The partial list shown in the figure starts out as a lone `listhead` node with a `next` member of `NULL` (no link).

The primary operations that can be performed on a list include the following:

- Insert a node into a list

- Delete the current node from a list

- Access a node for writing or reading

You need access to `list` nodes to assign values to data members of the nodes or to read their values. Access is also needed to traverse the list to find a particular node.

Figure 12-2 depicts the process of inserting a node into a singly-linked list. The process involves a sequence of steps that must be done in the order shown. The code for each step is shown in the figure.

1. Allocate a new node (dynamic allocation at run-time is shown, but static allocations at translation time can be used instead).

2. Make the new node's `next` member point to the node that will follow it in the list (the one pointed to by the current node before the insertion).

3. Make the `next` member of the current node point to the new node.

A list with no prefirst node is empty when there are no nodes at all, but only a pointer such as `head` with a `NULL` value, so that arranging the pointers is a more complex task that must take special cases into account. In a list with a prefirst node, the code for an insertion operation is easier to write because there is no need to accommodate special cases, as occur when you are inserting a node into an empty list.

Collecting the pieces together, here is code that inserts a node into a singly-linked list:

```
SNODE *
insert_node(SNODE *listp)
{
    SNODE *new;

    new = (SNODE *) malloc(sizeof (SNODE));
    if (new != NULL) {
```

```
        new->next = listp->next;
        listp->next = new;
    }
    return new;
}
```

Deleting a node from a singly-linked list involves the reverse process of inserting one, but with a twist. Because each node in a singly-linked list points only to the next node in a list, it is both inconvenient and inefficient to find out which node points to the current node. The code for delete_node() deletes the node *after* the one passed as an argument to the function.

```
void
delete_node(SNODE *listp)
{
    SNODE *tmp;

    tmp = listp->next;
     listp->next = listp->next->next;
    free(tmp);
}
```

The expression listp->next points to the node to be deleted (the "doomed" node) and the expression listp->next->next points to the one after it (NULL marks the end of the list).

Circular Singly-Linked Lists

The next pointer of the node at the end of a linear singly-linked list has a next pointer value of NULL because it doesn't point to another node. A circular list is one in which every node points to another node in the list. The last node points back to the head of the list completing the circle.

Having the prefirst node point to itself initially forms the basis of a circular list. As nodes are inserted, the list maintains its circular nature. The circular list simplifies operations such as searching from an interior node to any other part of the list with automatic wrapping around the ends of the list.

Figure 12-2: Inserting a Node into a Linked List

a)

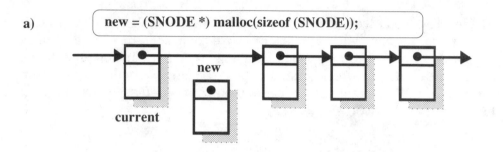

```
new = (SNODE *) malloc(sizeof (SNODE));
```

b)

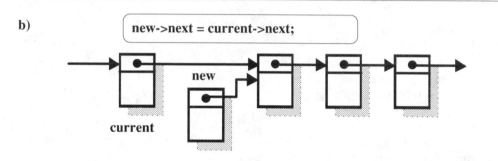

```
new->next = current->next;
```

c)

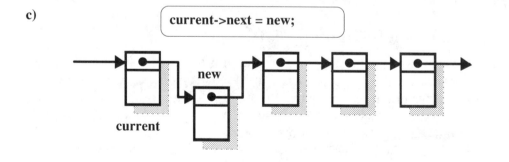

```
current->next = new;
```

The `listhead` node, pointed to by the `head` pointer, is made to point to itself by the statement:

```
head->next = head;
```

The expression `head->next` selects the forward pointer member of the node. This is a modifiable `lvalue`, so the value of a pointer of the same type (in this case `head`), can be assigned to it, forming an empty circular list.

Two key operations in list management are the allocation and deallocation of nodes. These operations can be based on either static or dynamic methods. In the static case, which allocates nodes at the time the program is translated and linked, typically declares arrays of nodes and links them together into a free list. A pointer designates the beginning of the array. As nodes are needed, they are removed from the head of the free list. As they are released they are inserted back into the free list.

A problem with static allocation is that you need some idea in advance of how many nodes are needed. In addition, you are faced with some inefficiencies caused by having space allocated that may not be used. Dynamic memory allocation, which takes place at run-time, provides a way around this. This brings us to the next topic.

Memory Management

Memory management involves requests from a process for additional memory resources. Whether such requests can be granted depends on the availability of memory in an area of memory commonly known as the heap, which is a region of unallocated memory that is made available to a process on demand.

Several memory managements functions are of particular help in list management functions. We will use `malloc()` to allocate blocks of memory and `free()` to release (deallocate) the memory when it is no longer needed. Here are the function prototypes for `malloc()` and `free()`:

```
void *malloc(size_t size);
void free(void *ptr);
```

The `malloc()` function does not alter the contents of the memory it allocates. Two other memory-allocation functions are `calloc()`, which initializes (clears) allocated memory , and `realloc()`, which attempts to alter the size of previously allocated memory blocks without altering their contents.

The `malloc()` function returns a curious looking pointer value: `void *`. What does that mean? The pointer type `void *` is a generic pointer. It is suitable for use as a pointer to an object of any type. A pointer to an object of any type can be converted to a generic pointer type and then back again without change. A pointer to `void` has the same alignment requirements as a pointer to `char`.

Pre-ANSI implementations of `malloc()` returned a `char *` pointer, treating its allocated memory as a sequence of bytes. When allocating memory with `malloc()`, it was necessary to cast the return value to a pointer to the type of the object being allocated. This is no longer a requirement because of the generic pointer return type, but I have shown the pre-ANSI form because most C translators still require the cast.

Programs frequently need to make an exact copy of a string. An example of this is gathering lines of input from the keyboard or a file. If you set up an array that is big enough to hold the largest expected input line, a lot of space will be wasted because most lines will be shorter than the statically allocated array. It would be better to allocate only the amount of memory that is needed to hold each line.

The standard libraries provided with many DOS-oriented C compilers provide a `strdup()` function that dynamically allocates a region of memory and copies a string into it. This function is not covered in the ANSI library description, so here is a version of `strdup()` that you can use if your C translator doesn't provide it.

```
/*
 * strdup()
 *
 * Create a buffer of appropriate size and
 * copy a string into the buffer.
 */

#include <stdio.h>
```

```
#include <stdlib.h>
#include <string.h>

char *
strdup(const char *str)
{
    char *new;

    new = (char *) malloc(strlen (str) + 1);
    return new == NULL ? new : strcpy(buf, str);
}
```

This function takes a string argument and uses `malloc()` to allocate a block of bytes that is big enough to hold a copy of the string, including the null byte [hence `strlen(str) + 1`]. The function returns either a pointer to the start of the newly created string or NULL to indicate an error. If an error occurs, it would be a failure to allocate the needed memory, indicating that the available memory resource is expended. The calling function should take appropriate action to respond to such errors, which are usually fatal unless there is a way to deallocated other memory allocations.

Use the `free()` function to deallocate memory previously allocated by a call to `malloc()`, `calloc()`, or `realloc()`. Attempting to free memory not previously allocated by the other memory-management functions is an error. Such attempts produce undefined behavior.

Example Program: cardfile

The **cardfile** program demonstrates the features of a singly-linked list and the functions that manage it. The program is a simple electronic version of a file of contact names and telephone numbers.

The supported commands are:

- Add a new card to the file

- Find a card based on a name search

- List the contents of the file

- Quit (save changes)

- Exit (abandon changes)

The **cardfile** program is a large one. You can place all of the code in one file, if you prefer, but it makes sense to organize it as a set of source files that are separately compiled and linked. Let's start with the code for the `main()` function, which consists of initialization code and the main program processing loop. Observe the data declarations and the function prototypes to get an idea of what the rest of the program contains.

```
/*
 * cardfile.c
 *
 * This is a highly simplified cardfile system that
 * demonstrates the use of linked lists and dynamic
 * memory allocation and deallocation techniques.
 */

#include <stdio.h>
#include <stdlib.h>
#include <string.h>

#define NBYTES 128
#define NAMESIZE 30
#define PHONESIZE 20

/* structure template */
typedef struct card_st {
      char name[NAMESIZE];
      char phone[PHONESIZE];
      struct card_st *next;
} CARD;

/* cardfile variables */
CARD listhead, *head, *current;

/* function prototypes */
static int add_card(void);
```

```
static int find_card(void);
static int list_cards(void);
static int read_file(char *);
static int write_file(char *);
CARD *insert_node(CARD *);
void error(char *);
static void prt_record(char *, char *);

char reply[NBYTES + 1];

int
main(int argc, char *argv[])
{
    int rc;
    FILE *fp;
    static char data_file[NBYTES + 1] = {
        "cardfile.dat"
    };

    /* check for user-supplied data file name */
    if (argc == 2)
        strcpy(data_file, argv[1]);

    /* set up the empty list  */
    current = head = &listhead;
    head->next = head;

    /* read data into buffer */
    rc = read_file(data_file);
    if (rc)
        error("Cannot read data file");

    /* print instructions */
    puts("CARDFILE commands:");
    puts("  a = add a new card to the file");
    puts("  f = find a card based on a name search");
    puts("  l = list the card file");
    puts("  q = quit (save changes)");
    puts("  x = exit without saving changes\n");
```

```c
        while (1) {
                /* get user's command */
                printf("Command (a, f, l, q, or x): ");
                gets(reply);

                /* process command */
                switch (reply[0]) {
                case 'a':
                case 'A':
                        add_card();
                        break;
                case 'f':
                case 'F':
                        find_card();
                        break;
                case 'l':
                case 'L':
                        list_cards();
                        break;
                case 'q':
                case 'Q':
                        /* save changes and exit */
                        write_file(data_file);
                        return EXIT_SUCCESS;
                case 'x':
                case 'X':
                        /* exit without saving changes */
                        return EXIT_SUCCESS;
                default:
                        /* ignore */
                        break;
                } /* end switch */
        } /* end while */

        return EXIT_SUCCESS;
}
```

The node data structure in this program is called CARD. The initial variables of this type are the listhead structure (the prefirst node), and the head and current pointers.

In the body of main() the command line is checked to see whether an alternative name for the data file has been typed by the user. If none is specified, the default name of **cardfile.dat** is used.

The program prints a brief instructional frame containing descriptions of the allowed commands. The switch prompts the user for commands and calls the functions that implement them.

One of the commands is "add a new card." The code for this command is in the function add_card():

```
/* add an entry to the list */
static int
add_card(void)
{
        int rc = 0;
        CARD *tmp;

        tmp = insert_node(current);
        if (tmp == NULL) {
                fprintf(stderr, "Out of memory");
                ++rc;
        }
        else {
                current = tmp;

                /* input person's name & address */
                printf("Name: ");
                gets(reply);
                strcpy(current->name, reply);
                printf("Phone: ");
                gets(reply);
                strcpy(current->phone, reply);
        }

        return 0;
}
```

If there is enough memory for a new `list` node, it is created (dynamically allocated) and linked into the list. Then the user is prompted for name and telephone number information to be stored in the card. If there is not enough memory to allocate a new card, that fact is reported to the calling function by the NULL return and a message notifies the user of the bad news.

The `find_card()` function checks to make sure that the list is not empty. Then it asks for a literal string as the search key and scans the list for a card that contains the string in the name field. The search begins at the node after the `listhead` node. This is the first node that contains contact data.

```c
/* find and print an entry */
static int
find_card(void)
{
        int  rc = 0;
        int  hits = 0;
        int  len;
        char *cp;
        CARD *tmp;

        tmp = head;
        if (tmp->next == head) {
                puts("List empty");
                return ++rc;
        }

        printf("Name to find: ");
        gets(reply);
        len = strlen(reply);
        while (tmp->next != head) {
                tmp = tmp->next;
                cp = tmp->name;
                while (*cp != '\0') {
                        if (strncmp(cp, reply, len) == 0) {
                                prt_record(tmp->name, tmp->phone);
                                ++hits;
```

```
                    }
                    ++cp;
            }
    }
    if (hits == 0)
            puts("Card not found");

    return rc;
}
```

Note the use of `strncpy()`, which compares only the specified number of characters (the third argument). The function returns zero if there is a match. The loop controlled by the character pointer `cp` moves along the `name` member of the card. You can, therefore, search for a substring in the `name` field rather than having to type the entire `name` field. If the card is found, its contents are listed and the current pointer is updated to point to the found card. If there is no match, `find_card()` prints a message and returns a nonzero value.

The `list_cards()` function simply traverses the list from the head to the last card and prints the contents of each card in the file. Again, a test is made to guard against trying to list an empty file.

```
/* list the entire data file */
static int
list_cards(void)
{
    int rc;
    CARD *tmp;

    tmp = head;
    if (tmp->next == head) {
            puts("List empty");
            ++rc;
    }
    else
            while (tmp->next != head) {
                    tmp = tmp->next;
                    prt_record(tmp->name, tmp->phone);
```

```
            }

        return rc;
}
```

The next two functions, `read_file()` and `write_file()`, provide the interface to the user's file system. When the program starts executing, `read_file()` attempts to open the specified data file or the default data file, **cardfile.dat**, and read in its contents. The file is closed immediately after the data is read in to avoid any unwanted changes to the file.

Here is the code for `read_file()`:

```
/* read data file into buffer */
static int
read_file(char *fname)
{
        char *cp;
        FILE *fp;
        char line[NBYTES + 1];
        int rc = 0;
        CARD *tmp;

        /* open the file for reading */
        fp = fopen(fname, "r");
        if (fp == NULL)
                return 0;           /* not an error */

        /* read the data into a buffer */
        while (fgets(line, NBYTES + 1, fp) != NULL) {
                /* remove NL */
                cp = line;
                while (*cp != '\n' && *cp != '\0')
                        ++cp;
                *cp = '\0';

                /* allocate a node and point to it */
                tmp = insert_node(current);
                if (tmp == NULL)
                        error("out of memory");
```

```
              current = tmp;

              /* copy data to card structure */
              strcpy(current->name, strtok(line, "\t"));
              strcpy(current->phone, strtok(NULL, "\t"));
       }

       /* close the file */
       fclose(fp);
       if (ferror(fp))
              error("Cannot close data file");

       return rc;
}
```

The format of the data file is one line per card record with a tab as a field separator. The data is read in a line at a time by the `fgets()` function, the newline character is removed, and the data fields extracted by successive calls to the `strtok()`, which copies tokens from a data stream. The tab is used as a field separator. The first call to `strtok()` contains the name of the array that contains the tokens to be copied. The second call to it uses `NULL`, which causes the token-copying activity to continue where it left off in the previous call.

The `write_file()` function is a bit simpler than `read_file()`. It calls `fprintf()` to print the records to the data file. As with `read_file()`, the data file is opened, accessed, and closed immediately.

```
/* write data in buffer to the data file */
static int
write_file(char *fname)
{
       FILE *fp;
       int rc = 0;
       char reply[NBYTES + 1];
       CARD *tmp;

       /* open the file for reading */
       fp = fopen(fname, "w");
```

```
    if (fp == NULL) {
          fprintf(stderr, "Cannot open %s\n", fname);
          return ++rc;
    }

    /* write the data into a buffer */
    tmp = head;
    if (tmp->next == head) {
          puts("List empty");
          ++rc;
    }
    else
          while (tmp->next != head) {
                tmp = tmp->next;
                fprintf(fp, "%s\t%s\n",
                      tmp->name, tmp->phone);
          }

    /* close the file */
    fclose(fp);
    if (ferror(fp))
          error("Cannot close data file");

    return rc;
}
```

The error() function is designed to print an error message and then exit immediately with an error exit code (nonzero). The message consists of a fixed part ("ERROR:") and a variable part provided by the parameter mesg.

```
/* print message and exit with failure indication */
void
error(char *mesg)
{
      fprintf(stderr, "ERROR: %s\n", mesg);
      exit(EXIT_FAILURE);
}
```

Here is the list-management function that actually inserts nodes. The function `insert_node()` receives a pointer to the current location in the list. It inserts the new node to the right of the current node.

```
/* insert a new node after the current position */
CARD *
insert_node(CARD *listp)
{
        CARD *new;

        /* allocate a new node */
        new = (CARD *) malloc(sizeof (CARD));
        if (new != NULL) {
                /* link the node into the list */
                new->next = listp->next;
                listp->next = new;
        }

        return new;
}
```

The `prt_record()` function is called by some of the card functions to print out (display) a node's contents. It takes two string arguments and formats them into columns.

```
static void
prt_record(char *s1, char *s2)
{
        printf("%-*s\t%-*s\n",
                NAMESIZE, s1, PHONESIZE, s2);
}
```

Notice how the * width specifier is used. It picks up the width from values in the argument list. This avoids having values for the column widths hard-coded in each `printf()` call. A width argument is placed in the list before the argument with which it is associated.

Doubly-Linked Lists

Singly-linked lists are not ideal solutions to many problems because it is difficult and inefficient to traverse the list backwards. That's why doubly-linked lists are used in text editors, window-management systems, and many other applications that require quick forward and backward positioning.

Figure 12-3 depicts a doubly-linked list. Such a list is distinguished by the pair of node pointer members that allow the nodes to be linked in both directions. The declaration of the DNODE type creates a new type name for the struct dnode_st type. The forward (next) and backward (prev) pointers each point to objects of the DNODE type.

Figure 12-3: A Doubly-linked List of Data Structures

DECLARATIONS

```
typedef struct dnode_st {
  struct dnode_st *next, *prev;
  /* ... */
} DNODE;
DNODE listhead, *head, *current;
```

GENERAL FORM OF DOUBLY-LINKED LIST

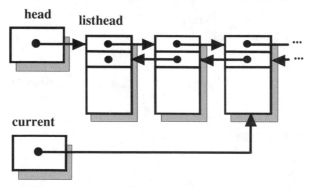

You can still have an auxiliary pointer to designate the head of the list and the current position, but the pointers must also be declared to be of the doubly-linked node type. Because of the double linking, you also need new functions for inserting and deleting nodes.

```
DNODE *
insert_dnode(DNODE *listp)
{
    DNODE *new;

    new = (DNODE *) malloc(sizeof (DNODE));
    if (new != NULL) {
        new->prev = listp;
        new->next = listp->next;
        listp->next->prev = new;
        listp->next = new;
    }

    return new;
}
```

If it is not immediately clear to you what is going on with the pointer assignments, draw yourself a picture of the insertion process that parallels the one for the singly-linked list and work through the function statements one at a time, following the links manually.

The code to delete a node is also complicated by the additional link per node. The advantage of the doubly-linked list delete function is that it deletes the current node instead of the next node in the list.

```
void
delete_dnode(DNODE *listp)
{
    listp->prev->next = listp->next;
    listp->next->prev = listp->prev;
    free(listp);
}
```

Circular Doubly-Linked List

A circular doubly-linked list follows the pattern of a circular singly-linked list, but the doubly-linked case requires that two pointers per node be used. Circular lists make nice control mechanisms for editing buffers in text editor programs and other situations in which convenient wrap-around at the buffer boundaries as needed.

Figure 12-4 depicts a circular doubly-linked list. The next pointer members of the node structures provide a circular forward chain of links and the `prev` members provide the circular backward chain of links.

The combination of a prefirst node and a circular list implementation prides a convenient and efficient dynamic storage mechanism. Functions that manipulate a circular list don't need to deal with special cases. Functions that traverse a circular need to deal only with the special case of skipping over the prefirst node when wrapping from the list tail to the list head, or the reverse.

Figure 12-4: A Circular Doubly-linked List

CIRCULAR LIST

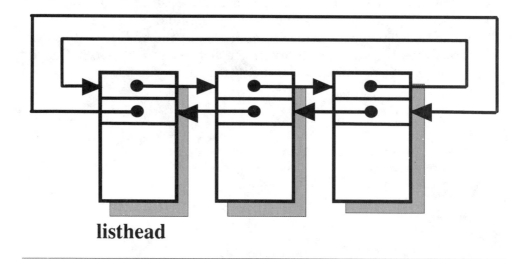

listhead

Summary

Data structures and algorithms are the heart and soul of computer programs. Try to obtain some books that address these areas of study and devote a fair share of your time to studying them and working with them. A good working knowledge of data structures, their associated processing algorithms, and a feeling for when to apply them is essential to your programming future.

This chapter introduced you to linked data structures including singly-linked and doubly-linked lists. It also described dynamic memory management techniques for allocating and deallocating memory while a program is running rather than depending on potentially inefficient static memory allocations. When you feel at ease with these linked data structures, investigate binary trees and other tree-like structures, priority queues, and other advanced data structures.

Questions and Exercises

1. What is a `list` node and how is it declared?

2. What are the characteristics of a singly-linked list?

3. Describe the process of inserting a new node into a list.

4. What is tricky about deleting a node from a singly-linked list.

5. True or false: stacks and queues can be implemented as linked lists.

6. Why is a prefirst node used in linked lists?

7. The code for examining a list to see whether it is empty occurs in many places in the cardfile code. Write a function `list_empty()` that returns a nonzero value if the list pointer passed to it is to an empty list.

8. What are some advantages of circular lists over their linear equivalents?

9. Write a declaration for a `list` node that contains forward and backward pointers, a pointer to a keycap legend string, a pointer to a help message

string, and an integer that can hold a unique key code in the range of -1 to 32,535.

10. As written, find_card() searches through the entire list, printing out the contents of every card that matches the search string. Rewrite the function so that it stops at the first matching card and updates the current pointer so that it points to the matched card node.

Additional Exercises

A. Add a delete_node() function to the **cardfile** program and revise the other code in main() to permit the user to delete the current card, which is selected by using the find command first. This task will require that you also write a delete_card () function. Be sure that you delete the current card and not the one after it.

B. Design a program that reads all the lines from a text file into a buffer and prints the lines out in reverse order. A doubly-linked list of line-control nodes is well suited to this problem.

C. Write a simple line-oriented file viewer that lets you display lines from a file in screen pages (typically 24 or 25 lines) with the ability to scroll forward and backward in the file with equal ease and speed.

D. Redesign the CARD data structure used in the **cardfile** program so that it contains members for the person's first and last names, company or other affiliation, and telephone number. Break the phone number into area code and base phone number components. Then rewrite the program so that searches can be based on the contents of any field. For example, running the find command with a field name of area_code and the seach string "303" would print out all cards for the northern Colorado calling area.

CHAPTER 13

COMMUNICATING WITH
THE OPERATING SYSTEM

To this point our programs have had a one-way communication with the operating system by returning exit codes that indicate success or failure. It is also possible for the operating system to pass data to running programs in a couple of ways.

This chapter explores the use of command-line arguments and environment variables as communication pathways from the operating environment to a running program.

Command-Line Arguments

Even under growing pressure from windowing interfaces and menu-driven systems, the command line is still an important feature of present-day operating systems. Both UNIX and DOS in their raw forms provide a Spartan prompt that invites the user to type a command.

It would be convenient to have commands that require only a simple command name, preferably short, and possibly a filename or two. Indeed, that was a goal of the original UNIX design, which emphasized the use of many single-purpose commands that could be combined in pipelines to provide ad hoc solutions to a wide range of computing and text-processing problems.

Over the years, many of these simple programs have accumulated new features, most of which are activated by command-line options. The **pr** program is an example of a program that started out as a simple egg and now looks more like a budding potato.

Here is a sample command line that uses the standard UNIX syntax:

```
$ look -c src/calc.c
```

The command invokes a program called **look** to list the contents of a file. Without the -c option, **look** simply lists the lines in the named file. When the -c option is used, the program puts special highlighting around the decimal codes of any control characters to make them stand out.

Figure 13-1 shows how a UNIX command line is accessed. The illustration depicts one way of storing the command-line text in a character array. Each space or tab is replaced by a null byte, effectively creating a set of separate strings. Pointer variables are assigned the addresses of the substrings created by this process.

Figure 13-1: Command-line Argument Count and Vector Table

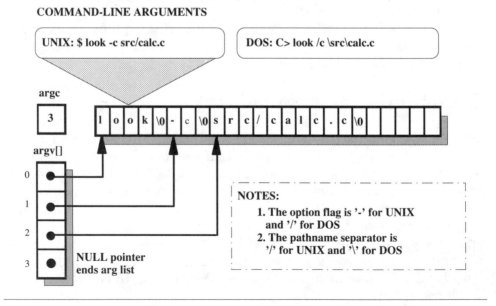

✍**Programmer's Notebook:**

As Figure 13-1 shows, DOS uses different conventions for command-line symbols. For compatibility with CP/M, the predecessor of DOS, the forward slash ('/') is used as the "switch character" or option flag. Because of this choice, the pathname separator is the backslash ('\'). This difference in command syntax is a chronic pain for those of us who regularly work with both DOS and UNIX.

The look Program

This is the program that was alluded to in Figure 13-1. The behavior of the **look** program is specified by the command-line option, -c, and controlled internally by the variable showControl. The connection between the external specifier and the internal variable is made by the parameters to main(), argc and argv, which you are seeing for the first time in this book. If the definition of main() has formal parameters, something must call main() with actual arguments. But we haven't written anything that calls main(), the entry point to our program. So what does call it?

The answer is the C run-time startup system. When a C program is translated, code is generated that, among other tasks, passes command-line arguments in a call to main(). The arguments provide values for argc, the argument count, and argv, which is an array of pointers to character strings.

The integer argc value includes the program name and any optional and required arguments typed by the user. The character pointer array, *argv[], contains one pointer for each argument that results from reading the command line and possibly expanding wildcards in filename specifications.

Here is the source code for the **look** program:

```
/*
 * look.c
 *
 * Demonstrate in a simple program how the operating
 * system passes data from the user command-line to a
```

```
 * program.
 */

#include <ctype.h>
#include <stdio.h>
#include <stdlib.h>
#include <string.h>

typedef enum { FALSE, TRUE } BOOL;

int
main(int argc, char *argv[])
{
        int ch;                 /* input/output character */
        BOOL showControl;       /* show control codes when TRUE */
        char *fname;            /* file name pointer */
        FILE *fp;               /* file pointer */

        /* process the command line */
        showControl = FALSE;
        if (argc < 2 || argc > 3) {
                fputs("Usage: look [-c] file\n", stderr);
                exit(EXIT_FAILURE);
        }
        switch (argc) {
        case 2:
                fname = argv[1];
                break;
        case 3:
                showControl = TRUE;
                fname = argv[2];
                break;
        }

        /* open the file for reading */
        if ((fp = fopen(fname, "r")) == NULL) {
                fprintf(stderr, "Cannot open %s\n", fname);
                exit(EXIT_FAILURE);
        }
```

```
/* copy the file to the standard output */
while ((ch = fgetc(fp)) != EOF)
      if (showControl == TRUE && iscntrl(ch))
            printf("<%i>", ch);
      else
            putchar(ch);
if (ferror(fp)) {
      fprintf(stderr, "Error reading %s\n", fname);
      clearerr(fp);
}

/* close the file and exit */
fclose(fp);
if (ferror(fp)) {
      fprintf(stderr, "Error closing %s\n", fname);
}
return EXIT_SUCCESS;
}
```

The second argument to main(), which is shown as:

```
char *argv[]
```

can be written as:

```
char **argv
```

with precisely the same effect. The first form is read as, "argv is an array of pointers to objects of type char." The second form is read as, "argv is a pointer to a pointer to an object of type char."

By convention, the first component of a command line is the program name (except DOS versions prior to 3.0). In operating environments that cannot make the program name available for any reason, an empty string ("") or some dummy name string is provided.

If you use **look** to list a file with the following contents, its normal output looks exactly the same:

```
Line 1
Line 2
Line 3
```

If you issue the `-c` option, the output changes to a sequence of bytes with all control characters represented by their decimal codes with their usual formatting effects turned off. Here is what the alternative output looks like:

```
Line 1<10>Line 2<10>Line 3<10>
```

Ambiguous Filenames

Filename arguments are handled differently by DOS and UNIX. If a filename argument contains wildcard characters, such as * and ?, they are expanded by a UNIX shell. Wildcards in a filename argument under DOS are not expanded by the COMMAND.COM processor, so a separate library module, typically called `setargv()`, must be linked with the C programs you create for use under DOS.

In addition to the * and ? wildcards understood by both DOS and UNIX, UNIX also accepts character classes, indicated by square brackets surrounding lists and ranges of characters. Thus, the filename arguments:

```
file?.c [A-Z]*
```

match files with names like `file1`, `filex`, `Alpha`, `Delta`, but not `file01`, `alpha`, and so on.

Environment Variables

UNIX, DOS, OS/2, and most other operating systems maintain "environmental" data as a list of variable/value pairs. The variables in the list are defined in configuration files controlled by a system administrator or by the user, either interactively or via a start-up file (**.profile** or **.login** under

UNIX; **AUTOEXEC.BAT** under DOS, and so on). Each defined variable has a string value that can be accessed by your programs.

The data items are usually available to a process in at least two ways. The first, but least reliable, is a third parameter, `envp`, to the `main()` function. The declaration of `envp` can be shown as:

`char *envp[]`

or:

`char **envp`

which is analogous to the way `argv` can be declared. The `envp` variable is an array of environment pointers. In this case, each pointer is provided with the address of a name/value pair in the environment space. If you set up a PATH variable in your environment, for example, you can use the environment pointer to search in the variable list for the name strings and then retrieve the value string by using string functions from the standard library, keying on the equal sign that separates the value from the name.

The `envp` parameter is only useful upon entering a program because the environment is subject to relocation as the program runs. A variable's value could change at any time and the locations of variable/value pairs can change. This problem occurs in an environment that supports a function called `putenv()`, which let's you make changes to your environment on the fly.

✍**Programmer's Notebook:**

When a program starts executing (becomes a process), it inherits a copy of the user's environment. Changes made to that copy have no lasting effect because they do not change the original environment.

The getenv() Function

A second and more reliable way to read environment values is to call the `getenv()` function. This function is called with a name string as its only argument. It returns a pointer to an array that contains the value string for the specified variable.

Figure 13-2 shows the use of `getenv()` to get the value of an environment variable. Given the environment depicted in the partial listing, a call to `getenv()` with the string "WIDTH" as an argument retrieves the associated value, "80", which is the character string representation of a number. The code for accessing the variable tests the function return value because NULL indicates that the variable could not be found.

If the variable is found, its value must be converted to the needed form. In this example, the string is converted to an integer by the call to `atoi()`, which is one of a set of data conversion functions in the standard library.

Figure 13-2: The getenv() Function

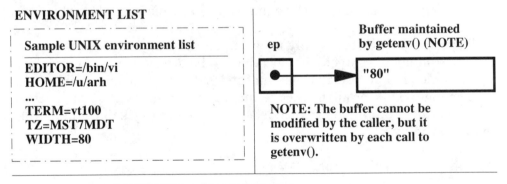

ENVIRONMENT LIST

Sample UNIX environment list

EDITOR=/bin/vi
HOME=/u/arh
...
TERM=vt100
TZ=MST7MDT
WIDTH=80

ep

Buffer maintained
by getenv() (NOTE)

"80"

NOTE: The buffer cannot be modified by the caller, but it is overwritten by each call to getenv().

ACCESSING A VARIABLE

```
char *ep;
int width;

if ((ep = getenv("WIDTH")) != NULL)
    width = atoi(ep);
```

The **envdemo** program demonstrates these two ways to access the environment. Here is the source code:

```
/*
 * envdemo.c
 *
 * List the variables defined in the user's
 * environment and their values.
 */

#include <stdio.h>
#include <stdlib.h>

#define MAXNAME 25

int
main(int argc, char **argv, char **envp)
{
        char *env;                  /* string pointer */
        char **ep;                  /* environment pointer */
#if defined(MSDOS)
        char *cp;
#endif

        /* input buffer */
        char varname[MAXNAME + 1];

        /* print the environment list */
        ep = envp;
        while (*ep++)
              puts(*ep);

        /* demo the use of getenv() */
        printf("Variable name: ");
        gets(varname);

#if defined(MSDOS)
        /* convert variable name to caps if OS=DOS */
        for (cp = varname; *cp != '\0'; ++cp)
```

```
            *cp = (char) toupper((int) *cp);
#endif

    if ((env = getenv(varname)) != NULL)
        printf("%s=%s\n", varname, env);
    else {
        fprintf(stderr,
            "Variable %s not found\n", varname);
        exit(EXIT_FAILURE);
    }
    return EXIT_SUCCESS;
}
```

The program contains some conditional processing directives. When translated for DOS, the program contains additional code to convert the name typed by the user to uppercase letters. The symbolic name MSDOS is usually defined by C translators for DOS-based systems. If it isn't, you can define it yourself by adding the directive:

```
#define MSDOS
```

to the source file or by using a translator command-line argument that produces the same effect.

Here is a sample of the output of **envdemo** when run on one of my DOS machines:

```
CONFIG=c:\init
CTINIT=c:\ctrm\ctrm.ini
NOSNOWCONTROL=true
UPDATEMODE=direct
TZ=MST7MDT
PWPLIB=c:\pwplib
PROMPT=$p$g
PATH=C:\QC2\BIN;C:\DOS4;C:\BIN;C:\BATCH;C:\WORD;C:\CTRM;C:\WI
NDOWS
INCLUDE=c:\qc2\include
LIB=c:\qc2\lib
TMP=c:\tmp
```

Here is a sample of **envdemo** output when run on my XENIX/386 system:

```
EDITOR=/bin/vi
HOME=/u/arh
HZ=50
MAIL=/usr/spool/mail/arh
PATH=/bin:/usr/bin:/usr/lbin:/u/arh/bin:.
SHELL=/bin/sh
TERM=vt100
TZ=MST7MDT
```

Portability

The last argument vector, `argv[argc]`, should be assigned a value of NULL according to the ANSI standard. Many pre-ANSI C translators have supported this convention, but some don't. Use the initial value of the `argc` parameter to find out where the end of the argument list is located rather than depending on finding a NULL as the last vector.

To obtain reasonable uniformity in the way command-line arguments are keyed in by the user and analyzed by a program, use the `getopt()` library function if it is available in your C translator's library. If it is not, as is the case for many DOS C translators, you can use the public domain version of `getopt()` that is included in one of my other books, *Proficient C* (Microsoft Press, 1987). Virtually all of the programs that accept command-line arguments in the book use `getopt()` to process the arguments in a consistent manner.

The set of environment variable names and values is implementation-defined. Interactions with the environment may also vary from one C-supporting implementation to another.

The use of a third argument to `main()` is not universally supported. Even if you can use `envp`, its value is valid only at program startup. Although some environments support the use of a `putenv()` library function, most do not.

If you write code that interacts with the user environment, put it in a separate translation unit to ease the burden of porting code among different operating environments.

Summary

Command-line arguments and environment variables each provide ways of getting external data into a program.

ANSI C supports two parameters to `main()` that permit ready access to the command-line arguments. The parameters, usually called `argc` and `argv`, are supported by hosted C translators. Because these parameters are local to the function `main()`, you can use other names for them if you wish.

A third parameter, called envp by most implementations that support its use, initially points to the start of the environment block. The environment block, a collection of variable/value pairs, can more reliably be accessed by calls to `getenv()`, which returns the value of the variable named as the argument or NULL if the variable is not defined in the environment.

Questions and Exercises

1. What is the purpose of the `argc` parameter to `main`?

2. If a program has five arguments in addition to the `name` argument, what is the range of `argv` array subscripts?

3. In environments that make the program name available, which argument vector contains the program name?

4. DOS does not expand ambiguous filename arguments into lists of filenames. UNIX does. How can you make DOS programs have the same command-line behavior as their UNIX equivalents?

5. Given the command line:

```
myprog -n file1 file2 file3
```

write a statement that prints each of the argument strings except the program name.

6. Why is the use of `envp` discouraged? What is a more reliable alternative for accessing environment variables?

7. Given the environment list shown in Figure 13-2, write a code fragment that reads and prints the value of the `EDITOR` variable. Design the code so that the default "/bin/ed" editor is used if the `EDITOR` variable is not defined.

8. In Figure 13-2, why is the function `atoi()` used in the code for accessing the `WIDTH` variable?

Additional Exercises

A. Modify the **look** program so that the output produced when the `-c` option is activated retains its line formatting while still showing all control codes graphically.

B. When a text file is transferred from a DOS system to a UNIX system, it might have extraneous carriage returns at the end of each line because of incorrect translation. Write a program, **rm_cr**, that removes extraneous returns from such a file. The program should get the name of the file to be processed from the command line and print the translated file to the standard output.

C. Modify the **look** program so that it displays error messages only if an environment variable called `VERBOSE` is defined to have a value of "TRUE". Test the program in separate test runs with the variable not defined in one and defined in the other. Also check what happens if the value of `VERBOSE` is "YES" instead of "TRUE". [NOTE: You can check your DOS or UNIX environment by typing the `set` command.]

CHAPTER 14

FILE CONVERSION UTILITIES

In preparing the material for this book, I used several UNIX-based and DOS-based systems. What follows is the analysis of a problem we encountered and a solution that saved the editors and me a lot of time. The solution will spare you the anguish of reading incorrectly transcribed program source listings because the process was automated.

Understanding the Need

The wordprocessing and document formatting was done on an IBM Personal Computer/AT running version 4.00 of PC-DOS. Wordprocessing was handled by Microsoft Word and document formatting by Ventura Publisher. Certainly other software could have done the job as well, but these programs and systems were available to both myself and my publisher.

A traditional approach to creating documents of this type is to have someone key in text and code from the author's drafts and printed listings of program sources. This is time-consuming and error-prone.

Given the availability of computer systems and software, we chose to automate the process. A complex task such as this involves not one, but many programs, including text editors, compilers, word processors, page-layout programs, illustration programs, and communications software.

The problem became one of making programs work together instead of against each other.

The manuscript for this book incorporates the source code of programs and functions from the original source files to avoid keying mistakes. This introduces a problem that is best solved by a computer program. The problem is one of conflict between symbols needed in the source files and formatting codes that execute commands in the word processing and desktop publishing software.

If you read source files into a Microsoft Word document, you need to process the raw text files to prepare them first. This requirement stems from the fact that a word processor treats each line of a source file, delimited by a newline character, as a paragraph. Line breaks within a paragraph are indicated by a special code, the vertical tab, in place of the newline.

Because Ventura Publisher uses the @, <, and > symbols in formatting commands, you must protect the symbols if they are to be seen as themselves within a VP document. As you know, the < and > symbols are used in preprocessor directives and relational expressions. If you don't protect them from processing, they are lost or interpreted as formatting commands, often with startling attribute changes and surprises.

Designing a Solution

The approach to solving this conversion problem involved examining the way each product worked. Although the documentation for these products is quite solid and comprehensive, I had to run numerous tests on files to see what codes were used for what purposes.

The **src2vp** program is the ad hoc solution I came up with. It converts all newline codes in a source file to the vertical tab code expected by Microsoft Word. With this conversion in place, you can select the source listing as a unit rather than as a collection of individual paragraphs.

The prescribed method of protecting a special symbol is to double the character. For example, @ must be changed to @@ to prevent it from being treated as a VP command. The **src2vp** program does this translation.

My first crack at a design, expressed in pseudocode, looked like this:

if the command-line argument count is not 2
  print a usage diagnostic and exit
open the specified source file for reading in text mode
if the open fails
  print a diagnostic message and exit
while a character remains in the input stream
  read it
  if it is a formatting code
    double it
  else if it is a newline
    convert it to a vertical tab
  else
    print it without change
if an I/O error occurred on the input stream
  print a diagnostic message and exit
close the file
if a close error occurs
  print a diagnostic message and exit
return to caller

The pseudocode describes the operation of the program without nailing down a particular coding of the solution. At this point we could use BASIC, Pascal, or some other language, but we'll stick with the plan and try coding it in C. But first...

The Manual Page

The operation of **src2vp** is best described by a manual page. I wrote the manual page before writing the program code so that it could serve as a design document. The pseudocode shown in the previous section was developed along with the manual page.

After coding the program, I found that a program to do the opposite task, converting a file in a document back to normal text form was also useful. In addition, I didn't know initially that the @ symbol was a problem until I wrote a test case that used the symbol. Therefore, changes were made to the manual page to document some things that were not part of the original design. Here is the final manual page in a UNIX-like reference manual format:

NAME
src2vp
vp2src

SYNTAX
src2vp *srcfile* [> *vpfile*]
vp2src *vpfile* [> *srcfile*]

DESCRIPTION

The **src2vp** utility program converts an ordinary program source file (text) into a form that is suitable for use in Microsoft Word and Ventura Publisher files. The program sends its output to the standard output stream, which you can optionally redirect to a file or other destination.

Word Conversion

You must process raw source files to prepare them for merging into documents prepared with Microsoft Word. Word treats all lines terminated by a newline character as separate paragraphs. The **src2vp** program converts newline codes to the vertical tab codes expected by Word.

Ventura Publisher Conversions

Because Ventura Publisher uses the @, <, and > symbols as formatting commands, you must protect the symbols if they are to be seen as themselves within a VP document. The prescribed method of protection is to double the character (for example, @ must be changed to @@) to prevent it from being treated as a VP command. The **src2vp** program does these translations.

The **vp2src** program provides the inverse translation. Use it to create a correct source file from material extracted from a document file. The file is assumed to have been extracted from a Ventura formatted file by using the "unformatted" save option of Word.

EXAMPLE
src2vp sample.c > sample.cvp

Converts a C source file and saves it in a separate file that can be read into Word (Transfer-Merge) and subsequently into Ventura Publisher.

NOTES

There may be other special codes supported by Word or Ventura that are not accounted for in this program, and publishers of those programs may add new features in the future that might affect the conversion process. So much for program descriptions. Let's get on with coding.

Coding the Programs

The C source code falls out rather easily from the pseudocode description. A technique I often use is to write the pseudocode as comments in what will become a source file. Having the framework of the program in the file makes it easy to place statements where they belong and to avoid forgetting a piece of the program. Here is the source for **src2vp**:

```
/*
 *   src2vp.c
 *
 *   Convert a program source code file to a form
 *   that is suitable for use with Ventura Publisher.
 *   The program handles these items:
 *     - protects @@, <, and > symbols by doubling them
 *     - changes hard line terminations (CR/LF) to a
 *       vertical tab code (VP = 11 dec, 0B hex).
 */

#include <stdio.h>
#include <stdlib.h>

#define E_CMD    1
#define E_SRC    2
#define E_READ   3
#define E_CLOSE 4
#define VT       11
/* function prototype */
extern void fatal(char *, int);
```

```c
int
main(int argc, char *argv[])
{
        int ch;
        FILE *fp;

        /* Check the command line syntax */
        if (argc != 2)
                fatal("Usage: src2vp src_file", E_CMD);

        /* Open the file for reading in text mode */
        fp = fopen(argv[1], "rt");
        if (fp == NULL)
                fatal("Error opening the source file", E_SRC);

        /* Copy the source file to the standard output */
        while ((ch = fgetc(fp)) != EOF) {
                /* apply required translations */
                switch (ch) {
                case '@@':
                case '<':
                case '>':
                        /* these codes need to be doubled */
                        putchar(ch);
                        break;
                case '\n':
                        /*
                         * convert hard line terminations
                         * to vertical tabs
                         */
                        putchar(VT);
                        continue;
                }
                putchar(ch);
        }

        /* error check */
        if (ferror(fp))
                fatal("Error reading the source file", E_READ);

        /* close the file */
        if (fclose(fp) != 0)
                fatal("Error closing the source file", E_CLOSE);
```

```
      return EXIT_SUCCESS;
}
```

Most of what you see in the source is similar to the file-oriented programs in Chapter 9. The essence of the processing task is embedded in the `switch` statement. If one of the three formatting command codes is encountered, it is printed once by the `putchar()` statement in the case body and again by the statement following the `switch` statement. If a newline is encountered, it is thrown away and a vertical tab printed in its place. The `continue` statement forces the next iteration of the loop, bypassing the `putchar()` following the `switch` statement.

In the code for the **src2vp** program are several calls to the `fatal()` function. It is defined in a separate source file called **fatal.c**:

```
/*
 *   fatal()
 *
 *   Print an error message and exit with a specified
 *   status to flag the error to the calling program.
 */

#include <stdio.h>
#include <stdlib.h>

void
fatal(char *message, int status)
{
        fputs(message, stderr);
        exit(status);
}
```

The reason for separating `fatal()` from the `main` program is that it is used in the **vp2src** program and can easily be called by other programs. Try to break your programs into modules as much as possible. You can combine many useful functions into libraries (use `LIB` under DOS and `ar` under UNIX), which you can link with your programs as needed.

One advantage of this approach to program design is the creation of reusable routines. You effectively force yourself to generalize routines for wider use than you would if you design for single-use situations. Another advantage is program translation time is reduced. You translate the source once and then link the object modules when you need them. Only parts of your code whose sources have changed need to be retranslated.

You can use the **make** program under UNIX or a variety of make-like utilities available for DOS C translators. Using the Microsoft QuickC 2.0 compiler for this example, here's the "makefile" that assembles the pieces:

```
PROJ    =SRC2VP
DEBUG =1
CC      =qcl
CFLAGS_G      = /AS /W3 /Za
CFLAGS_D      = /Zi /Zr /Od
CFLAGS_R      = /Od /DNDEBUG
CFLAGS        =$(CFLAGS_G) $(CFLAGS_D)
LFLAGS_G      = /CP:0xffff /NOI /NOE /SE:0x80 /ST:0x800
LFLAGS_D      =
LFLAGS_R      =
LFLAGS        =$(LFLAGS_G) $(LFLAGS_D)
RUNFLAGS      =
OBJS_EXT =
LIBS_EXT =

all:  $(PROJ).exe

src2vp.obj: src2vp.c

fatal.obj:  fatal.c

$(PROJ).exe:       src2vp.obj fatal.obj $(OBJS_EXT)
      echo >NUL @@<<$(PROJ).crf
src2vp.obj +
fatal.obj +
$(OBJS_EXT)
$(PROJ).exe

$(LIBS_EXT);
<<
      ilink -a -e "link $(LFLAGS) @@$(PROJ).crf" $(PROJ)

run: $(PROJ).exe
      $(PROJ) $(RUNFLAGS)
```

You don't have to write this file. The QuickC compiler does it for you. When you read in the **src2vp.c** source file, the compiler asks whether you want to load the makefile. Say yes by pressing Return (Enter on a PC). Turbo C and other DOS-based C compilers and interpreters have similar capabilities.

The inverse conversion called **vp2src** is also handy. Occasionally, I have keyed in the code for a needed function while editing and formatting in Ventura Publisher and wanted to verify that it would translate and run correctly. Rather than type it all over again in a source file, I extract the code while running the word processor (using unformatted output) and convert the resulting VP file to standard text format by using **vp2src**. The source code for **vp2src** is more complex than **src2vp** because stripping out protection is not as straightforward as putting it in.

```
/*
 *  vp2src.c
 *
 *  Convert a program extracted from a Ventura Publisher or
 *  Microsoft Word file to a standard ASCII form.
 *  The program handles these items:
 *    - unprotects @@, <, and > symbols by replacing each
 *       doubled symbol with a single equivalent symbol.
 *    - changes vertical tab line terminations (VT) to a
 *       newline character.
 */

#include <stdio.h>
#include <stdlib.h>

#define E_CMD    1
#define E_SRC    2
#define E_READ   3
#define E_CLOSE  4
#define VT       11

void fatal(char *, int);

typedef enum state_e { COPYING, CHECKING } STATE;

int
```

```
main(int argc, char *argv[])
{
      int ch, savedChar;
      FILE *fp;
      STATE cpState = COPYING;

      /* Check the command line syntax */
      if (argc != 2)
            fatal("Usage: vp2src filename", E_CMD);

      /* Open the file for reading in text mode */
      fp = fopen(argv[1], "rt");
      if (fp == NULL)
            fatal("Error opening the source file", E_SRC);

      /* Copy the source file to the standard output */
      while ((ch = fgetc(fp)) != EOF) {
            /* Apply required translations */
            switch (ch) {
            case '@@':
                  switch (cpState) {
                  case COPYING:
                        putchar(ch);
                        savedChar = ch;
                        cpState = CHECKING;
                        break;
                  case CHECKING:
                        if (savedChar != '@@')
                              putchar(ch);
                        cpState = COPYING;
                        break;
                  }
                  break;
            case '<':
                  switch (cpState) {
                  case COPYING:
                        putchar(ch);
                        savedChar = ch;
                        cpState = CHECKING;
                        break;
                  case CHECKING:
                        if (savedChar != '<')
                              putchar(ch);
```

```
                        cpState = COPYING;
                        break;
                }
                break;
        case '>':
                switch (cpState) {
                case COPYING:
                        putchar(ch);
                        savedChar = ch;
                        cpState = CHECKING;
                        break;
                case CHECKING:
                        if (savedChar != '>')
                                putchar(ch);
                        cpState = COPYING;
                        break;
                }
                break;
        case VT:
                /* Line-termination character */
                putchar('\n');
                break;
        default:
                putchar(ch);
                break;
        }
    }

    /* error check */
    if (ferror(fp))
        fatal("Error reading the source file", E_READ);

    /* close the file */
    if (fclose(fp) == EOF)
        fatal("Error closing the source file", E_CLOSE);

    return EXIT_SUCCESS;
}
```

The heart of this program is a simulation of a finite state machine
(FSM). The machine state is controlled by the variable cpState, which
has type STATE. Essentially, the program is either routinely copying its

input to its output (`cpState` is `COPYING`) or looking at the next character to see if it is part of a set of identical twins—a protected code (`cpState` is `CHECKING`).

When one of the special codes is seen, it is sent to the output stream and a copy of it is preserved in the `savedChar` variable while the program gets the next character from the input. If the previous character and the current character match, the current one is thrown away. Otherwise it is sent to the output stream.

Programming Exercises

1. The programs require that you type the source filename and then another name for the destination file. Rewrite at least one of the programs so that it creates a destination name that uses the base filename from the source file specification as the basis of a destination filename. Have the program automatically write its output to that file. Be sure that the file doesn't already exist before opening it for writing.

2. An additional step in the direction of user-friendliness is to let the programs take a list of files and have them convert each named file rather than having to feed the program a file at a time. Change the command-line argument processing to accept a list and the internal workings to accommodate this mode of operation. A missing file should not cause the program to quit. Just report the missing file's name and continue processing other files.

3. Files of text that contain control codes other than newlines and tabs can cause problems for terminals running off a UNIX system. Write a filter program that makes any control codes (except NL and TAB) visible in some way. For example, you might show control-K as ^K. Challenge yourself by adding an optional command-line argument, -s, that lets the user strip out these unwanted codes.

APPENDIX A

KEYWORDS AND RESERVED IDENTIFIERS

The C standard specifies the set of 32 keywords listed in Table A-1. The keywords are part of the definition of C language itself.

Table A-1: Standard Keywords

auto	double	int	struct
break	else	long	switch
case	enum	register	typedef
char	extern	return	union
const	float	short	unsigned
continue	for	signed	void
default	goto	sizeof	volatile
do	if	static	while

You cannot use these names for any other purpose in a C program.

Reserved Identifiers

A large body of "standard" routines has been developed to handle many common tasks. The tables below summarize the standard C library. Functions and macros are grouped according to purpose. Each section shows the name of the header in which related function prototypes or actual macro definitions occur. The reserved identifers are the names of routines in the standard library. In addition, the following headers contain some other needed values:

<errno.h> —Contains macros that are used in error reporting.

<float.h> and **<limits.h>** —Macros in this header specify translation limits.

<stddef.h>—Contains common `typedef` statements and macro definitions.

Diagnostics
<assert.h>

Table A-2: Diagnostics	
ROUTINE	**DESCRIPTION**
assert	Put diagnostic information into a program

Character Handling
<ctype.h>

Table A-3: Character Handling	
ROUTINE	**DESCRIPTION**
isalnum	Test for an alphanumeric character
isalpha	Test for a letter
iscntrl	Test for a control character
isdigit	Test for a digit
isgraph	Test for a printable character (except space)
islower	Test for a lowercase letter
isprint	Test for any printable character
ispunct	Test for a punctuation character
isspace	Test for a white-space character
isupper	Test for an uppercase letter
isxdigit	Test for a hexadecimal character
tolower	Convert a character to lowercase
toupper	Convert a character to uppercase

Localization
\<locale.h\>

Table A-4: Localization

ROUTINE	DESCRIPTION
localeconv	Set components of a locale conversion data structure
setlocale	Set or query a program's locale

Mathematics
\<math.h\>

Table A-5a: Trigonometric

ROUTINE	DESCRIPTION
acos	Arc cosine
asin	Arc sine
atan	Arc tangent
atan2	Arc tangent (2 parameters)
cos	Cosine
sin	Sine
tan	Tangent

Table A-5b: Hyperbolic

ROUTINE	DESCRIPTION
cosh	Hyperbolic cosine
sinh	Hyperbolic sine
tanh	Hyperbolic tangent

Table A-5c: Exponential and Logarithic

ROUTINE	DESCRIPTION
exp	Exponential
frexp	Break a floating-point value into its mantissa and exponent

Table A-5c: Exponential and Logarithic

ROUTINE	DESCRIPTION
ldexp	Multiply a floating-point value by an integral power of 2.
log	Natural logarithm
log10	Base-10 logarithm
modf	Break a floating-point value into its integer and fractional parts

Table A-5d: Power

ROUTINE	DESCRIPTION
pow	Raise a value to a power
sqrt	Square root

Table A-5e: Nearest Integer

ROUTINE	DESCRIPTION
ceil	Ceiling
fabs	Absolute value of a floating-point value
floor	Floor value
fmod	Floating-point modulus (remainder)

Non-Local Jumps
<setjmp.h>

Table A-6: Non-local Jumps

ROUTINE	DESCRIPTION
longjump	Return from a non-local jump
setjmp	Prepare for a non-local jump

Signal Handling

Table A-7: Signal Handling

ROUTINE	DESCRIPTION
raise	Send a signal to the running process
signal	Define system interrupt handling

Variable Arguments
<stdarg.h>

Table A-8: Variable Arguments

ROUTINE	DESCRIPTION
va_arg	Rewind argument list (UNIX only)
va_end	Reset argument pointer
va_start	Rewind argument list (ANSI only)

Input and Output
<stdio.h>

Table A-9a: File Operations

ROUTINE	DESCRIPTION
remove	Delete a file
rename	Rename a file or directory
tmpfile	Create a temporary binary file
tmpname	Generate a unique temporary filename

Table A-9b: File Access

ROUTINE	DESCRIPTION
fclose	Close an open stream
fflush	Flush (empty or clear) a stream buffer
fopen	Open a file
freopen	Close the current file associated with a stream and assign another file to the same stream

Table A-9b: File Access

ROUTINE	DESCRIPTION
setbuf	Control buffering type for a stream
setvbuf	Control buffering type and buffer size for a stream

Table A-9c: Formatted I/O

ROUTINE	DESCRIPTION
fprintf	Format and print a series of characters and values to a stream
fscanf	Read data from a stream into buffers
printf	Format and print a series of characters and values to standard output
scanf	Read data from standard input and format items into buffers
sprintf	Format and store a series of characters and values into a buffer
sscanf	Read data from buffer
vfprintf	Format and print a series of characters and values to a stream
vprintf	Format and print a series of characters and values to standard output
vsprintf	Format and print a series of characters and values to a buffer

Table A-9d: Character I/O

ROUTINE	DESCRIPTION
fgetc	Read a single character from a stream
fgets	Read a string from a stream
fputc	Write a single character to a stream
fputs	Write a string to a stream
getc	Read a single character from a stream
getchar	Read a character from standard input
gets	Read a string from a stream
putc	Write a single character to a stream
putchar	Write a character to standard output
puts	Write a string to standard output
ungetc	Push back the last character read froma stream

Table A-9e: Direct I/O

ROUTINE	DESCRIPTION
fread	Read a block of bytes from a stream
fwrite	Write a block of bytes to a stream

Table A-9f: File Positioning

ROUTINE	DESCRIPTION
fgetpos	Get a stream's file-position value
fseek	Move a streams's file-pointer
fsetpos	Set a stream's file-position indicator
ftell	Get the current position of a stream's file pointer
rewind	Move a stream's file pointer to offset 0

Table A-9g: Error Handling

ROUTINE	DESCRIPTION
clearerr	Reset stream's error and EOF indicators
feof	Check end-of-file status of a stream
ferror	Check I/O-error status of a stream
perror	Map an error number to an error message

General Utilities
<stdlib.h>

Table A-10a: String Conversion

ROUTINE	DESCRIPTION
atof	Convert a string to double
atoi	Convert a string to integer
atol	Convert a string to long
itoa	Convert an integer to a string
strtod	Convert a string to double
strtol	Convert a string to a long

Table A-10a: String Conversion

ROUTINE	DESCRIPTION
strtoul	Convert a string to an unsigned long

Table A-10b: Pseudo-random Sequence Generation

ROUTINE	DESCRIPTION
rand	Random number generator
srand	Seed random-number generator

Table A-10c: Memory Management

ROUTINE	DESCRIPTION
calloc	Allocate and initialize a block of memory
free	Deallocate a block of memory
malloc	Allocate a block of memory
realloc	Change the size of a previously allocated block of memory
sbrk	Reset the memory "break" value

Table A-10d: Communication with the Environment

ROUTINE	DESCRIPTION
abort	Abort with an error message
atexit	Add a function to the exit list
exit	Terminate after closing files
getenv	Get the value of an environment variable
system	Pass a string to the command interpreter

Table A-10e: Searching and Sorting

ROUTINE	DESCRIPTION
bsearch	Run a binary search on a sorted array
qsort	Sort an array of items using the quick-sort algorithm

Table A-10f: Integer Arithmetic	
ROUTINE	**DESCRIPTION**
abs	Absolute value of an integer
div	Divide integers yielding a quotient and a remainder
labs	Absolute value of a long
ldiv	Divide longs yielding a quotient and a remainder

String Handling
<string.h>

Table A-11a: Copying	
ROUTINE	**DESCRIPTION**
memcpy	Copy bytes from one buffer to another
memmove	Same as memcpy but ensures that over-lapping regions are copied correctly
strcpy	Copy a string
strncpy	Copy the initial portion of a string

Table A-11b: Concatenation	
ROUTINE	**DESCRIPTION**
strcat	Concatenate strings
strncat	Append a specified number of characters from a string onto another string

Table A-11c: Comparison	
ROUTINE	**DESCRIPTION**
memcmp	Compare bytes in two buffers
strcmp	Compare strings
strcoll	Compare strings with locale-specific collation
strncmp	Compare initial portions of two strings
strxfrm	Transform a string

Table A-11d: Search

ROUTINE	DESCRIPTION
memchr	Find a character in a buffer
strchr	Search for a character in a string
strcspn	Find the first substring in a string composed of characters not in another string
strpbrk	Find any character in one string that occurs in another string
strrchr	Reverse search for a character in a string
strspn	Return the offset into a string of the first character found that is not in a set specified by another string
strstr	Return a pointer to the first occurrence of a string within another string
strtok	Extract tokens from a string

Table A-11e: Miscellaneous

ROUTINE	DESCRIPTION
memset	Set bytes in a buffer to a character
strerror	Map an error number to a message string
strlen	Get the length of a string

Date and Time
<time.h>

Table A-12: Date and Time

ROUTINE	DESCRIPTION
asctime	Convert a time structure to a characterstring
clock	Tell how much processor time is used
ctime	Convert a time_t value to a character string
difftime	Compute a time difference
gmtime	Convert a time_t value to a GMT-based time structure
localtime	Convert a time_t value to a local time structure
mktime	Convert a local time structure into a calendar value (time_t)

APPENDIX B

C LANGUAGE OPERATORS

The following tables summarize the C operators, precedence, and associativity.

C Operators

Table B-1: Complement and Unary Plus Operators

OPERATOR	DESCRIPTION
-	Unary minus
~	Bitwise complement
!	Logical negation
+	Unary plus

Table B-2: Indirection and Address-of Operators

OPERATOR	DESCRIPTION
*	Indirection
&	Address of

The sizeof Operator

The `sizeof` operator (it is not a macro or function) yields the storage requirement of an identifier or a data type, expressed as a cast, in bytes.

Table B-3: Multiplicative Operators

OPERATOR	DESCRIPTION
*	Multiplication
/	Division
%	Modulus

Table B-4: Shift Operators

OPERATOR	DESCRIPTION
<<	Shift left
>>	Shift right

Table B-5: Relational Operators

OPERATOR	DESCRIPTION
<	Less than
>	Greater than
<=	Less than or equal to
>=	Greater than or equal to
==	Equal to
!=	Not equal to

Table B-6: Bitwise Operators

OPERATOR	DESCRIPTION
&	Bitwise AND

Table B-6: Bitwise Operators	
OPERATOR	DESCRIPTION
|	Bitwise inclusive OR
	Bitwise exclusive OR

Table B-7: Logical Operators	
OPERATOR	DESCRIPTION
&&	Logical AND
||	Logical OR

Sequential-Evaluation Operator

The "comma" operator enforces a left-to-right evaluation of its operands [op1,op2].

Conditional Operator

The conditional operator (op1?op2:op3) is C's only ternary operator. It evaluates op1 and yields the value of op2 if the first is logically TRUE (non-zero) or the value of op3 if it is FALSE.

Table B-8: Unary Increment and Decrement Operators	
OPERATOR	DESCRIPTION
+	Unary increment
--	Unary decrement

Table B-9: Assignment Operators	
OPERATOR	DESCRIPTION
=	Simple assignment
*=	Multiplication assignment

Table B-9: Assignment Operators	
OPERATOR	**DESCRIPTION**
/=	Division assignment
%=	Remainder assignment
+=	Addition assignment
-=	Subtraction assignment
<<=	Left-shift assignment
>>=	Right-shift assignment
&=	Bitwise-AND assignment
| =	Bitwise-inclusive-OR assignment
	Bitwise-exclusive-OR assignment

Operator Precedence and Associativity

In the following table, entries closer to the head of the table have the highest precedence. Most operators associate left to right, but a few associate right to left in expressions involving two or more operators at the same precedence level.

Table B-10: Operator Precedence and Associativity		
OPERATOR	**DESCRIPTION**	**ASSOCIATIVITY**
( ) [ ] -> .	Function call Array index Structure pointer Structure member	Left to right

Table B-10: Operator Precedence and Associativity

OPERATOR	DESCRIPTION	ASSOCIATIVITY
- + ++ -- ! ~ * & sizeof (type)	Unary minus Unary plus Increment Decrement Logical negation Bitwise complement Indirection Address Object size Type cast (explicit conversion)	RIGHT TO LEFT
* / %	Multiplication Division Modulus	Left to right
+ -	Addition Subtraction	Left to right
<< >>	Shift left Shift right	Left to right
< <= > >=	Less than Less than or equal Greater than Greater than or equal	Left to right
== !=	Equal Not equal	Left to right
&	Bitwise AND	Left to right
	Bitwise XOR	Left to right
|	Bitwise OR	Left to right
&&	Logical AND	Left to right
||	Logical OR	Left to right
?:	Conditional	RIGHT TO LEFT

Table B-10: Operator Precedence and Associativity

OPERATOR	DESCRIPTION	ASSOCIATIVITY
= += -+ *= /+ %= &= |= ^= <<= >>=	Assignment	RIGHT TO LEFT
, (comma)	Sequence	Left to right

APPENDIX C

Control Codes

The characters listed in Table C-1 are called control characters. They provide line and page formatting, communications between data terminal and data communication devices, and various other services. Some computer systems, such as IBM Personal Computers, provide "graphic" symbols when the characters are displayed, but most terminal devices do not.

Table C-1: ASCII Control Characters

DEC CODE	HEX CODE	NAME	TYPE
0	00	NUL	Null character (CC or FE)
1	01	SOH	Start of heading (CC)
2	02	STX	Start of text (CC)
3	03	ETX	End of text (CC)
4	04	EOT	End of transmission (CC)
5	05	ENQ	Enquiry (CC)
6	06	ACK	Acknowledge (CC)
7	07	BEL	Bell

Table C-1: ASCII Control Characters

DEC CODE	HEX CODE	NAME	TYPE
8	08	BS	Backspace
9	09	HT	Horizontal tabulation (FE)
10	0A	LF	Linefeed (FE)
11	0B	VT	Vertical tabulation (FE)
12	0C	FF	Formfeed (FE)
13	0D	CR	Carriage return (FE)
14	0E	SO	Shift out
15	0F	SI	Shift in
16	10	DLE	Data link escape (CC)
17	11	DC1	Device control #1
18	12	DC2	Device control #2
19	13	DC3	Device control #3
20	14	DC4	Device control #4
21	15	NAK	Negative acknowledgment (CC)
22	16	SYN	Synchronous idle (CC)
23	17	ETB	End of transmission block (CC)
24	18	CAN	Cancel
25	19	EM	End of medium
26	1A	SUB	Substitute
27	1B	ESC	Escape
28	1C	FS	Field separator (IS)
29	1D	GS	Group separator (IS)
30	1E	RS	Record separator (IS)
31	1F	US	Unit separator (IS)
127	7F	DEL	Delete (CC or FE)

Printable 7-Bit ASCII Characters

Table C-2 lists the printable ASCII character set.

Table C-2: Printable Character Table		
DEC CODE	**HEX CODE**	**KEY OR SYMBOL**
32	20	(space)
33	21	!
34	22	"
35	23	#
36	24	$
37	25	%
38	26	&
39	27	'
40	28	
41	29	
42	2A	(
43	2B	)
44	2C	*
45	2D	+
46	2E	,
47	2F	/
48	30	0
49	31	1
50	32	2
51	33	3
52	34	4
53	35	5
54	36	6
55	37	7
56	38	8

Table C-2: Printable Character Table

DEC CODE	HEX CODE	KEY OR SYMBOL
57	39	9
58	3A	:
59	3B	;
60	3C	<
61	3D	=
62	3E	>
63	3F	?
64	40	@
65	41	A
66	42	B
67	43	C
68	44	D
69	45	E
70	46	F
71	47	G
72	48	H
73	49	I
74	4A	J
75	4B	K
76	4C	L
77	4D	M
78	4E	N
79	4F	O
80	50	P
81	51	Q
82	52	R
83	53	S
84	54	T
85	55	U

Table C-2: Printable Character Table

DEC CODE	HEX CODE	KEY OR SYMBOL
86	56	V
87	57	W
88	58	X
89	59	Y
90	5A	Z
91	5B	[
92	5C	\
93	5D	]
94	5E	
95	5F	_
96	60	'
97	61	a
98	62	b
99	63	c
100	64	d
101	65	e
102	66	f
103	67	g
104	68	h
105	69	i
106	6A	j
107	6B	k
108	6C	l
109	6D	m
110	6E	n
111	6F	o
112	70	p
113	71	q
114	72	r

Table C-2: Printable Character Table

DEC CODE	HEX CODE	KEY OR SYMBOL
115	73	s
116	74	t
117	75	u
118	76	v
119	77	w
120	78	x
121	79	y
122	7A	z
123	7B	
124	7C		
125	7D	}
126	7E	-

THE C PREPROCESSOR

The C preprocessor is conceptually the first pass of a C translation system. A preprocessor directive is an instruction to the C preprocessor, which recognizes the directives listed in Table D-1.

Table D-1: Preprocessor Directives	
IDENTIFIER	**DESCRIPTION**
#define	Associate an identifier with a definition text.
#undef	Remove the definition of an identifier.
#if	Start a conditional branch
#else	Alternate conditional branch
#endif	End a conditional branch
#elif	Combined #else and #if directives
#ifdef	Test whether an identifier is defined
#ifndef	Test whether an identifier is not defined
#include	Include the text of a named file
#line	Line control
#error	Produce diagnostic message
#pragma	Cause an implementation-defined behavior

Preprocessor Operators

The operators listed in Table D2 are used with preprocessor directives.

Table D-2: Preprocessor Operators	
OPERATOR	**DESCRIPTION**
#	A macro parameter is treated as a quoted literal string.
##	Concatenate tokens in macro parameters ("token pasting").
defined	Unary conditional operator

Predefined Macro Name

The macros listed in Table D-3 are defined by the implementation. These macros are not subject to modifications by `#define` or `#undef` directives.

Table D-3: Predefined Macro Names	
MACRO NAME	**DESCRIPTION**
__LINE__	Current source file line number (decimal constant)
__FILE__	Current source file name (string literal)
__DATE__	Date of translation (if available)
__TIME__	Time of translation (if available)
__STDC__	Flag to indicate standard C, if applicable

APPENDIX E: Answers

Chapter 2

1. There is no `main()` function, `test()` needs an integer return value, and `puts()` requires the inclusion of the `<stdio.h>` header.
2. Standard library functions are prewritten and translated subprograms. Many high-use processing tasks are encapsulated in library functions.
3. Before executing a C program, you must translate it and possibly link it.
4. It is possible to write a program on a single line, but it makes the program hard to read.
5. Answer d is correct.
6. An in-line comment is commonly used to explain a single statement. A block comment is more commonly used to describe the workings of an entire function or block of code.
7. The statement declares an array of 20 characters: `name[0]` to `name[19]`.
8. A `#define` directive associates a name with a definition text, repeating a macro. The macro can be either parameterless or have one or more parameters.
9. The `#include` directive effects file inclusion.
10. `puts()`   Print a string to the standard output stream
    `gets()`   Reads a string from the standard input stream
    `printf()`   Formats and prints a text string to standard output
11. Command-line arguments are values and options provided by the user on the command line. These arguments control program behavior and provide data.
12. Return values provide a way to pass valueS from a function to its caller. Such return values can indicate success or failure.

Chapter 3

1. RAM is fast and directly accessible to CPU, but data is lost when power is removed. ROM is also fast. It retains its data in the absence of power, but it cannot be written. Secondary memory, (disks and tapes) is permanent data storage, but slow.
2. The range is two and the values are 0 and 1.
3. The range is four and the values are 1, 2, 3, and 4.
4. They are, in order, 0, 1, 6, 8, and 10.
5. They have a leading zero.
6. They are, in order, 0, 1, 6, 8, 10, 10, 12, and 15
7. Hexadecimal numbers have a leading 0x.
8. 9540
9. Keywords must be typed in all lowercase letters.
10. `junk`, `number`, `ExtendLine`, and `Nextpage` are valid internal names.
11. Names that are not keywords, but are six letters or less in length are valid.
12. It specifies a regular character called cat, sets the value to the character constant 'D' and displays the value to the screen.
13. The code of a character constant may vary from system to system.
14. String literals produce a null character at the end of the array, character constants represent an integer value of the string. String literals use double quotes, character constants use single ones.
15. Escape sequences allow users to represent non-visible characters such as returns.

16. `int`—plain integer; `unsigned int`—nonnegative integer; `long`—long integer; `unsigned long`—nonnegative long integer; `short`—short integer; `unsigned short`—nonnegative short integer (signed is assumed for int, long, and short).
17. They are used to present data in the desired form.
18. The `printf()` function accepts the conversion specifier `%s`.
19. `float`, `double`, and `long double`. They differ in precision.
20. `<limits.h>` specifies sizes and limits for integral numbers, and `<float.h>` does the same with floating point numbers.
21. The answer is b.
22. It converts an integral value form a single line argument.
23. You can do this by using the `scanf()` function.

Chapter 4
1. An operator in C, as in other programming languages, specifies an operation to be performed on an operand or a set of operands.
2. An expression is a combination of operators and operands that performs a computation or produces a side effect. The expression m – n is one.
3. a = b + c;
4. Other C statement types: labelled, compound, selection, iteration, and jump.
5. The precedence chart specifies the precedence and associativity of operators and how expressions involving more than one operator are evaluated.
6. The expression a = b * c + d is ambiguous. The default evaluation is a = (b * c) + d because multiplication has a higher precedence than addition.
7. Associativity.
8. The valiable offset is promoted to unsigned long before the addition is done.
9. c = 12 / 5 = 2 (integer division) d = 12 / 5 = 2 (remainder)
10. False because `sizeof` is an operator.
11. For variables a = 9 and b = 3: a < b is false; a >= b is true; a == b is false; a != b is true.
12. For integers a = 10, b = 3, c = 7 and d = 20: (a = b) && (c d) -> result is true (both subexpressions are true); (a < b) || (c <= d) -> result is true.
13. Short-circuit evaluation means that the evaluation of a logical expression, proceeding left to right, stops as soon as the result is known. Example (using values in 12): result = (a > b) || (c > d);
14. Starting value: 0xF0. Bit pattern: 11110000—bits >> 4   -> 00001111—bits & 0x2F -> 00100000—~bits   -> 00001111—bits | 0x04 -> 11110100
15. `count += delta;`
16. Values of n and x after the statements are executed (shown in comments): short n, x; n = 5;   /* n = 5, x undefined */—x = ++n; /* n = 6, x = 6 *—n = 11;   /* n = 11, x = 6 */—x = n++; /* n = 12, x = 11 */

Chapter 5
1. The `if` statement provides conditional branching. If the controlling test expression is true (arithmetically nonzero), the statement body is executed. If the expression is false (arithmetically zero), the statement body is bypassed.
2. An `else` clause can be added to the simple `if` statement to provide statement bodies for both the true and false branches.
3. This code will test the value of the variable `door`. If `door` has a value of OPEN, its value is changed to CLOSED. Conversely, if `door` has a value of CLOSED, it is assigned a value of OPEN. This behavior is called "toggling."
4. If none of the test conditions in earlier statements is true, a must be greater than b so it is not necessary to test for this condition.
5. Fall-through is the passing of execution control from the statements associated with one case label to those of the next case label. This behavior occurs automatically if no break statement is used to terminate the statement block following a case label.
6. while   Tests the expression at the top of the loop.
   for   Same as a while loop, but has three expressions: Middle expressions controls the looping. The other expressions are used for initializations.
   do   Executes the statement body first, then tests the expression.

7. Iteration statements are used to transfer control of a program to an earlier statement, causing a block of enclosed statements to be repeatedly executed.
8. The null statement means "do nothing." All loops must have a statement body.
9. The `goto` statement provides an absolute jump to a label in the same function.

Chapter 6
1. Functions divide the work of a program among a set of related subprograms, each of which does one job well. In addition, functions provide a means of hiding information by carefully controlling access to variable.
2. Yes. It's bad programming unless the program is small and uncomplicated.
3. By name.
4. External linkage provides a way of connecting names declared in one program module with the definitions of the names in other modules.
5. A function prototype is a forward declaration that tells the translator what to expect when the function is called before being completely defined.
6. Definition

```
int Add(int a, int b)
{
    return a + b;
}
```

Prototype

```
int Add(int, int);
```

7. A function prototype specifies the function return type, its name, and the number and types of formal parameters (void if none).
8. Formal parameters are used in a function definition to specify types and local names of function inputs. Actual arguments are values passed to a function in a function call.
9. False. Call-by-value is the default parameter-passing mechanism in C.
10. Answers b and c.
11. Recursion is the ability of a function to call itself either directly or indirectly through another function.
12. Iteration.
13. `int x = 6, y = 11;`
    `Add(x, y);`
14. Answers b and c are true.
15. The "extra" parentheses in the following define directive are needed to prevent unwanted side effects:
    `#define abs(x) (((x) 0) ? -(x) : (x))`

Chapter 7
1. Answers a and c are correct.
2. False for an ANSI-conforming translator. Pre-ANSI translators required that arrays be declared static if the declaration was internal to a function.
3. The `static` keyword in this context places the message array in a part of program memory that is "permanent."
4. A multidimensional array is actually an array of arrays.
5. ??? (question doesn't have a declaration).
6. A pointer is a variable that holds an address.
7. The following create an integer and pointer and establish the pointer to the integer:

```
        int i, *ip;
        ip = &i;
```

8. `char ch, *cp;  /* declare character and pointer variables*/`
   `cp = &ch;      /* point to the variable */`
   `*cp = 'Q';     /* assign value 'Q' to the storage location */`
   `putchar(ch); /* print out the value of ch (*cp), which is 'Q'.`
9. Operations a and c are permitted on pointers to the same object.
10. Convert all letters in a string to lowercase:

```
        char*cp;
        cp = text; /* or cp = &text[0]; */
        #include <ctype.h>
        . . .
        while (*cp != '\0'){
                *cp = tolower(*cp);
```

```
                        ++cp;
    }
```
11. `double (*dp) ();`

Chapter 8

1. Answers a and c are correct.
2. A structure is a collection of variables hat are referred to by a common name. Possible structures: card in file, birth certificate, driver's license, entries in a telephone directory.
3. False.
4. The amount of storage used is enough for three integers, which is a machine-dependent value. On a 16-bit machine, six bytes; on a 32-bit machine, 12 bytes.
5. Declare a variable and assign it values: struct time_st now; now.hour = 14; now.minute = 18; now.second = 0;
6. Only the needed amount of storage is used rather than wasting some fixed amount of space for each string.
7. An array is not a modifiable lvalue, so it cannot be assigned. Use a standard copy function: `strcpy(person[22].first_name, "Fran");`
8. `strcpy(p->last_name, "Jones");`
9. `strcpy((p+3)->last_name, "Williams");`
10. Answer is correct.
11. False. A `typedef` statement creates a new data type name.
12. `CARD cards[10], *cardptr;`
13. `typedef enum { READING, WRITING, PROCESSING, IDLE } MSTATE; MSTATE state; state = IDLE;`
14. Answers b and c are true.
15. Declare and assign a union variable:
```
        union mixed_u {
            char c;
            int i;
            long l;
        } value;
        value.float = 326.19;
```
16. Value ranges of bitfield variable: a: 0 to 7 (eight values); b: 0 to 31 (32 values); c: 0 to 3 (four values); d: 0 to 61 (64 values)
17. `bits.b = bits.d / 2; printf("bits.b = %d\n", bits.b);` The statement prints out 18 due to integer arithmetic.

Chapter 9

1. A stream is a named sequence of bytes. Streams provide a uniform, easily manipulated input and output mechanism.
2. Buffering is used to improve system performance by avoiding the costly character-at-a-time behavior of unbuffered I/O.
3. The `stderr` stream is unbuffered so that error messages appear at the user's terminal or console immediately instead of being held in a buffer.
4. `$ random > numbers`
5. A pipeline command is a series of commands that are connected together. UNIX example: `$ cat filename | sort | pg`   DOS example: `C> dir | more`
6. Text translations accommodate differences such as end-of-file treatment and CR/LF versus NL end-of-line treatment.
7. The `more` command overwrites the contents of the named file and waits for keyboard input, which is redirected to the file. The less-than sign should be used for input redirection.
8. The FILE data structure contains information about a file. A pointer to a structure of this type obtained by a call to `fopen()` is used to access a file.
9. `FILE *f_in;   /* FILE pointer */`
   ...
   `fopen(filename, "r");`
10. The `const` qualifier in a function parameter list says that the actual argument will not be affected by the function call.
11. The "rb" open type request binary read access. No text translations take place.

12. The plus sign means "update" mode, which requests interleaved read and write access.
13. A NULL return from `fopen()` flags an error that could be caused by a file-naming error, a missing floppy disk, etc.
14. False. Your program might need to close files to free pointers for accessing other files.
15. Line buffering.
16. The `getc()` function reads only from standard input while `fgetc()` can read form any opened input stream.
17. Reading a line of input: `fgets(line, stdin);` The line contains a new-line character, if one was read.
18. Use `feof()` to check a specified stream if an ambiguous EOF code is returned from an I/O function such as `fgetc()`, `getchar()`, and so on.

Chapter 10

1. (You're on your own with this one, folks.)
2. Pseudocode for `StringUpper()`:

> *point to start of string with a temporary pointer while the current character is not a null byte*
> > *if character is lowercase, convert it to uppercase [toupper()]*
> > *increment the pointer*
> *return the address of the string*

3. Pseudocode for the **pal** program:

> *point to the start of the string with pointers p and q*
> *find the end of the string with q (NOTE)*
> *while p is less than q*
> > *if lowercase equivalents of the characters don't match break the loop*
> > *increment p*
> > *decrement q*
> *if p is less than q*
> > *return 0 (string is not a palindrome)*
> *else*
> > *return 1 (string is a palindrome)*

4. Pseudocode for the **showtab** program:

> *while the next character read is not at end-of-file*
> > *if the character is a tab*
> > *print the special symbol ("-" or other)*
> > *else*
> > *print the character unchanged*
> *if an i/o error occurred*
> > *print an error message*
> > *exit with an error indication*
> *return success*

Chapter 11

1. A stack is a last-in, first-out data type. Items are pushed onto and popped off of the stack. Only the item at the top of the stack is directly accessible.
2. Handling a telephone call while in the middle of a meeting causes the meeting to be suspended while the call is in progress (pushed onto your activity stack). The meeting resumes when the call stops (is popped from your activity stack).
3. The stack is empty when the top index is the same as the base of the array.
4. Additional RPN calculator operations:

Add a and b:	Divide a by b:	Subtract b from a:
push(a)	push(a)	push(a)
push(b)	push(b)	push(b)
push(pop(), pop())	tmp = pop(), tmp = pop()	push(pop() - pop())
	push(pop() / tmp)	

5. A queue is a data type that has first-in, first-out sequencing. Objects of a queue type are used for buffering of data, especially between devices of differing processing speeds.

6. The read index lags one behind the write index in an empty circular queue.
7. The read - write (adjusted for wraparound) is 2, the queue is full.
8. Eventually, there is no room left in the queue for more data.
9. 19. One array element is wasted to differentiate the full and empty conditions.

Chapter 12

1. A node is an object of a structured type that contains one or more pointers to objects of identical type.
2. A singly-linked list contains one pointer for making forward links. The nodes of such a list are chained together in one direction.
3. Inserting a node involves: a) Creating a new node and establishing a temporary pointer to it; b) Assigning the current node pointer value to the new node pointer; c) Assigning the temporary pointer value to the current pointer.
4. You can't easily find the previous node, so you delete the node after the current node.
5. True.
6. A prefirst node simplifies list management tasks and prevents an empty list from being a special case with extra code to handle the condition.
7. The `list_empty()` function:
```
int list_empty(SNODE *listp)
{
    if (listp->next == listp)
        return 1;
      else
          return 0;
}
```
8. A circular list simplifies the code needed to wrap around the boundaries of the list, easing the code needed to search for text in a buffer of a text editor, for example.
9. List node declaration:
```
typedef struct dnode_st {
    struct dnode_st *next, *prev;
    char *legend;        char *help;
    short keycode;
} DNODE;
```
10. Use the code as it with the following changes: a) Remove the hits variable. It is not needed.; b) Within the innermost loop in the if statement, add a the following statements: `current = tmp;`   `break;`

Chapter 13

1. The `argc` parameter receives the number of command-line arguments when control is transferred to `main()` at program startup.
2. The range of `argv` subscripts is 0 to 4. An additional vector at subscript 5 should contain a NULL pointer, many C translators do not follow this convention yet.
3. `argv[0]`
4. Link the program with the module `setargv` or an equivalent that does wildcard expansions (check your translator's documentation).
5. Print arguments beyond program name:
```
int i;
for (i = 1; i < argv; ++i)
    printf(:argv[%d] = %s\n", i, argv[i]);
```
6. The `envp` pointer (a double indirect) is only valid upon entry and will not reflect any changes to the environment that occur at runtime.
7. Checking the `EDITOR` variable:
```
char editor[NAXSTR];
if (strcpy(editor, getenv("EDITOR")) == NULL)
    strcpy(editor, "/bin/ed");
```
8. The `WIDTH` variable is obtained in the form of a character string and must be converted to it numeric equivalent.

& , 76, 77
% , 70
- , 63, 69
- - , 83-84
+ , 63, 69-70
+ + , 83-84
" ->" , 213
[ ] , 125, 156, 164
, (comma), 66, 85
* , 85, 204
= , 67, 81-82
= = , 75
~ , 80
! , 76
> , 225
< , 224
( ) , 64, 66-67, 74, 91, 111,
    142, 143, 145, 182
; , 62, 106, 111
':' , 191

A

Absolute jump statements, 4
Actual arguments, 126, 127-
    128
Actual parameter, 126
Addition assignment, 82
Addresses, 32, 33-35
Address operator, 84
*Advanced C Programming
    for OS/2* (Hansen and
    Vernon), 7
Aggregate, 153
Alteration, 93

Ampersand (&), as logical
    connective, 76, 77
AND
    as bitwise operator, 79,
        80
    truth tables for, 77
ANSI C standard, 7, 126,
    147, 159, 193, 207
A.out, 10, 17
Argc, 295, 303
Arguments. *See* Command-
    line arguments; Filename
    arguments
Argv, 295, 299, 303
Arithmetic operators, 67-73
    data conversions, 70-72
    integer arithmetic, 73
    memory manipulation,
        68, 69
    modulus operator (%), 70
    on pointers, 169
    precision, loss of, 72-73
    promotion, 73
    unary minus (-) operator,
        69
    unary plus (+) operator,
        69-70
Arrays, 46
    accessing elements, 159-
        162
    automatic array, 156,
        157, 159, 164
    day-of-week calculation
        example, 175-176

declarations, 154-155
    storage class specifi-
        ers in, 158-159
    elements of array, 153-
        154
    elements and size, 154
    to implement stacks,
        254, 255
    to implement queue, 261
    initialized with literal
        string, 172
    initializing elements,
        156, 164
    integer array example,
        154-155
    memory space saving,
        175-176
    multidimensional ar-
        rays, 162-165
        accessing array, 164-
            165
        adding dimensions,
            163
        initializing array,
            164
        two-dimensional ex-
            ample, 163-165
    object as buffer in, 57
    pointers and, 170-176
        arrays of pointers,
            174-176
        C string, 170-173

pointer to access
array elements,
173-174
subscripted arrays,
174
portability and, 185
in program creation, 21
ragged-array approach,
174-176
static array, 156, 157,
159, 164
string literal as, 40-41
strings, 47
subscripts, 159, 163,
165, 174
tally program example,
160-162
ASCII character set, 40, 106,
107
Assignment operators, 61,
67, 81-83
types of, 82
Atof ( ) library function, 101
Atoi ( ) function, 54, 99, 162,
300
AUTOEXEC.BAT, 299
Automatic array, 156, 157,
159, 164
Automatic storage duration,
156, 157

B

Big-endian storage, 35
Binary digit. *See* Bits
Binary operators, 63
Bit fields
bit-field object, 33
" ->" notation and, 213
concept of, 211-212
declarations, 212
use of, 212-213
Bits, 28-31
bit patterns, 29-30
byte, 32-33

decimal values, 30, 31
hexadecimal values, 31
least significant bit, 33
most significant bit
(MSB), 33
octal values, 30
states of, 8
Bitwise-AND assignment, 82
Bitwise-exclusive-OR assignment, 82
Bitwise-inclusive-OR assignment, 82
Bitwise operators, 78-81
AND, 79, 80, 82
OR, 79, 80, 82
shift operators, 80-81
Block scope, identifiers, 157
Blocks. *See* Compound statements
Boxtext program, 121-122,
132-134, 147-148
Braces ([ ])
initializers of array elements list, 156, 164
statement body, 125
Brainstorming, program design, 248
Branching, multi-way, 97-101
Branching statements, 4
conditional expressions
and, 95
Break statement, 4, 91, 102,
114
Buffer, 21, 232-234
in array, 57
full buffering, 233
input/output, 232-234
line buffering, 233
setbuf ( ) function, 233-
234
unbuffered streams, 233
See also Queues; Stacks.
Byte, 32-33
byte order, 35

high byte, 33
low byte, 32
number of bits in, 32

C

C0, C1 and C2, 10
Calc.c program, 114-116
Calculator program
four-function calculator,
100-101, 114-116
Reverse Polish Notation
(RPN), 101
Call-by-reference technique,
132, 177
Call-by-value parameter
passing, 131-132
Calloc ( ) function, 276, 277
Call/return mechanism, 5
Cardfile program, 277-287
Carriage return, 223
Case labels, 4
switch statement in,
102, 103-104
Case of letters, UNIX and, 10
Cat program, 229
Cc command, 10, 131
Cc program, 11
Central processing unit
(CPU), 27
Char, character types, 39-43
Character constants, com-
pared to, string literals, 41
Character-oriented input/out-
put, 234-237
wrtfile program exam-
ple, 235-236
Character sets
ASCII, 40
EBCDIC, 40
line-feed character, 107
Character types, 39-43
character constants, 40
declaring character ob-
ject, 39

escape sequences, 41-43
plain character, 39
printing, 39-40
string literals, 40-41
value in variable, 39-40
Circular doubly-linked lists, 290
Circular queue, 262
Circular singly-linked lists, 273-275
C Language
compilers, 6, 7
elements of, 3
features of, 2
flow-control statements, 4-5
as free form language, 19
interpreters, 7
programming environments, 6-7
programming tools, 6
size of, 3
subprograms, 5
subroutine library, 5-6
translators, 7
Closing file, 232, 238
CL, 12, 17
Coding, 249-250
Comma (,), sequence operator, 66, 85
COMMAND.COM, 298
Command-line arguments
accessing UNIX command line, 294
argc, 295, 303
argv, 295, 299, 303
filename arguments, 298
look program example, 294-298
in program creation, 23
Comments
long comments, 21
in program creation, 20-21

program readability and, 20
short comments, 20
styles of, 21
Compare.c, 97
Compare program, multi-way branching, 97-99
Compilers, 3, 6, 7
Microsoft C.50 Optimizing Compiler, 11, 13
MS-DOS, 11-13
QuickC, 11, 12, 13
separate compilation, 123-124
translation units, 123
Turbo C, 11, 12-13
UNIX, 11
Compound statement, 63
Computer memory
addresses, 32, 33-35
bits, 28-31
bytes, 32-33
Intel architecture, 34-35
Motorola 68000 architecture, 35
objects, 33
Conditional expressions, branch statements and, 95
Connective operators, 77-78, 95
Continue statement, 4, 91, 102
while statement and, 107-108
Control passes, to functions, 125
Conversion specifiers
conversion characters, 45
flag characters, 51
floating types, 50-52
integer types, 44-45
precision values, 51, 52
Counting, characters/lines/words, 247, 249

C program creation
array of characters, 21
command-line arguments, 23
comments, 20-21
in DOS, 17
greeting program example, 15-24
layout of program, 19
main ( ) function, 16, 18-19, 23
preprocessor directives, 22
return values, 23-24
standard library routines, 22
in UNIX, 16
See also Program development.
Cptr program, 168-169
Ctrl+Break, 114
Ctrl-Z code, 224
Ctype.h, 162

D
Data conversions, computations and, 70-72
DATACONV program, 71, 73
Data input, 53-57
numeric data, 54-57
readnum program, 54-55
scanf ( ), 56-57
as strings, 54-55
text strings, 54
Data-low diagrams, 248
Date program, 195-199
Debuggers, 6
Decimal values, bits, 30, 31
Declarations
arrays, 158-159
bit fields, 212
file pointer, 227
functions, 123-125

pointers, 165-167
structures, 190-191
unions, 210
Default behavior, 3
Default label, 4, 90
switch statement in, 101, 102
Default parameter passing
call-by-reference, 132, 177
call-by-value, 131-132, 177
#define directive, 140
define directive, 147
DEL, 114
Dequeue ( ), 261, 265
Dereferenced pointers, 167, 169
Dereferencing operator (*), 85, 204
Derived data types
size problem of, 206
typedef statement and, 206-207
Destination array, size of, 192
Directory, in UNIX, 9
Disk files, 222
Division assignment, 82
DNODE type, 288
Do loop, 111-113
basic form of, 111
example of use, 111-113
input/output and, 112-113
DOS. *See* MS/DOS
Do statement, 90
Dot operator, selecting structure member with, 204
Doubly-linked lists, 188-189
circular, 290
Do...while statements, 4
Dynamic memory management, 275

E
EBCDIC character set, 40
Ed, 8
Else clauses, 90
Else if, 93-94
multi-way branching, 96-97
Emacs, 8
End-of-line (EOL) treatment, UNIX compared to DOS, 223-224
Enforcers, 85
Enqueue ( ), 261, 265
Enumerations
enum keyword, 208-209
enum/typedef combination, 209
member names in, 209
Envdemo program, 301-303
Environment variables, 298-303
envdemo program example, 301-303
getenv ( ) function, 299-300
portability, 303-304
putenv ( ) function, 299
reading environment variables, 299-300
Equality (= =), 75
Equals (=), 67, 81-82
Equivalent/similar ~ operator, 80
ERR ( ) macro, 144-145
Error ( ) function, 286
Error handling
end of function return, 238
feof ( ) macro, 238
ferror ( ) macro, 238
input/output, 237-240
lwc program, 238-240
Escape sequences, character types, 41-43

Eventst program, 143-144
Exception, 62
Exclamation point (!), to negate logical expression, 76
EXIT_FAILURE, 138, 205
Exit ( ) function call, 102
Exiting programs, 114
EXIT_SUCCESS, 24
Expressions
evaluation order, 62
exception and, 62
forcing evaluation by compiler, 66-67
function of, 62
parentheses and, 64, 66-67
scalar expressions, 91
Expression statement, 62-63, 63
External linkage, identifiers, 158
External names
identifiers and, 36
and linkages, 124

F
Factorial ( ) function, 136-137, 140
Fall-through, switch statement in, 102-103
Fclose ( ) function, 232, 236
Feof ( ) macro, 238
Ferror ( ) macro, 238
Fflush ( ) function, 229, 233
Fgetc ( ) function, 231, 234, 235
Fgets ( ) function, 237
Fields. *See* Bit fields
FIFO storage, queues, 261, 262
File input/output, 226-234
file pointer, 227-228
opening file, 228-234
Filename arguments, 228

in MS/DOS, 298
in UNIX, 298
wildcards in, 298
File operations
remove ( ) function, 240
rename ( ) function, 240
tmpfile ( ) function, 240
tmpnam ( ) function, 240-
241
File-positioning functions,
229
Files
disk files, 222
function of, 222
text files, 222-224
File scope, identifiers, 157
Flag characters, conversion
specifiers, 51
Float.h, 52
Float.c, 49
Floating types, 48-52
conversion specifiers, 50-
52
float program, 49-50
IEEE format, 48
obsolete long float type,
48
precision, 48
preserving fractions, 73
printing, 48-50
Flowcharts, 248
Flow control statements, 4-5
branching statements, 4
looping statements, 4
Fopen ( ) function, 228, 229,
231
For loop, 108-111
basic form of, 108
as equivalent while
statement, 109-110
infinite loops, 110-111
with three loop-control
expressions, 108, 109
Formal arguments, 126

Formal parameters, func-
tions, 126-127
Formatted input/output, 234
For statement, 4, 90
Four.c, 100, 103
Fprintf ( ) function, 234
Fputc ( ) function, 235
Fputs ( ) function, 236, 237
Fractional truncation, 73
Free ( ) function, 275
Freopen ( ) function, 232
Fseek ( ) function, 229
Fsetpos ( ) function, 229
Full buffering, 233
Function calls, 4
Function-like macros, 142-
145
basic form of, 142
ERR ( ) macro example,
144-145
eventst program exam-
ple, 143-144
identifier_list compo-
nent, 142
parentheses in, 142, 143,
145
white space characters
in, 142
Functions, 5
actual arguments, 126,
127-128
in boxtext program, 121-
122, 132-134
call-by-value parameter
passing, 131-132
control passes to, 125
declarations, 123-125
external names and link-
ages, 123-124
formal parameters, 126-
127
function-call hierarchy,
121, 122
function definition

elements of, 124
form of, 124
function header, 124,
125, 128-129
function/macro tradeoff,
146
function prototype, 128-
131
function prototypes, por-
tability and, 147
information hiding and,
122-123
main ( ) functions, 119
naming of, 125
one per task in program-
ming, 121
pointers and, 177-185
functions returning
pointers, 178-181
pointer as formal pa-
rameter, 177-178
pointers to a func-
tion, 181-185
purpose of, 119-120
statement body, 125
structures and, 195-200
date program exam-
ple, 195-199
functions to return
structures, 199-
200
passing structures
as function pa-
rameter, 195-199
subprograms as, 120
Function scope, identifiers,
157

G
Getchar ( ) function, 234
Getc ( ) macro, 234, 235
GetKey ( ) function, 110
Gets ( ) function, 16, 22, 54,
237

Goto statement, 4, 90, 157
    alternatives to, 113
    basic form of, 113
Greater than (>), output redirection, 225
Greeting program, creation of, 15-24

H
Hbars program, 127-128, 129
Header files, 8-9, 22, 24, 52
    function header, 124, 125, 128-129
Hexadecimal values, bits, 31
Hiding information, functions, 122-123
High byte, 33

I
Identifier_list component, function-like macros, 142
Identifiers, 35-37
    external linkage, 158
    internal/external names and, 36
    internal linkage, 159
    invalid identifiers, 36-37
    scope of, 157
    structure of, 35-36
IEEE format, floating types, 48
If statements, 4, 90, 91-99, 231
    basic form of, 91
    and control expression, 92-92
    with else clause, 93-94
    example of use, 92-93
    flowchart for, 92
    nesting of, 95-98
    parentheses, 91
INBUFSIZE, 101
Increment operator, 83

in prefix/postfix notation, 84
Indirection operator, 85
    pointer declaration, 165
Infinite loops, 110-111
Initializers, array elements, 156, 164
Input errors, scanf ( ) function and, 202
Input/output (I/O)
    buffering, 232-234
    character-oriented input/output, 234-237
    and C language, 219-220
    error handling, 237-240
    file I/O, 226-234
    formatted input/output, 234
    physical devices of, 220
    redirection, 224-226
    stream I/O, 220
    subroutine library and, 220
    system I/O, 220
Inrange ( ) function, 141
Int.c, 43
Integer arithmetic, 73
Integer types, 43-47
    conversion specifiers, 44-45
    integer constants, 45-46
    long integer, 43, 45
    plain integers, 43
    printing, 43-44
    short integer, 43, 45
    strings, 46-48
    unsigned integers, 45
Integrated compiler (TC), 12
Intel architecture, memory of, 34-35
Internal linkage, identifiers, 159
Internal names, 124
    identifiers and, 36

Interpretation, 3
Interpreters, 7
Ints, 43, 45
Isdigit ( ) macro, 162
Iteration statements, 63, 89, 90
Iterative solutions, recursion and, 138

J
Jump statements, 63, 89, 90-91
    goto statement, 113

K
Keyboard buffer, as circular queue, 262
Keywords, types in C language, 35

L
Labeled statement, 63
Layout of program, in program creation, 19
Ld, 10
Least-significant bit, 33
Left-shift assignment, 82
Less than (<), input redirection, 224
LIFO storage, stacks, 253
Limits.h, 52
Line, 54
Line buffering, 233
Line-drawing characters, 134
Line-feed character, 107, 223
Linkage editor, UNIX, 10
LINK command, 131
Linked lists
    circular doubly-linked lists, 290
    circular singly-linked lists, 273-275
    doubly-linked lists, 288-289

singly-linked lists, 270-271

Linker, 6

  instruction source, 131

Listfile program, 229-234, 234, 235, 237

Lists

  linear lists, 273

  list nodes, 272

  operations on list, 272

  operations in list management, 275

  See also Linked lists.

Literal strings, to initialize array, 172

Little-endian storage, 35

Logical operators, 75-78

  connective operators, 77-78

  to negate logical expression, 76

  short-circuit evaluation, 78, 84

  truth tables for, 76-77

Login, 298

Long integer, 43, 45

Look program, 294-298

Loops, 4

  do loop, 111-113

  for loop, 108-111

  while statement, 104-107

Loop-termination test, 172-173

Low byte, 32

Lwc program, 238-240, 247, 249

M

Macros, 5

  function-like macros, 142-145

  function/macro tradeoff, 146

  gets ( ) macro, 22

object-like macros, 140-142

side effects, 143, 145

See also Function-like macros; object-like macros.

Main ( ) function, 127, 128, 136, 148

  in program creation, 16, 18-19, 23

Maintenance of program, 251-252

Malloc ( ) function, 275, 276, 277

Memory

  primary memory, 27

  random-access memory (RAM), 27

  read-only memory (ROM), 28

  secondary memory, 28

  See also Computer memory.

Memory management

  calloc ( ) function, 276, 277

  cardfile program example, 277-287

  free ( ) function, 275

  malloc ( ) function, 275, 276, 277

  realloc ( ) function, 276, 277

  strdup ( ) function, 276-277

Microsoft C.50 Optimizing Compiler, 11, 13

  advantages to use, 13

Minus (- -), decrement operator, 83-84

Mode argument codes, 228-229

Modulus operator (%), 70

Most significant bit (MSB), 33

Motorola 68000 architecture, memory of, 35

MS/DOS, 6, 7, 11-14

  command line syntax, 295

  compilers, 11-13

  compiling C programs, 11-12

  filename arguments, 298

  greeting program, 17

  pipelines and, 225

  standard streams, 221-222

  text files, 223-224

Multidimensional arrays, 162-165

  accessing array, 164-165

  adding dimensions, 163

  initializing array, 164

Multiplication assignment, 82

Multi-way branching

  compare program, 97-99

  else if, 96-97

  switch statement, 99-101

N

NBYTES, 21, 22

Negation

  of logical expressions, 76

  truth tables for, 76

Nesting if statements, 95-98

  compare program and, 97-99

  else if and, 96-97

  in false branch, 96

  in true branch, 95-96

Newline character, 42, 54, 106, 107, 223, 237

N memb parameter, 184

Nodes

allocation and dealloca-
tion of, 175
deletion in singly-linked
list, 273
inserting in singly-
linked list, 272, 274
list management and,
275
Null byte, strings and, 170
Null character, 40, 42, 54
Null statement
character-reading loop
and, 107
example of use, 106
while statement and,
106-107

O

Object-like macros, 140-142
basic form of, 140-141
on more than one line,
141
PROMPT macro exam-
ple, 141-142
Objects, 33
addresses, 32, 33-35
bit-field object, 33
elements in arrays, 153-
154
Octal values, bits, 30
Opening file, 228-234
filename argument, 228
file-positioning func-
tions, 229
fopen ( ) function, 228,
229
listfile program exam-
ple, 229-234
mode argument codes,
228-229
update modes, 229
Operands, 61
Operating system

command-line argu-
ments, 294-298
environment variables,
298-303
See also MS/DOS and
UNIX.
Operators, 3
address operator, 84
arithmetic operators, 67-
73
assignment operator, 61,
67
assignment operators,
81-83
binary operators, 63
bitwise operators, 78-81
decrement operator, 83
expressions created
from, 62
increment operator, 83
indirection operator, 85
logical operators, 75-78
precedence and associa-
tivity, 64-67
relational operator, 74-75
sequence operator, 66, 85
sizeof operator, 74
ternary operators, 63
unary operators, 63
OR
as bitwise operator, 79,
80
truth tables for, 77

P

Parameter list, in function
header, 125, 127
Parameter passing
call-by-reference, 132-
177
call-by-value, 131-132,
177
Parentheses ( )

declaring pointer to function and, 182
and expressions, 64, 66-
67
if statements, 91
in macros, 142, 143, 145
semicolon at end of test
expression, 111
and sizeof operator, 74
Passes, 9
Pgm.c, 8, 10
Phases, 9
Pipelines
to connect programs,
225-226
MS/DOS, 225
sink in, 226
UNIX, 225
Plain integers, 43
Plus (+ +), increment operator, 83-84
Pointers, 46, 57, 84
accessing data and, 167-
169
address of, 167
arithmetic operators on,
169
arrays and, 170-176
arrays of pointers,
174-176
C string, 170-173
pointer to access
array elements,
173-174
subscripted arrays,
174
basic form of, 165
with characters, cptr program example, 168-169
confusion with integers,
167
declarations, 165-167
dereferenced pointers,
167, 169

file pointer, 227-228
functions and, 177-185
    functions returning pointers, 178-181
    pointer as formal parameter, 177-178
    pointers to a function, 181-185
portability and, 185
size, scaling of, 169
structures and, 200-205
    resistor program example, 200-205
    selecting structure member with pointer, 204
Pop ( ) function, 254, 258
Portability
    arrays and, 185
    environment variables, 303-304
    example of, 147-148
    function prototypes and, 147
    pointers and, 185
    structures and, 214
Precedence and associativity, operators, 64-67
Precision
    floating types, 48
    loss of, 72-73
Precision values, conversion specifiers, 51, 52
Preprocessor
    preprocessor directives in program creation, 22
    text-replacement capacity, 140, 141
    UNIX, 10
Primary memory, 27
Printf ( ) function, 22, 42, 44, 46, 47, 56
Printing
    character types, 39-40

floating types, 48-50
integer types, 43-44
Processing directives, 22, 302
Profile, 298
Program development
    coding, 249-250
    maintenance, 251-252
    problem analysis, 245-247
        illustration of, 246-247
    program design
        brainstorming, 248
        graphic methods, 248
        pseudocode, 248-249
    testing, guidelines for, 250-251
Programming environments
    MS-DOS, 6, 7, 11-14
    UNIX, 6, 7, 8-11
Programming tools, 6
Promotion, computations and, 73
PROMPT macro, 141-142
Prototypes, function prototypes, 128-131, 147
Pr program, 294
Pseudocode, program design, 248-249
Push ( ) function, 254, 258
Putchar ( ) function, 42, 235
Putenv ( ) function, 299
Puts ( ) function, 236, 237

Q
QC, 12
QCL, 12, 17
'Q' command, 114
Qsort ( ) function, 184, 185
Qsrtdemo program, 182-184
Queues
    array implementation of, 261
    circular queue, 262

data type, 261
dequeue ( ), 261, 265
enqueue ( ), 261, 265
FIFO storage, 261, 262
queue program example, 262-266
QuickC, 11, 12, 13, 17

R
Ragged-array approach, 174-176
Random-access memory (RAM), 27
Readnum program, 54-55
Read-only memory (ROM), 28
Realloc ( ) function, 276, 277
Rectangular array, 162-165
Recursion
    ifact program, 138-140
    iterative solution, use of, 138
    negative attributes of, 135, 138
    rfact program, 135-138
    termination condition and, 138
    uses of, 135
Redirection
    (< and >) in, 224, 225
    input redirection, 224-225
    output redirection, 225
    pipelines in, 225-226
Relational operator, 74-75
Remainder assignment, 82
Remainder operator, 70
Remove ( ) function, 240
Rename ( ) function, 240
Resistor program, 200-205
Return eater, 116
Return key, 107
Return statements, 91, 99
Return values, in program creation, 23-24

Reverse Polish Notation (RPN), 101
Rewind ( ) function, 229
Right-shift assignment, 82

S

Scanf ( ) function, 234
   input errors and, 202
   numeric data and, 56-57
Scope
   block scope, 157
   file scope, 157
   function scope, 157
   of identifiers, 157-158
Secondary memory, 28
Selection statements, 63, 89, 90
   else clauses, 93-94
   if statement, 91-99
   switch statement, 99-103
Self-referential data structure, 269
Semicolon (;)
   null statement, 106
   parenthesized test expressions and, 111
   as statement termination, 62
Separate compilation, 123-124
Sequence operator, 66, 85
Setargv ( ) function, 298
Setbuf ( ) function, 233-234
Setvbuf ( ) function, 233
Shift operators, 80-81
Short-circuit evaluation, 78, 84
Short integer, 43, 45
Side effects, macros, 143, 145
Singly-linked lists, 270-271
   circular, 273-275
   deleting node in, 273
   inserting node in, 272, 274

Sink, pipelines in, 226
Sizeof operator, 74, 237
SLIBCE.LIB, 131
SNODE type, 270-271, 274
Source code, compressing, 19
Source files, 8, 9
Sprintf ( ) function, 234
Stacks
   array implementation of, 254, 255
   code for management of, 254
   data type, 253-254
   LIFO storage, 253
   pop ( ) function, 254, 258
   push ( ) function, 254, 258
   stack program example, 256-260
   usefulness of, 253, 260
Standard library routines, 22, 178, 238
Standard streams
   MS/DOS, 221-222
   standard error, 221
   standard input, 221
   standard output, 221
   stddaux stream, 222
   stdprn stream, 221-222
   UNIX, 220-221
Statement body, functions, 125
Statements
   compound statement, 63
   expression statement, 62-63
   order of execution, 62
   semicolon and, 62
   syntax of, 63
States, of bits, 28-29
Static array, 156, 157, 159, 164
Static memory management, 275

Static storage duration, 156, 157
Stdio.h, 8, 22, 131, 227, 228, 236
Stdlib.h, 24
Storage class, specifiers in declaration statement, 158-159
Storage duration
   automatic storage duration, 156, 157
   static storage duration, 156, 157
Storage requirements, 52-53
Strcpy ( ) function, 192
Strdup ( ) function, 276-277
Streams
   I/O, 220
   redirection, 224-226
   standard streams, 220-222
String-handling functions, 178
   String Copy ( ) function, 178-181
   string ( ) function, 127
   strncopy ( ) function, 283
String literals
   as array of characters, 40-41
   compared to character constant, 41
   concatenation of, 41
Strings, 46-48
   arrays of characters, 47
   numeric data as, 54-55
   pointers and, 170-173
   printf ( ) statement, 47
   strings program, 46-47
   str program example, 171
   text strings, reading, 54
Str program, 171
Strtest program, 181

Strtok ( ) function, 285
Structure member operator
  ('.'), 191
Structures
  basic form of, 190
  bit fields, 211-214
  declarations, 190-191
  enumerations, 207-209
  functions and, 195-200
    date program exam-
      ple, 195-199
    functions to return
      structures, 199-
      200
    passing structures
      as function pa-
      rameter, 195-199
  pointers and, 200-205
    resistor program ex-
      ample, 200-205
    selecting structure
      member with
      pointer, 204
  pointers in, 193-195
  portability, 214
  self-referential data
    structure, 269
  strcpy ( ) function and,
    192
  structure member opera-
    tor ('.'), 191
  template for, 190-191
  typedef statement and,
    206-207
  unions, 210
  usefulness of, 189, 191-
    193
  varname, 190, 192
Subprograms
  as functions, 120
  functions, 5
  macros, 5
Subroutine library, 5-6

Subscripts, arrays, 159, 163,
  165
Subtraction assignment, 82
Support.c, 8
Switch statement, 4, 90, 99-
  103
  basic form of, 99
  case labels in, 102, 103-
    104
  default case in, 101, 102
  fall-through in, 102-103
  multi-way branching, 99-
    101
Syntax checkers, 6

T
Tally program, 160-162
TCC, 17
Template, structure tem-
  plate, 190-191
Temporary file names, 240-
  241
Ternary operators, 63
Testing program, guidelines
  for, 250-251
Text editor, 8, 15
Text files, 222-224
  DOS, 223-224
  UNIX, 223-224
Tmpfile ( ) function, 240
Tmpnam ( ) function, 240-241
Toggling, 93, 95
Translation, 3
Translation units, 123
Translators, 7
  function prototype, 128-
    131
Tree program, 129-130
Truth tables
  for AND, 77
  logical operators, 76-77
  for negation, 76
  for OR, 77
Turbo C, 11, 12-13, 17

command-line compiler
  (TCC), 12
Two-dimensional array, 163-
  165
Typedef statement
  combined with enum,
    209
  structures and, 206-207
Types
  character types, 39-43
  floating types, 48-52
  function types, 38
  incomplete types, 38
  integer types, 43-47
  object types, 38
  sizes, 52-53

U
Unary minus (-) operator, 63,
  69
Unary plus (+) operator, 63,
  69-70
Unbuffered streams, 233
Unions
  caution about, 210
  declarations, 210
  use of union variables,
    210-211
UNIX, 6, 7, 8-11
  case of letters in, 10
  cc program, 11
  command line argument,
    294
  command line syntax,
    295
  commands, style of, 293-
    294
  compiler, 11
  compiling C programs, 8-
    10
  directory in, 9
  filename arguments, 298
  greeting program, 16
  header files, 8-9

linkage editor, 10
pipelines and, 225
preprocessor, 10
source files, 8, 9
standard streams, 220-
221
text files, 223-224
Unsigned integers, 45
Update modes, 229
/usr/include, 9
/usr/include/sys, 9
/usr/lib/llibc, 131

V

Values
bytes, 33
value ranges, 52-53
Variables
declaring variable, 37
naming of, 37
scope, 157-158
storage duration, 156-
157
Varname, structures, 190,
192
Varnier-Orr diagrams, 248
Vertical bar, (|), 225
Vi, 8, 15
VOID, 148

W

Wc program, 238
While statement, 4, 90, 104-
107, 231
basic form of, 104
continue statement and,
017-108
desired behavior, exam-
ple of, 104-105
equivalent for loop for,
109-110
input/output and, 105-
106

null statement and, 106-
107
White space characters, function-like macros in, 142
Width
as number or asterisk, 51
width specifier, 287
Wildcards, 298
Wrtfile program, 235-236,
238

X

XENIX, 7